FROM SHAKESPEARE TO O. HENRY

FROM SHAKESPEARE
TO O. HENRY

STUDIES IN LITERATURE

BY

S. P. B. MAIS

PR99
.M23

ESSAY INDEX

REVISED EDITION

Essay Index Reprint Series

90293

 BOOKS FOR LIBRARIES PRESS

FREEPORT, NEW YORK

Revised Edition First Published 1923
Reprinted 1968

LIBRARY OF CONGRESS CATALOG CARD NUMBER:

68-16952

PRINTED IN THE UNITED STATES OF AMERICA

TO
MY WIFE

CONTENTS

I desire to thank the editors of " The Nineteenth Century," " The Fortnightly Review," " The Journal of Education " and " The Parents' Review," for permission to reprint here six of the following essays. The remainder are now published for the first time.

I

SHAKESPEARE [1]

i

THERE has never been an age so prolific of Shakespearean criticism as our own. There can be no doubt that the studies of Brandes, Ten Brink, Taine, Raleigh, Bradley, Frank Harris, Masefield and Dowden have opened up new roads of thought, each of them different from the other, but each converging on the one end we would all attain, the heart of Shakespeare.

We recognise now, for instance, that Wordsworth was far more of a seer than Browning, and more probably right when he suggested that in the Sonnets we have the real living Shakespeare : " with this key Shakespeare unlocked his heart." The theory that we know little or nothing of the dramatist's own life [2] or point of view is exploded, we may hope, for ever : the truth is that we know more, not less, about the actual details of his life than we do about any other dramatist of his time, owing to the energy of Sir Sidney Lee, Professor Wallace and others ; and, as Bagehot says, Shakespeare is, after all, his own biographer. Surely no man could desire a better Boswell. As it was one of Shakespeare's most notable gifts to be able to make

---

[1] Mainly derived from Frank Harris and Bradley.

[2] Sir George Greenwood's theory that Shakespeare the actor and "Shakespeare" the playwright were two different men does not come within the scope of this paper, but cannot be neglected.

11

a fictitious character live more really than many people with whom we have been intimately connected all our lives, so when he comes to portray his own idiosyncrasies we find that we know Shakespeare better almost than anybody else in the whole world. It has been said, of course, that it is the business of the dramatist to treat his art objectively, to stand right outside it and so far to obliterate his own point of view as to be able to step into the very body and soul of his *dramatis personæ* and, for the time being, to become them : to see life from their particular niche and to utter sentiments (which may be totally opposed to his own) which fit their character. This is a quite true and sound criticism, but when Homer nods, when the character for some inexplicable reason gratuitously emphasises points in his character which rather tend to retard than to develop the action, we may justifiably begin to think that at these times the personality of the author is unconsciously obtruding itself and is, in a word, his own temperament giving voice to its likes and dislikes.

Again, when a dramatist returns time after time to the same peculiarities in his major creations, it is obvious that he is at any rate interested in those peculiarities, either because they are his own obsessions or are possessed by his most intimate friends. No man can depict what he fails to understand, nor does he usually attempt to draw what never interests him ; Shakespeare, for instance, nowhere gives us a living portrait of the zealous Puritan fanatic reformer, or the shop-keeping, middle-class citizen : neither type interested him.

Two types alone stand out among his delineations of men. As Doctor Johnson shrewdly remarks, Shakespeare has no heroes ; his best pictures of men are those which depict them as creatures of obvious human failings like unto ourselves, and they stand out, very clear-cut, in two main groups.

First there is the group which we identify as like in nearly all points to Shakespeare himself—the Hamlet, Biron, Vincentio, Orsino, Prospero, Jaques, Macbeth, Posthumus, Richard the Second type. These men are amazingly alike even when, by all the laws of drama, they ought not to be. They all love solitude, are far too much given to introspection and thinking too precisely on the event, it is their great failing that their native hue of resolution is sicklied o'er by the pale cast of thought, they all find solace in music, they are gentle, almost too gentle, " too full of the milk of human kindness," in all of them their imaginative faculty is developed at the expense of all their other faculties. They may, in some cases, describe themselves as " plain, blunt men," but as a matter of fact they delude themselves when they say so ; the truth is that they are all poets ; they never speak anything but the purest poetry ; they are simply Shakespeare, Shakespeare himself speaking through the lips of these kings and princes and dukes, Shakespeare the gentle, the passionate, the irresolute. After all, if we take Leonardo da Vinci's opinion to be worth anything, we should expect this. " For the form," he says, " we go to Nature and use our observations, for the soul we look into our own hearts and paint ourselves."

This it is that seems to me to account for Shakespeare's failure when we begin to analyse his depiction of the second broad group—the men of action. For who are Shakespeare's men of action ?

Othello ? He begins as man of action and ends as a man of action, but in the middle of the play he is the poet, imaginative, given to much thinking (it is almost a *sine qua non* that our men of action should not be overburdened with intellect ; it is just because they don't waste time in overmuch thinking that we admire them), a bad judge of character (where your man of action is almost infallible), suspicious to an extraordinary degree. He talks too much.

Macbeth ? He is superstitious, lily-livered in his fear of blood, more a poet, and far more sensitive of soul, than Othello.

Henry the Fifth ? As a king he may compel admiration, but as a man he is almost beneath contempt ; he is a low, common cad who deserts his friends, butchers his enemies and makes love like a savage.[1]

Hotspur ? His masterpiece of the man of action is a medley of contrarieties, who hates " mincing poetry " and yet employs it *ad nauseam*, losing himself in mistimed philosophic reflection when he ought to be the brave, blunt hero.

Richard the Second ? Heavens, no ! Falconbridge ? He is slavishly copied from *The Troublesome Raigne.*

Search the plays through and through and you will find that Shakespeare mars in some particular all his men of action.[2] The truth is that he is not sufficiently interested in them to understand them. How otherwise can we explain the fact that he never took the trouble to depict a Raleigh, a Hawkins, a Frobisher, a Drake or a Sir Philip Sidney ? He had models enough near at hand ; he must have come into intimate contact with men of this famous breed ; he nowhere portrays them any more than he portrays the zealous Puritan or the middle-class shopkeeper. He had nothing in common with them. He had, truly, the finest experiencing nature ever given to man ; his mind

[1] Masefield's idea.   [2] Coriolanus ought, I think, to be excepted.

was like a highly sensitive photographic plate. Consequently, he has immortalised types which will live for ever in tragedy and comedy. His Falstaff, about whom it has been said that if anyone were to garner up all the humour and gaiety of his entire life it would amount to about the worth of one sentence of the immortal knight; his Nurse in *Romeo and Juliet*, who remains ever fresh when all our real nurses are forgotten; his Dogberry, who contains the essence of all the policemen we have had the misfortune to know; his Shallow, whose humour Masefield compares to an apple-loft in some old barn where the apples of last year lie sweet in the straw—all these are in the world's great portrait gallery. Yet it must not be forgotten that, in spite of these, Shakespeare had his limitations, and this failure to depict the man of action was one of the most noticeable. He seems himself to have been a man obsessed with a horror of bloodshed. He can never quite rise to an adequate description of courage—as Frank Harris says, when we want to see this side of life faithfully rendered we have to turn to Bunyan : Valiant-for-Truth, with his "I fought till my sword did cleave to my hand and when they were joined together as if a sword grew out of my arm, and when the blood ran through my fingers, then I fought with most courage," is quite beyond the scope of Shakespeare.

But, as Professor Saintsbury says in his *Peace of the Augustans*, "it is not a sin for a potato not to be a peach or not to be sorry because it is one " : it is not Shakespeare's fault if he left us no picture of the modern Public School boy or drew the happy warrior less happily than Wordsworth; what is sinful is for us to pretend that he did what he did not do. "For the soul we look into our own hearts and paint ourselves."

So when Shakespeare came to portray womanhood I believe he painted those whom he knew, and sometimes idealised them to such a degree that they became lifeless abstractions.

Hazlitt's dictum that "Shakespeare's heroines (though they have been found fault with as insipid) are the finest in the world," like most of Hazlitt's judgments, hits the nail on the head.

When suddenly we are asked to pick out our favourite heroines in fiction we are hard put to it to think of any with whom we would willingly spend our days. Scott once, in Jeanie Deans, painted a real live girl, Meredith again and again; but few other writers have succeeded in pleasing us. Shakespeare certainly has left the best we know, but with many even of his we are prone to find fault.

Who, for instance, would willingly marry an Ophelia ? She is scarcely more than a puppet. There are times when we are so tortured in *Othello* that we long for any girl of our acquaintance to change places for half-an-hour with Desdemona. There would have been no tragedy had a flesh-and-blood girl been in her situation; it is Desdemona's dumbness, Desdemona's ethereal qualities that allow a tragedy which strains the probabilities almost to breaking-point.

In Cordelia, however, Shakespeare rises to his highest; though she speaks barely a hundred lines she lives for us for ever; her foolish obstinacy, her show of temper as she leaves her sisters, her amazing filial devotion, all endear her to us, so that she stands out far above all the other women whom Shakespeare depicted.[1] The truth is that Shakespeare was always painting ideal portraits of girls : in Rosalind, in Portia, in Beatrice, in Juliet. Again and again we have the same sprightly,

[1] Middleton Murry makes out an excellent case for Virgilia.

witty, loose-talking, boyish girl who is like no one we ever met, but in some points like the girl of our dreams.

Occasionally we get a picture of a shrew, as in Adriana, Katherine, or Constance (in the earlier scenes), and from hints that Shakespeare drops from time to time we may well believe that he was here depicting that unfortunate Anne Hathaway, the wife who was eight years older than her husband, to whom the second-best bed was his last bequest. In Volumnia, that splendid Roman matron, he has paid a grand tribute to mothers, and it is quite on the cards that in the bloodless abstractions with which he occupied himself in his closing years, in Perdita, Marina and Miranda, he may well have had in mind his daughter Judith. But it none the less remains true that he never succeeded in painting any type of womanhood so successfully again as he did in Cleopatra. No other woman in Shakespeare is worthy to compare with her ; she is astoundingly alive and real. She has the power of making us feel that had we been Antony we should have done what Antony did, and in rereading the play it seems impossible to imagine that Shakespeare drew entirely from his imagination when he conceived such a character. Frank Harris's theory that Cleopatra and Cressida are both portraits of the Dark Lady of the Sonnets, that Shakespeare's great tragedy was his unbridled passion for this lady, call her Mary Fitton or whom you will, is at least plausible, and becomes more and more likely as we follow up the threads of his argument.[1]

That Shakespeare personally experienced deep suffering of some sort seems to be obvious ; it is inconceivable that he should have written *Hamlet, Lear, Macbeth* and *Othello* had he not himself been in the depths ; what that experience was we cannot now know for

---

[1] Clemence Dane makes no bones about it—Mary Fitton it is.

certain, but, judging from what we do know of him, it appears more likely to have been an agony of love, of treachery and baseness in love than anything else. The story of the friend being deputed to make love to the girl for the hero does not occur, be it remembered, only in the Sonnets ; we have the same story retold in *Much Ado About Nothing* and in *Twelfth Night.* It is an absurd story for a dramatist so versatile as Shakespeare to harp on, but he somehow cannot get away from it, as he would not, were he recalling an episode in his own life. When we recollect how often Shakespeare inveighs against the sin of ingratitude, to him obviously the worst offence imaginable, it lends colour all the more strongly to the theory that Shakespeare sent the young Herbert to plead his cause with Mary Fitton, only to discover that she succumbed to the attractiveness of the friend and betrayed Shakespeare by giving herself to that friend.

Whatever the truth of this may be, there is at least no doubt that Shakespeare was more successful in his portraiture of women when he was painting the coquette, the wanton Cleopatra (whom he seemed to know right down to the utmost depths) than he was in depicting any other type of womanhood at all. Even Ruskin noticed that nearly all Shakespeare's women were faultless, but he does not conclude, therefore, as we do, that they were, for this very reason, inhuman and untrue to life.

ii

It has been said that Shakespeare spent his life in two places : in the Court, mingling with the young gallants who had taken him up and found his witty, sunny disposition to their liking ; and in the taverns, with Ben Jonson and Marlowe, where he met the

Bardolphs, Falstaffs and Quicklys of life. The middle of humanity he never knew, but only the extremes. This may be due to all sorts of reasons; one certainly was that he was inherently an aristocrat; by a strange paradoxical irony, apparently he was also a snob. Somehow in the light of this it is easier to understand the way in which Mary Fitton treated him, " now she would and now she wouldn't "—always keeping him on the tenterhooks alternately of hope and despair, until she finally married for the second time and left London for ever. Genius was ever unhappy in its relations with the opposite sex, and it appears unlikely that Shakespeare was an exception to a rule which has scarcely ever been broken, except in the case of the Brownings.

It has been the fashion for many years now to extol Shakespeare's sense of humour as almost the most perfectly developed which we possess; but Doctor Johnson noticed what many of us nowadays feel : that many of his so-called comic scenes are intolerably dull, owing to the eternal playing upon words in which the characters indulge. Just as Euphuism was a passing phase, a fashion of the moment, so this habit of punning, so dear to the heart of Shakespeare, once it reaches its zenith in Sidney Smith, ceases to have any claim upon our attention : it has become the very lowest form of wit—cheap, vulgar, relegated to the less desirable type of music hall. No fashion changes more quickly than the fashion of fun, the criterion of what is or what is not humorous ; it is this that so surprises us in Johnson's other statement when he says that in his comic scenes Shakespeare seems to produce without labour what no labour can improve ; Hazlitt strikes a truer note when he says that we prefer Shakespearean tragedy to Shakespearean comedy for the simple reason that tragedy is better than comedy. Nothing, for instance, could be more tedious or more wooden to modern ears than the opening scene of *Romeo and Juliet*, with its silly talk about " choler," " collier " and " collar." It is now almost painful to have to attribute such drivel to the pen that created Sir Andrew Aguecheek, Sir Toby Belch and Bottom.

Shakespeare's failures in the world of humour are more noticeable than any other man's, for the simple reason that he was more richly endowed with the precious gift than any other man ; as Meredith truly points out, from Mother Earth

> " Came the honeyed corner of his lips,
>   The conquering smile wherein his spirit sails
> Calm as the God who the white sea-wave whips,
>   Yet full of speech and intershifting tales,
> Close mirrors of us : thence had he the laugh
>   We feel is hers."

There was in his life a summer-time when his innate capacity for sunny gaiety came to full expression in the golden comedies of *Twelfth Night, A Midsummer Night's Dream* and *As You Like It*.

How different is his success in the ever-famous Nurse and in Bully Bottom and their likes, all of whom he saw with loving observation, from his pictures of men of action : very rarely does his humour become sardonic or contemptuous : rather is it closely allied with Meredith's Comic Spirit — sympathetic, harmless and beautiful as summer lightning. As Meredith says of him :

" Shakespeare is a well-spring of characters which are saturated with the Comic Spirit ; with more of what we call blood-life than is to be found anywhere else : and they are of this world, but they are of the world enlarged to our embrace by imagination and by great poetic imagination."

So much for the particular. But it is when Meredith generalises on the Comic Spirit that he gives us the truest picture of Shakespearean humour :

" It has the sage's brows, and the sunny malice of a faun lurks at the corners of the half-closed lips drawn in an idle wariness of half-tension. It shows sunlight of the mind, mental richness rather than noisy enormity. Its common aspect is one of unsolicitous observation, as if surveying a full field and having leisure to dart on its chosen morsels, without any fluttering eagerness. Men's future upon earth does not attract it ; their honesty and shapeliness in the present does : and whenever they wax out of proportion, overblown, affected, pretentious, bombastical, hypocritical, pedantic, fantastically delicate ; whenever it sees them self-deceived or hoodwinked, given to run riot in idolatries, drifting into vanities, congregating in absurdities, planning short-sightedly, plotting dementedly ; whenever they are at variance with their professions and violate the unwritten laws binding them in consideration one to another ; whenever they offend sound reason, fair justice : are false in humility, or mixed with conceit, individually or in the bulk— the Spirit overhead will look humanely malign and cast an oblique light on them, followed by volleys of silvery laughter."

iii

We should have thought, from the fact that Shakespeare must have met many hundreds of boys on the stage, that he would have left us one deathless portrait at least of the human boy, but by a strange paradox he has left no picture of the living boy we know. All Shakespeare's boy characters are precocious and almost girlish in their ways. Arthur is far the best of them, and may well stand as a type for all the others. There is no question of his being alive : he holds a very dear place in our hearts among the gallery of Shakespeare's most successful characters, but he is scarcely the boy as we know him ; he is all angelic love, a woman-child in his unselfish sympathy, exceedingly tender and sweet of heart, almost perfect and yet quite natural, never mawkish or sentimental ; it is a wonderful creation, tear-compelling in his pathetic helplessness, just as are the prattling Princes or Macduff's son.

So then we see, whether we are discussing Shakespeare's heroes, heroines, humour or boy characters, broadly defined some of his own peculiar idiosyncrasies : his gentle, forgiving, almost feminine mind stands out at every phase of his life's journey and betrays him to us. It remains for us to fill in the portrait by noting in a careful rereading what other qualities he seems to place in the category of good or bad.

First and by far the most noticeable is his love of music ; all his favourite characters, from Orsino to Cleopatra, call for music on the slightest pretext ; he even goes out of his way to condemn the man who has no music in his soul, though we know well enough how false a judgment that is. It is on a par with the " love me, love my dog " theory, and incidentally in this connection it is worthy of remark that Shakespeare always derides dogs : for him they seem always to be synonymous with some vice ; he is, if there ever was one, a dog-hater, which is all the more strange when we think of his love for the open air and the country, and his knowledge of hounds. No man ever described the chase from the point of view of the hare so well as

Shakespeare; no man ever described a hound so well.

That he was generous and liberal-minded is clear to anyone who has read *The Merchant of Venice*; everyone in the play (except Shylock) seems to look on money as dirt, and miserliness is, to Shakespeare's mind, certainly only a lesser crime than ingratitude. I have touched on his snobbishness before; it is, of course, a national trait, but Shakespeare seems to have suffered from the malady badly; it is strange indeed to think that so great a man should have worried to appeal to the Heralds' Court to be assigned a coat of arms as befitted a gentleman; that he was a gentleman and an aristocrat is obvious, but none the less, he seems delighted always to portray himself as a duke or prince whenever possible.

With regard to his politics we may be sure that he sided with law, order and the Constitution. It is not always remembered that he wrote in Tudor times—it would have been strange indeed had he sided otherwise, constituted as he was—he was certainly not the man to understand Jack Cade; Piers Plowman would have left him cold. It has been pointed out frequently that in *The Tempest* he damned the Socialistic point of view for ever, but it may well be doubted whether, had he been living now, he would have taken even the trouble to do that.

"Shakespeare has nowhere drawn the religious type of man in his plays": so runs the famous indictment of the great critic, and for many years the general reader has agreed complacently without taking the trouble to forage for himself and prove the truth or falsity of this sweeping generalisation.

It all depends upon what you mean by the word religious: in an age which no one in his senses could call tolerant, Shakespeare stands out without a trace of bigotry. It was scarcely likely that he would extol the Roman Catholics : on the other hand, he has nowhere left a living picture of the fanatic Puritan, ready to burn for his principles if need be, obsessed by the zeal of his faith which could remove mountains : it would have been so easy for a genius who had only (apparently) to observe a man to become him to have drawn an imperishable portrait of the finest type of Puritan : but no ; the truth must be confessed : Shakespeare, like Homer, had his blind side : to put it shortly, the type did not interest him ; the middle-class shopkeeper, together with the zealot, failed to attract him. Shakespeare was for ever depicting the highest and the lowest ; he seemed not to see the vast millions who lay in between : that was part and parcel of his aristocratic temperament.

That he was contemptuous, in a quite minor degree, both of ordinary citizens and of the Puritans, was natural when we think how both these types combined to oppose the acting of plays, and even petitioned Elizabeth to banish theatres to the suburbs, but it is absurd to take Sir Andrew Aguecheek's opinion as Shakespeare's :

" *Maria.* Marry, sir, sometimes he is a kind of Puritan.

Sir Andrew. O, if I thought that, I'd beat him like a dog.

Sir Toby. What, for being a Puritan ?   Thy exquisite reason, dear knight ?

Sir Andrew. I have no exquisite reason for't, but I have reason good enough."

Incidentally it is to be noticed à propos of Malvolio that Maria replies to this : " The devil a Puritan that he is, or anything constantly but a time-pleaser."

It was certainly not for his Puritanic leanings that Shakespeare thought fit to make Malvolio "a most notorious geck and gull."

The above dialogue reflects altogether on the foolishness of Sir Andrew, and not at all on the Puritans as a body. It might with more justice be urged that Shakespeare is here paying the Puritans a very high compliment.

No : the truth is that we may search Shakespeare through and through in vain to discover any sectarian point of view held up to admiration or ridicule. But religion, to all except the few, is not sectarian. The point at issue rather is, does or does not Shakespeare propound a theory to explain the riddle of life ? Does he praise virtue and condemn vice ? Is he, in the broadest and only true sense, religious ? I answer, without the shadow of a doubt, yes !

It must, however, first of all be remembered that the dramatist's first duty is, like the novelist's, to attract and amuse his audience. He must not obtrude his own personality or moralise upon his *dramatis personæ*. His business is to show you the unfolding of character, not to tell you what to think of the character as if he were the editor of a school edition of his own plays. He is also bound to depict life as he sees it, not as it ought or ought not to be.

Hence to the dullard it is quite possible that Shakespeare seems to have no ulterior moral purpose. We have tragedy after tragedy in which the corpses of righteous and vicious alike lie side by side, in that indiscriminating way which, as the Psalmist saw, is so true to life. The righteous man may beg his bread, and appear to all intents and purposes forsaken, while the wicked man obviously flourishes like a green bay-tree. But that is not all : we are most distinctly left with a sense (never mentioned in so many words, but plainly hinted at again and again) that this world is not all, and that even in this world the purpose of its progress is towards virtue, for it is evil that violently disturbs our ordered path; hence it follows that nature is not indifferent between evil and good, but is quite definitely on the side of the angels. The whole theory of Shakespearean tragedy is a proof of Shakespeare's sane, broad-minded, religious point of view.

What could be more definite, more succinct, more noble, than the whole attitude of Edgar towards life, summed up in this one immortal phrase :

> " men must endure
> Their going hence, even as their coming hither :
> Ripeness is all."

Or, again, his dictum that

> " The gods are just, and of our pleasant vices
> Make instruments to scourge us."

Or,

> " Think that the clearest gods, who make them honours
> Of men's impossibilities, have preserved thee."

It would be easy to multiply instances from his lips to prove that Edgar, for one, was deeply religious. To come to a far more famous instance, who would deny that Hamlet was instinct with a very real sense of religion ?

" Not a whit, we defy augury ; there is a special providence in the fall of the sparrow. If it be now, 'tis not to come ; if it be not to come, it will be now : if it be not now, yet it will come : the readiness is all. Since no man has aught of what he leaves, what is't to leave betimes ? Let be."

It is no argument to the contrary to quote that, on
the other hand, Macbeth talks about " the way to dusty
death," life itself being " but a tale, told by an idiot,
full of sound and fury signifying nothing." To those
whose obsessions have perverted their true nobility,
and degraded them below the level of normal man, it
is but natural that they should turn fatalist at the end.
Shakespeare, in all his tragedies, but emphasises the
truth of the wise Greek saying that " Character is
destiny," and in no case is this so clearly shown as in
the character of Banquo in the same play. Banquo
was a man with a devout sense of religion if there ever
was one, and should alone convince any fair critic of
the untruth of my opening quotation :

> " In the great hand of God I stand, and thence
> Against the undivulged pretence I fight
> Of treasonous malice."

He is one who, determined to play the part of a brave
and honest man, when his turn comes, fails to do anything of the kind, and is made to suffer in a manner
which seems quite out of proportion to his offence.
What Shakespeare appears to have on his mind here
is the incalculability of evil; once start a train of
evil factors and you can never guess at the damage
which such a procedure entails. All you can be sure
about is the impossibility of your escape from the
consequences.

Banquo, be it remembered, prays to be delivered
from temptation :

> " merciful powers,
> Restrain in me the cursed thoughts that nature
> Gives way to in repose ! "

like the God-fearing man he was, but it is all of no avail. He succumbs, and swift retribution follows.

Shakespeare lovers will scarcely need to be reminded of the innate sense of religion which is so outstanding a characteristic of Horatio as well as Hamlet :

> " *Hamlet.* There's a divinity that shapes our ends
> Rough-hew them how we will.
>   *Horatio.*   That is most certain."

But what is more important than these isolated cases is the general sense and unanalysable impression from all Shakespearean tragedy. As Bradley very truly says :

> " Sometimes from the very furnace of affliction a conviction seems borne to us that somehow, if we could see it, this agony counts as nothing against the heroism and love which appear in it and thrill our hearts. Sometimes we are driven to cry out that these mighty or heavenly spirits who perish are too great for the little space in which they move, and that they vanish not into nothingness but into freedom. Sometimes from these sources and from others comes a presentiment, formless but haunting and even profound, that all the fury of conflict, with its waste and woe, is less than half the truth, even an illusion, ' such stuff as dreams are made on.' "

And just because Shakespeare felt so deeply and sympathised so keenly with suffering humanity, his religion could not bear to be confined within the narrow limits of one strait sect, least of all of that sort of sect which, in a few years, was to banish the maypole and all gaiety, and substitute a horrible repression of all natural outlets for the emotions of the people.

His was the religion of weekdays as well as of
Sundays :

" ' Dost thou think because thou art virtuous that
there shall be no more cakes and ale ? '
' Yea and by St Anne, ginger shall be hot i' the mouth
too.' "

No man without a very real religion would ever have
possessed in such an accentuated degree that almost
divine gift of forgiveness. In all the later plays we
find that Shakespeare pockets all his grievances and,
God-like, pardons his enemies :

" The rarer action is
In virtue than in vengeance : they being penitent,
The sole drift of my purpose doth extend
Not a frown further."

Posthumus with all the reason in the world to give
over Iachimo to the death exclaims :

" The power that I have on you, is to spare you :
The malice towards you, to forgive you : Live,
And deal with others better."

No one will convince me that the man who coined
those two phrases was devoid of the religious
temperament.

Shakespeare did not shrink from heaping scorn on
to the heads of ecclesiastical hypocrites, when it was
necessary, any more than he ever refrained from showing up abuses in any branch of the State, even to the
delineation of such a man as Angelo, but he is likewise
not ashamed to put simple, sincere prayers into the
mouths of his soldier-kings, Henry V. and others, which
come straight from the heart of the dramatist himself. And, finally, to anyone who yet doubts, I would

recommend a close perusal of all that is to be found about Brutus in *Julius Cæsar*.

Shakespeare always leaves us on a note of hopefulness. We are never depressed by any of his tragedies as we are by the work of so many of the moderns. As Meredith so wonderfully puts it :

" How smiles he at a generation ranked
    In gloomy noddings over life ! They pass.
Not he to feed upon a breast unthanked,
    Or eye a beauteous face in a cracked glass.
But he can spy that little twist of brain
    Which moved some weighty leader of the blind,
Unwitting 'twas the goad of personal pain,
    To view in curst eclipse our Mother's mind,
And show us of some rigid harridan
    The wretched bondmen till the end of time.
O lived the Master now to paint us Man,
    That little twist of brain would ring a chime
Of whence it came and what it caused, to start
Thunders of laughter, clearing air and heart."

Tragedy is to Shakespeare a consequence of some obsession : in Hamlet the consequence of irresolution following upon too much thinking ; in Lear the consequence of a foolish inability to understand human nature ; in Coriolanus the consequence of too overweening a pride ; in Othello the consequence of a too credulous mind ; in Antony the consequence of an unbridled passion. In every case man suffers in a way totally disproportionate to the wrong done ; the point to notice is that in each case the calamities do not simply happen, nor are they sent : they proceed mainly from actions : the protagonist sets the wheels of Fate in motion and nothing can prevent their revolving to the inexorable end, the death, after intolerable suffering, of the hero. The tragedy lies in the fact that, once having started the course of events, man is no longer able to calculate the results nor to control them ; the interest lies entirely in the inward struggle ; but we are never depressed, simply because we never get the feeling that man is but a poor, weak creature. On the contrary, in most cases he puts up a magnificent fight and has so much greatness that we are led to dwell rather upon the grand possibilities of human nature than upon its downfall in this particular case, and, most important of all, we notice that the main source of the suffering in tragedy is evil. If, therefore, it is evil that violently disturbs the order of this world, this order cannot be friendly to evil or indifferent between evil and good.

This leads us to a consideration of Shakespeare's villains, among whom, of course, Iago takes precedence, much as Falstaff does among his men of humour. Ever since the day when Coleridge coined his magic phrase of " motiveless malignity," opinion with regard to Iago's temperament has differed almost as much as it has about Hamlet. There is no quarrel about Iago's intellectual gifts : he had not a stupendous intellect, but, within limits, he most certainly had a finely working brain ; it is almost as if Shakespeare had embodied his own intelligence in him. He is critical, but, strangely enough, not maliciously so. Think for a moment of his picture of the women. " You're pictures out of doors, bells in your parlours, wild cats in your kitchens," and so on. What could be wittier or fairer ? But Shakespeare almost immediately impales himself upon the horns of a dilemma from which there is no escape. Having endowed his puppet with brains, he then strives to make him concrete, which is a contradiction in terms, for intellect is never entirely maleficent ; perfect pitiless malignity is as impossible for man as perfect innate goodness. Again and again the reader asks himself why Iago is so venomous ; again and again Iago strives valiantly (in soliloquy) to provide us with a reason ; he adduces many : not one of them will hold water for an instant.

In the end Othello himself asks piteously :

" Will you, I pray, demand that demi-devil
Why he hath thus ensnared my soul and body ? "

Iago refuses to answer ; in any case, whether he would or would not, he could not, for the simple reason that he literally did not know. Iachimo is but the pale shadow of Iago, and even less of a real person. Edmund alone of the villains has gaiety, and is more or less to be understood. He is Shakespeare's only portrait of the adventurer pure and simple, though by no means destitute of feeling. He certainly lives for us, being neither all black nor all white, as so many of the dramatist's characters are.

There is one other point in connection with Shakespearean tragedy which is not the least important part of its hold upon our imagination. I mean the continual use which Shakespeare makes of irony, particularly in *Macbeth*, irony on the part of the author himself, ironical juxtapositions of persons and events, and especially that species which we call " Sophoclean," whereby a speaker is made to use words bearing to the audience, in addition to his own meaning, a further and ominous sense, hidden from himself and, usually, from the other persons on the stage.

Macbeth's first words—

" So foul and fair a day I have not seen "—

are a famous example of this, echoing, as they do, the witches' " Fair is foul, and foul is fair."   " Fail not our feast," says Macbeth, later, to Banquo, who is about to be murdered. " My lord, I will not," is his blood-curdling reply—and he keeps his promise.

Instances of this will occur at once to all readers of the tragedies ; this device is extremely useful for contributing to excite the vague fear of hidden forces operating on minds unconscious of their influence ; added to this, and far more potent, of course, is the machinery of the unseen world and the spirit of evil, to the Elizabethan audiences a far more real dread than it is to us.

iv

Both in the tragedies and comedies it is essential that we take into account the audiences for whom Shakespeare wrote : their credulity (if we can call it so) was extraordinary ; witchcraft was treated with respect, as we discover in Reginald Scot's *Discoverie of Witchcraft* (1584). Fairy lore and astrology occupied the serious attention of vast numbers of the populace—but far more important than this, from our point of view, is the insatiable thirst for poetry, which was almost the most pronounced characteristic of these rough, bloodthirsty men who thronged, afternoon after afternoon, in the theatres, fresh from the Spanish Main or the battle-fields in Flanders. Men were beginning to use their language and extend their vocabulary ; new ideas of amazing import were penetrating their senses daily. They began " to go crazy " over poetry ; they all wrote it, they all demanded it from their favourite playwrights. Shakespeare, as usual, gave the public what the public wanted ; it is a noteworthy feature of his genius that he seemed to pander to the public taste by giving them all their old favourite machinery while changing this machinery in the crucible of his mind into the undying individual men and women we now know. For example, the audience demanded a fool and he gave them Feste and the Fool in *Lear*. They demanded a Jew who should be baited and he gave them Shylock. They demanded witches and he gave them *Macbeth*. They demanded blood and he gave them *Othello* and *Hamlet*. Most of all they demanded poetry, and he gave them thirty-seven plays so steeped in magic that he caused the English language to become the chief instrument of civilisation, the world-speech of humanity at large.

Shakespeare found the blank-verse form a powerful vehicle of dramatic elocution as used by Marlowe and perfected it until in his years of maturity almost unwittingly he seemed to coin a new heaven and a new earth of language; here as elsewhere, however, it is as well to recognise that he was no innovator as Wordsworth was; he did not invent the blank-verse form any more than he invented the plots for his plays: he took whatever he found to be grist for his mill, as all geniuses do, from the store-cupboard of all the writers who had lived before him—discarding here, adding there, with no thought but of benefiting from them and improving upon their mistakes. He must have been an omnivorous reader, much of the same type as Doctor Johnson, who tore the hearts out of books ruthlessly in order to extract the honey from them expeditiously. The fact that Shakespeare was an actor surely helped him enormously; knowing as he did the exigencies of the stage, he would in his remodelling of old plays know exactly how to adapt them to meet the popular demands, and we shall do well to bear in mind the eight features that Coleridge noted when he tried to particularise on Shakespeare's peculiarities.

First he notices that Shakespeare gains his effect always by expectation in preference to surprise; this is ever the way of genius; his business lies in the unravelling of character. Your interest as reader or playgoer is in the development of character, not in sudden surprises. In *Macbeth*, for instance, we are led gradually to expect the murder of Duncan; that is not the climax of the play; it is the result of the murder upon Macbeth's inner consciousness that so holds our attention that we scarcely dare to draw a breath until the last scene; so it is with *Hamlet*. It is the strange, unaccountable reluctance in the hero to take the obvious way that so enthralls us; we feel how extraordinarily natural it all is and yet how desperately tragic; the excitement is all the more tense because we are led to expect various things; we don't want the cheap substitution of surprise for expectation.

Secondly, Coleridge notices how Shakespeare adheres to the law that opposites attract, a point not even now sufficiently recognised by those who study the psychology of the human race. What was it that attracted the energetic, highly intellectual Hamlet in the anæmic, spiritless doll, Ophelia? What was it that so endeared the gentle Desdemona to the warrior Othello? Why ever did Emilia marry Iago or Imogen Posthumus? What had Henry the Fifth in common with Falstaff or Falstaff with him? Again and again we see this trait in Shakespeare, only explicable at all if we remember how extraordinarily true it is in real life that opposites have a strange attraction for each other.

The third point is that Shakespeare always keeps on the high road; he has no innocent adulteries, no sentimental rat-catchers, no æsthetic butchers; he does not penetrate the obscure corners of life. This

is the same feature which Meredith recognised when
he said :

" He probed from hell to hell
   Of human passions, but of love deflowered
His wisdom was not for he knew thee [Mother Earth]
   well.

There is no " sick philosophy " in Shakespeare as there
has been in so much of our modern writing ; he had
no leanings towards an inverted morality which would
prove immorality moral and all morality immoral. It
is with a sense of getting back to clean, fresh air, after
having been immured in a cesspool, that we read
Shakespeare after some of our latter-day prophets.

Shakespeare's fourth peculiarity is his absolute independence between the dramatic interest and the plot :
the plot is simply the canvas, nothing more ; it is quite
secondary to and independent of the main purpose
—the unfolding of character. This explains once again
why Shakespeare never troubled to invent a plot ; the
fifth peculiarity follows from the fourth, and is
the independence of the interest on the story as the
groundwork of the plot.

The sixth feature is the interfusion of the lyrical with,
in and through the dramatic. Songs, Coleridge noticed,
in Shakespeare are introduced as songs only ; and yet
how he heightens the humour, tightens the intensity
and more forcibly brings home to us the point of view
he would have us carry away. His personal love of
music to a great extent, of course, accounts for this,
but it is as well to remember how here again he takes
the old machinery and turns it to his own good purpose.

The seventh point is perhaps the most important of
all : it is that the characters of the *dramatis personæ*,
like those in real life, are to be *inferred* by the reader ;

they are not told to him. This is the reason why we come to so many different conclusions in our readings of the different characters; for years we are content to take other men's opinions, and then, suddenly, waking up from our lethargic acquiescence in their views, we re-read the play again for ourselves and find, perhaps, that Henry the Fifth was not the model man of valour we had been led to think him, nor Falstaff so much of a coward as we had been led to believe. We find that many of his later heroines are scarcely more than milk and watery abstractions, where we had before thought them glorious specimens of perfect English girlhood at its best.

Lastly, Coleridge would have us notice how every-thing, however heterogeneous, in Shakespeare is united, as it is in Nature; in other words, passion is that by which the individual is distinguished from others, not that which makes a different kind of him. These eight peculiarities are specially important for us to notice as we pass along, trying to build up for ourselves the complete picture of our Shakespeare. So far as he goes, Coleridge is seldom in the wrong, but there are several points still to be touched on before we can hope to have gained an all-round view.

V

For instance, Coleridge never mentioned the brilliant way in which Shakespeare introduced his very neces-sary stage directions into the text. When we take into account the absence of all scenery and the fact that these plays were acted in broad daylight, in theatres open alike to sun and rain, we begin to realise with what almost insurmountable difficulties the playwright had to cope, we are lost in admiration at the natural way in which the poet intersperses his hints about the time of day, the attitude and dress of the character, almost unnoticeably in the text. How often, for instance, in the churchyard scene in *Romeo and Juliet,* does Shakespeare lay stress upon the fact that it is pitch dark ! The opening words attune our ears to the general gloom :

> "Give me thy torch, boy : hence and stand aloof,
>   Yet put it out, for I would not be seen,"

says Paris. Romeo, after he has killed him, pretends that he has not been able to see his opponent's face : "Let me peruse this face." When Friar Laurence enters he begins :

> "What torch is yond', that vainly lends his light
>   To grubs and eyeless skulls ? "

Paris's page on his re-entry with the watch says :

> "This is the place : there, where the torch doth burn."

But Shakespeare not only introduces these very necessary hints into the poetry, but he sometimes, with magical success, makes his stage direction have a real bearing on the plot. The most famous instance of this is, of course, in *Othello* :

> " Put out the light, and then put out the light "—

when Othello comes in to murder Desdemona.

In *Julius Cæsar,* when Brutus and Cassius are communing apart, Shakespeare seizes the opportunity to emphasise the time of day by making the rest of the conspirators argue :

> " *Decius.* Here lies the east : doth not the day break here ?
> *Casca.* No.

Cinna. O, pardon, sir, it doth : and yon grey lines,
That fret the clouds, are messengers of day.
Casca. You shall confess that you are both deceived.
Here, as I point my sword, the sun arises :
Which is a great way growing on the south,
Weighing the youthful season of the year."

How extraordinarily it adds to the poignancy of
Macduff's suffering to hear Malcolm's

"What ! man, ne'er pull your hat upon your brows."

It visualises the scene exactly ; you feel that you
are really there, a spectator of the sad sight of the
strong man bowed with grief, unable to do anything
to assuage it.

Shakespeare more than any other man in the world
seems always to have the exact word or phrase at his
command with which to captivate our attention.
How graphic is that touch of "crying" in Prospero's
description of his wandering with Miranda in an open
boat in her infant years : "Me and thy *crying* self,"
or that wonderful use of the word "inly" in "the
inly touch of love."

Everyone will recall the "*hoary* leaves of the willow"
which were showing in "the glassy stream" where
Ophelia drowned herself, and Cleopatra's

"He's speaking now,
Or murmuring 'Where's my serpent of old Nile?'"

His language seems always to have been, as Hazlitt
said, hieroglyphical ; it translates thoughts into visible
images, so that you not only see and understand what
he describes but are yourself transported there. Think
of this description : "Light thickens and the crow
makes wing to the rooky wood." No other words

would do, nothing else call up quite the image which we visualise when we read this.

Strangely enough, when his characters are acting under the stress of great emotion, they have a wonderful habit of coining words. By far the best-known instance is the

> " No ; this my hand will rather
> The multitudinous seas *incarnadine*,
> Making the green one red "

of Macbeth.

It is here particularly that we congratulate ourselves on the fact that Shakespeare was unacademic and had no conventional prejudices to outgrow ; he would have no natural repugnance against coining a fresh word if his vocabulary failed him at a particular point. What he did possess was an unerring ear for music, so finely developed that words seem to come at his beck and call straight from heaven. It is this that makes us gasp at the pure magic of such a lyrical outburst as :

> "O ! my love ! my wife !
> Death, that hath sucked the honey of thy breath,
> Hath had no power yet against thy beauty :
> Thou art not conquer'd ; beauty's ensign yet
> Is crimson in thy lips, and in thy cheeks,
> And death's pale flag is not advanced there."

He had this gift from the very start. Think of the stupendous sonnet which begins :

> " Full many a glorious morning have I seen
> Flatter the mountain tops with sovran eye,
> Kissing with golden face the meadows green,
> Gilding pale streams with heavenly alchymy."

Could ever passionate love find more exquisite expression in fewer words than in the

> " O thou weed that are so lovely fair
> That the sense aches at thee "

of Othello ?

Or was ever a picture of Nature's beauties drawn that would parallel Perdita's

> " Daffodils
> That come before the swallow dares and take
> The winds of March with beauty : violets dim
> But sweeter than the lids of Juno's eyes
> Or Cytherea's breath . . . " ?

Milton's attempts, fine as they are, induce the criticism which Bagehot invented. " Why," he says, at the conclusion of a long description of natural phenomena in *Paradise Lost*, " you could draw a map of it."

This, then, is the secret of Shakespeare's greatness ; not only had he, owing to his experiencing nature, his large catholic sympathies, his ever-roaming, ever-interested eye, the power of visualising man's characteristics, but superimposed upon that he had the faculty for clothing his myriad thoughts in the most perfectly fitting expressions that it has been the good fortune of any genius to own.

It is easy to sum up his limitations, for they are almost trivial ; he does not seem to have been interested in novelties (he never mentions potatoes or tobacco ; we get a better insight into the common life of the Elizabethans by reading the contemporary drama of Dekker, Jonson and the rest of them). He had a supreme contempt for misers, Puritans and the middle classes ; he may have been a bit of a snob, and was probably sensuous—his faults only make him the more

human, the more lovable. What we do know about
him is that he was sunny, gentle, richly endowed with
a sense of humour which, in all probability, saved him
in the years when he probed from hell to hell the human
passions, but we know that he emerged serene in the
latest years, having discovered that

> "The rarer action is
> In virtue than in vengeance."

The power of being able to forgive your adversary
Shakespeare ranks as almost the most priceless attribute of man. He can even find it in him to forgive
Iachimo. "What an inhuman world," some modern
philosopher once said, "it would be without the old."
Youth is apt to be astonishingly cruel from the days
when in earliest infancy it deprives the fly upon the
window-pane of its wings, "just for fun." Shakespeare seems to have been the great exception to this;
he had a very real horror of all kinds of cruelty. He
was almost womanish in his dislike of harsh words or
blows; we feel that he could never have been a soldier;
he shrank instinctively from bloodshed as he shrank
from crowds, whom he did not understand but only
loathed, as sensitive people so often do. He was never
so happy as when he was in solitude or in the country,
where he could people the air with his fancies, yet he
took a delight in the material world or he would never
have been able to float those bubbles in the air or to lift
the land into mountain slopes so naturally, so entirely
without effort, as Emerson says :

"He had the faculty of being able to change places
at will with all humanity, turning the globe round for
his amusement : it is not that he seeks to edify us, he
wishes rather to amuse both himself and us . . . the

dreams of childhood, the ravings of despair were alike
the toys of his fancy."

His was not that cloistered virtue which Milton held
so much in contempt, which refused to sally forth and
seek its adversary; rather at times did gentle Shakespeare suffer horrible tortures amid the dust and heat
—"sed non sine pulvere palma." Through tribula-
tion he came to know men better, and out of the fire
he came purified seven times, so that he left behind,
as his testament to mankind, poetry so rich and full
of multitudinous beauties that the language in which
it was written has become the noblest in the world, a
gallery of portraits of men and women whom we know
more intimately than our nearest and dearest, and
thoughts couched in the most inspiring, unforgettable
phraseology that ever man could desire to solace and
refresh him in the arid deserts of life.

When we want to laugh, to cry, to be quiet, to be
boisterous, to find a friend, or be alone, whatever our
mood, Shakespeare can enter into it and provide us
with exactly the companion we most need. Of all
men who have really lived he is the first to whom
we turn when in trouble or joy; he halves our sorrows
and doubles our delights, for he is the most human,
the readiest to understand, the quickest to soothe our
troubled senses. It is the greatest privilege that we
enjoy as Englishmen that this man was of our blood,
an Englishman for the English. It is by far the
greatest achievement that we as a nation have yet
wrought that we have produced Shakespeare.

> "A rarer spirit never
> Did steer humanity."

II

THE EIGHTEENTH CENTURY [1]

NO century has received more neglect than the eighteenth; no century ever deserved neglect less. From 1700 to 1798 is a period full of good things, all specifics for our present-day malady. It is just a case of having given the dog a bad name and the name has most unjustly stuck. It will therefore be, perhaps, a good thing first of all to clear the ground and state exactly what the eighteenth century set out to do; how far it attained its aim; what it did not pretend to achieve, and wherein lies the difference between our own age and that of the earlier Georges. The whole century was given over to the cult of common-sense; it viewed any tendency towards such a thing as *Enthusiasm* with suspicion; clarity of diction, sparkling wit, sound material-mindedness, the avoidance of any exaggerated notions about idealism or other abstract " highfalutin " words, were conspicuously present in all its writers. Nothing could have been further removed from Shakespeare and Milton on the one side or the Romantic revivalists on the other. The field it set before itself to cover was a small one. The point to remember is that it covered it perfectly; it never failed to achieve its purpose, whether in prose, poetry, satire, the writing of letters, or the more gigantic feat of composing novels. It had no conception of " the desire of the moth for the star " theory, and Keats and

[1] A review of George Saintsbury's *The Peace of the Augustans*.

Shelley were right outside its ken. It had no dealings with the sublime, and it descended but rarely to the ridiculous. There was a robust sanity about it which compels admiration at all times, and it was rarely dull.

Now everyone will allow that the tendency to-day is all towards introspection, a state of continual hustle as we search after whatever chimera for the moment attracts us. Some of us believe (Mr Saintsbury is not among the number ; he seizes every opportunity to be rude to this fledgling century of ours) that the last few years have been productive of good poetry, lasting novels, and even of some signs of a sane dramatic re-vival. However that may be, the point rather lies in the fact that we have much to learn from an age when enthusiasm was regarded as a vice, and the end of knowledge, the habit of moderating the passions. It is a truism that our best work is done when we are " calm, cool and collected," as the nerve doctors say. Most of us suffer from too highly strung nerves, and consequently splash our canvas with all manner of colours, careless of co-ordination, of shadows and lights, only pleased that such and such a patch looks beautiful. There is to-day a very noticeable lack of method, a kind of neurasthenic irritability in the work of even the best men, which indicates the need for a long rest cure among the Augustans. In a word, our enthusiasms, excellent in intention as they are, need the tempering that can only be gained by a course of Swift, Johnson, Addison, Pope and the rest of a school who rarely suffered their passions to get the upper hand.

It is good for us to renew our acquaintance with Sir Roger de Coverley, Will Honeycomb and all the adorable bevy of bepatched beauties—Chloe, Clarissa, Vanessa, Flavia and so on, of *The Tatler* and *Spectator* ; to turn over the pages of Addison's or Steele's *Essays*,

and to watch Sir Roger at the play, in church, in Westminster Abbey, with the gipsies, at the Quarter Sessions
—to enter again into that life where ladies are laughed
out of their petty foibles and vain fancies, to read
Addison's Saturday sermons or his criticism on *Paradise
Lost*, interleaved with his sly reprimands to the oglers
and street-criers, the antics of the fan-wavers and the
members of the Trumpet and other clubs. It is all very
quiet, always witty, never heavy or dull, and, what is
most important, as different as possible from our life
to-day. And after Addison, Swift. Most wretched
in his own life, he never lifted the veil too far. It
was, as he himself said, only mankind in the mass
that he hated ; individual members of society he loved,
and, for all the carping of less understanding critics,
Gulliver's Travels does stand out as one of the most
humorous books ever written. Lacking, indeed, in the
comic spirit must that man be who is unable to be
tickled inwardly at the innumerable funny things in
Lilliput and Brobdingnag, or intellectually fed with the
amazing genius that went to the making of *A Tale of a
Tub*. It is all part and parcel of the scheme of the
century that Swift was so far able to control his passions
that he could write so sweetly (yes, sweetly) that children are kept from their play by the delights of Gulliver
and grown-up men and women can find refection
in the finest satire that has ever been written. But
it is to *The Journal to Stella* that we ought most surely
to turn if we want comfort and rest. Here we have a
slice of important history, a sketch of manners delightful
in themselves, a gazette in miniature, mingled pathos,
humour and love, pride and jealousy, all written not
in ink, but blood, making up a marvellous and quite
genuine autobiography. It is doubtful wehther, when
we require pure reereation, there is any author so

capable of gripping our attention and holding us as the man who wrote not only the above, but *Polite Conversation*, *A Modest Proposal*, *The Drapier Letters* and *The Battle of the Books*, to satisfy our aching senses.

Pope's place in literature has long been decided, but, because it has been granted that he is not a poet of the Wordsworthian order, it has somehow followed that he has been little read of late. We acknowledge his lack of originality, his insincerity and shallowness of thought, but his positive qualities more than outweigh these deficiencies. He is always witty, always polished and urbane, and never devoid of an intellectual quality that is not to be analysed, but is always felt and appreciated by all but the most meticulously romantic critics. The man or woman who fails to derive a very real pleasure from that consummately artistic mock-heroic epic, *The Rape of the Lock*, is sincerely to be pitied, while the *Essay on Criticism* and the *Essay on Man* sum up, in the most compact and charming style, aphorisms that have become the commonplaces of our everyday speech. The couplet about " true wit " is not the less valuable because it has suffered from too much bandying about. But we ought to reread not only Pope, but the sunny, honey-tongued Prior, Gay, Akenside, Churchill, Thomson and Young, all of whom contributed poetry of a kind that is at once direct, soothing, witty and polished. For far too long have these poets suffered an undeserved neglect and been chastised for daring to be limited in scope and execution. They form a very definite link in the history of English poetry. If they did nothing else they knocked a real sense of regular rhythm into the English head, and for this alone we ought to be devoutly thankful. But it is when we arrive at the birth of the novel proper in

Richardson, Fielding, Smollett and Sterne that we stand on the surest ground.

I by no means agree with Mr Saintsbury's estimate of our own age when he complains of the poverty of our modern novelists, but I readily acknowledge that, for pure rest and refreshment, Fielding, the perfecter of the direct narrative type of fiction, is better. There is so much searching of heart, so much dwelling on sordid details in the novelist of to-day, that we become troubled and " nervy " ourselves after a dose of their work. Fielding, on the other hand, enchants us. We are not in the least perturbed by the many accidents by flood and field that befall Tom Jones or Joseph Andrews; we watch the rapidly moving events as if in a kinema. We are transported to an age in which we most decidedly would not choose to live, but which is still picturesque, real, robust and full of sound common-sense and good humour. Partridge and Parson Adams are an everlasting joy, and give us as much real rest and happiness as any of Shakespeare's characters. I am convinced that no better prescription could be devised for those who would forget for a few hours the woes of to-day than a course of eighteenth-century novel-reading—not only all Fielding, *Pamela*, *Humphrey Clinker* and *Tristram Shandy*, but *John Buncle*, *The Spiritual Quixote*, *The Castle of Otranto*, *Vathek*, *Peter Wilkins* and *Moll Flanders*. All these novels are written with the one idea of *amusing* their readers and interesting them by excitement, suspense, pathos, sarcasm—by whatever means their authors could devise. That they succeeded for their own immediate readers is well known ; that they are less read to-day casts an unworthy aspersion on our critical faculties. For the by no means to be despised gift of story-telling, this age has never been approached, and it is this lost art that we now so much deplore and so much need to comfort and console us in our leisure hours.

Lord Rosebery only echoed an opinion held by very many cultivated men of taste when he declared that there was no bed book in the world to compare with Boswell's *Life of Johnson*, no other book which could compete with it as a solace for the convalescent. I myself can put on record that, when I had six months of forced indolence after a somewhat serious illness, Boswell was my constant companion and contributed more than anything to my ultimate recovery. And, as everyone has pointed out, Doctor Johnson is the eighteenth century in epitome ; no other age could have produced him. In him is wrapt up all the Augustan splendid sanity—its intolerance of cant, its magnificent common-sense (tempered in his case by a melancholy wisdom) ; its inimitable humour and avoidance of dullness ; its direct vision, which has been mistaken more often than not for platitudinising ; its habit of saying outright what pleased and what displeased it, regardless of quaint rulings of other ages ; its inflexible rigidity of principle, combined with a very real charity ; its wide knowledge, which has no sort of affinity with pedantry ; its curiosity, mingled with a wholesome scepticism ; its indomitable courage, coupled with that mysterious charm which so many of us for so long a time have held up to ridicule or scorned as being too childish for these latter days of wisdom.

Doctor Johnson is John Bull as we like to fancy him, not as travestied in the Press—superstitious, weak-kneed, maudlin or scandalmongering—but steadfast, robust, intellectual, religious, and not ashamed of being thought so ; companionable, witty and courteous (I repeat, courteous ; think of the Doctor's famous epigram to Mrs Siddons or his treatment of the inmates of his house); and it is not only Johnson the man whom we meet in Boswell, but the Johnson of *The Rambler*, of *The Vanity of Human Wishes*, of *Rasselas*, of *The Lives of the Poets* and *The Preface to Shakespeare*; Johnson the writer, with whom Mr Saintsbury would have us intimate. The legend that it is the man, and not the writer, who is able to afford us such a perfect rest and refreshment is radically erroneous. We ought to reread his works as well as to listen to his inimitable remarks. I would go even further and suggest that we no longer deride Johnson as a critic. Within his very obvious limitations he is not only a good, but a great, critic. I know few more illuminating, and no more refreshing, pieces of criticism than his remarks on Shakespeare. That he disliked blank verse is very plain—-he admits it; and, after all, every man is entitled to his own opinion. The question is, taking all his idiosyncrasies into account, whether or not he does shed light upon the works of the man whom he discusses. I answer unhesitatingly—yes.

Of Johnson's companions, Goldsmith, of course, stands out most prominently. For amusement and refreshment it would, indeed, be hard to name a more ideal companion. The most lovable of men in himself, his prose style has been the never-ending charm of all generations since; its perfect simplicity, its pellucid clarity and light humour have been the envy of all writers since. It is impossible to analyse it; it is sheer gossamer. But it is Goldsmith's versatility that is so amazing. He will write you a comedy, over which even a schoolboy will smirk as he reads it to himself; verses polished, descriptive, direct and even poignant; essays for which we cannot find high enough praise; a novel which still pleases and amuses every reader of whatever age; and even histories of

various kinds, which are a constant joy to anyone who
is ever lucky enough to unearth one in a second-hand
bookshop.

You can be sure of amusement, of absolute recreation and of perfect rest, whenever you pick up any
of the works of this astonishing Irishman. And so
we come to a branch of literature which even the most
blasé and " modernist " of the moderns will allow to be
the eighteenth century's peculiar gift—the art of letter-
writing. There must be something more than the
modern restlessness and hurry, the invention of telephone and telegraph to account for the rapid decay
of this fascinating department of the kingdom of
literature. Whatever the cause, it is an established fact
that never before nor since, in any age, have we had
letters to compare with those of Lady Mary Wortley
Montagu, Swift, Pope, Horace Walpole, Chesterfield,
Cowper and Gray. What a magnificent orgy is con-
jured up by the mere mention of these names ! We
take up a volume of any one of them, and hours afterwards may still be found glutting ourselves with their
witticisms, their pictures of the life and manners of
their times, their delightful anecdotes and the thousand
and one things about them that attract us. Lady
Mary, with her wonderful description of life in Turkey
and admonitions about her husband's prospects ; Lord
Chesterfield, with his never-failing Attic salt and
acumen, trying to model a perfect man of the world ;
Horace Walpole (to me the most interesting of all, and
to Mr Saintsbury so important that he recommends
these ten volumes as a " thirdsman " to the Bible and
Shakespeare), with his abounding vitality and endlessly
refreshing kaleidoscope of current events, portraying
the history of his time more exactly than any historian
could ever hope to ; Gray, with his scholarly and

scientifically inclined investigations, keeping his eye on the object like the true poet that he was ; and Cowper, most popular of all, with his pen pictures coined from nothing at all, able to interest us quietly, sedately, yet withal amusingly, about Olney, his garden, or a hare, the most exquisite small-beer—all these afford us a garden with never-ending pleasances and arbours, to which we can retire with absolute certitude that we shall return to the whirl of our daily round reinvigorated, full of new ideas, all our tangled skeins unravelled, and quietly confident because of our new-found peace. And wherein lies the magic of these peculiarly eighteenth-century letter-writers ? Is it not in the unfailing good sense, the inevitable good temper, the obvious leisured ease of the authors and the genuine interest betrayed and aroused in all sorts of different things ? Nowhere did the century find so natural an outlet for its genius as in this art, and to neglect these letter-writers is to miss a very considerable portion of the spice of life.

Of Gibbon and Burke Mr Saintsbury says but little ; he recognises the refreshing qualities of *The Decline and Fall*, but he by no means does justice to the gorgeous rhetoric of our noblest statesman. Lawyers invariably tell me that they always look on a man who doesn't know his Burke as only half educated, and certainly I have derived more considerable æsthetic refreshment from the speeches on India, France and America than in any writers of a like kind in any language. To some extent a novel depreciation of Sheridan has of late set in. There were better things written between 1700 and 1798 than his three plays, and critics wax angry because we don't read them ; but that ought not to blind them to the fact that in their class these comedies stand alone, and have been the constant delight of all

playgoers and readers ever since. No one in his senses
would deny that he gains a very definite sense of rest
and refreshment after seeing or rereading the comedies of
Sheridan or Goldsmith ; the stage, without these two in
this century, would have been poor indeed. But all this
time there has been an undercurrent of revolt against
the tenets of the Augustan school ; *The Fugitives from
the Happy Valley* were headed, of course, by Gray and
Collins, who, in spite of their personified abstractions,
handed on a very definite torch to Wordsworth himself.

Collins, in particular, had that peculiar dream quality,
that touch of pure lyrical softness, which haunts us in
the later romantics. He at least breaks with a school
which aims at neatness and polish and common-sense
above all else. *How Sleep the Brave* and the *Ode to
Evening* need no relative eulogy ; they are absolute,
final, ineffably graceful and sweet. Macpherson's
Ossian is, I fear, still caviare to the general, but its
popularity and influence were once widespread throughout Europe. The point is that this verse-prose, with
its breath of the blue mountains of Skye and the
Hebrides and magic vagueness, shows yet another
cleavage from the school of Pope. But it is when we
come to Percy's *Reliques* (1765), the most epoch-
making book that appeared between 1700 and 1798, that
we see the first real glimmerings of the great dawn of
the Romantic revival. How good it must have been for
the eighteenth century to read *Sir Cauline, Sir Patrick
Spens* and *The Nut Brown Maid*. It would, we feel, have
been worth while to have lived at that period, ordinarily
ignorant, and suddenly to have come across a copy
fresh from the press. No wonder Scott raved so about
it. I never met anyone, boy or man, who was not in
raptures over it when it was first brought to his notice.

It is difficult to analyse the charm which ballad

poetry exercises over us; the fact remains that we would part with many precious heritages before we would consent to lose *Chevy Chase, The Battle of Otterbourne, Young Waters* and so on. It is hardly necessary at this time of day to recommend people who are in need of rest and refreshment to go back to the ballad, but it is worth noticing that it is to the eighteenth century that we owe its revival and consequent popularity. Chatterton's *Ballade of Excellent Charity* and Smart's *Song to David* will never fail to provide restful pleasure to all who have eyes to see and ears to hear, but their place at this time of day is also well assured. And so we arrive at the setting of the Augustan sun. Cowper, almost as versatile as Goldsmith, we already know as a letter-writer. His hymns stand out as the finest we possess, his *John Gilpin* and *The Task* scarcely need mention here, but it is perhaps permissible once more to draw attention to the importance of *Yardley Oak*, which certainly contains matters entirely foreign to the earlier writers in the century. Here we have the imaginative visualising of everything, the half-pantheistic feeling of the community of man and Nature and God, which is so perfectly developed later on in Wordsworth. In all his poems, however, there is the same peacefulness and quiet humour which are so necessary for those in search of rest.

We feel, on laying down *The Peace of the Augustans*, that Mr Saintsbury has conferred upon the State a real benefit, for there never was a time when we all of us so sorely needed all that the eighteenth century has to give us—level-headedness, a sense of humour, a sense of quiet, even though oppressed and weighed down by innumerable troubles, robust strength, an avoidance of thinking too precisely on the event—all these and many more are the gifts which this age has to bestow.

It is all the more difficult when we feel so grateful for such a piece of criticism to have to comment adversely on many features, but, in common fairness to ourselves, a word must be added on the reverse side.

Never before can there have been such an astute literary critic who wrote so queer a language as Mr Saintsbury. His style has long been recognised as almost as bad as his criticisms are good, but in this book he has " out-Saintsburyed Saintsbury," which must weigh with university lecturers before they take the responsibility of advocating this book as a text-book of criticism. Furthermore, he is a Tory of the Tories, and obviously prefers a political fight to all the literature there ever was. Like many others of his belief, he is unable to understand the moderns, and consequently reviles them unjustly. Lastly, and most important of all, we close this book with a feeling that he himself does actually *prefer* the low-lying levels of the Augustan poets to the sublime heights of Keats, Shelley and Wordsworth. We feel that we have been cheated by a very clever counsel, who insidiously recommends that, for our sanity's sake, we should try his prescription of eighteenth-century literature ; and, when he has us in his clutches, he would have us leave all our glories of sea and sky and mountain, and stay with him in this field of very limited vision for ever.

The clever reader will take Mr Saintsbury's advice gladly *for a cure*, but, when he is rested, he will rise again like a giant refreshed with wine and come back to the present age, ready to fight afresh for the new ideals and the twentieth-century theory of life and letters, which anyone less biased than Mr Saintsbury will allow are in some ways finer than those of the nineteenth and certainly beyond the ken of the very earthy schemers of the eighteenth century.

III

SOME MODERN POETS

WHEN Mr Marsh first collected the poems most representative of his age in 1912, he kindly provided the critic with a beacon-light by quoting the following passage from Lord Dunsany :—

" Of all materials for labour, dreams are the hardest ; and the artificer in ideas is the chief of workers, who out of nothing will make a piece of work that may stop a child from crying or lead nations to higher things. For what is it to be a poet ? It is to see at a glance the glory of the world, to see beauty in all its forms and manifestations, to feel ugliness like a pain, to resent the wrongs of others as bitterly as one's own, to know mankind as others know single men, to know nature as botanists know a flower, to be thought a fool, to hear at moments the clear voice of God."

This brave venture appeared just at a time when there was no sale for poetry, when Richard Middleton was driven to commit suicide because he could make no headway in an age given over to materialism. It seemed that so far as the general public was concerned poetry was at its nadir ; the poet was, in Dunsany's words, truly thought to be a fool ; yet Mr Marsh persisted, and, as we now know, took the tide on its turn ; by May 1914 this slender volume had gone into its tenth edition : poetry had come into its own again.

56

Cambridge published its own productions in verse, Oxford followed suit ; quite normal citizens waited impatiently for fresh issues of " New Numbers," so that they might glut themselves with the poetry of Wilfrid Gibson, Lascelles Abercrombie and John Drinkwater ; where previously John Masefield alone had been able to create a public for his long narrative poems, now every new poet had a following, a coterie of devoted adherents. Then the war came, and with it the inevitable reaction. A writer of doggerel in one of the papers welcomed a new age of action which should cause us to turn aside from this foolish cult of reading and making poetry ; Mr Birrell publicly announced that it would be as well to give poetry the " go-by " until after the war ; publishers found that money lay in war books ; only in *The Times* did the dying Muse dare to assert herself, and there rarely with distinction ; silence would have been a sweeter swansong, but with the passage of days the public became discontented with *Secrets of the Prussian Court*; they longed for some seductive writer who would carry them away from the war and lure them back to an age when we were obsessed by less weighty problems, back to a time when destruction was not the world's united aim. Reprints of the great masterpieces began to sell again ; poetry, which but a little time ago was shunned by every publisher, is now being sought by them ; it is not easy to discover why.

Most of us can, of course, understand the reason for Rupert Brooke's enormous success ; he was typical of his age. Everything about him attracted something in each of us ; his intellect captivated some, his realism others, his sense of beauty ensnared the most perhaps, his poetry lives as the epitome of all our cravings and our strange perplexities ; we are like blind children in

the dark, and we cling to a slightly stronger brother
who can yet, for all that, give voice to our agony :

> " Who want and know not what we want and cry
>   With crooked mouths for Heaven and throw it by."

There is no doubt, too, that the manner of his death
enticed the great public to start buying and even
reading his work.

Most of the present-day critics are loud in their pro-
testations against this new school ; they say that in the
passionate revolt against the Romantic movement
they are rapidly working into a groove of mechanical
reaction ; that there is a danger lest their convention
become only a worse convention than that of the
Victorians, who drew beauty for its own sake as if it
were interesting quite apart from what is made of it ;
worse in that the young poet now draws ugliness for
its own sake, though it neither points a moral nor
adorns a tale.

This seems to be the one handle which the critic
turns unceasingly : Rupert Brooke was attacked for
his realism in *Jealousy, Menelaus and Helen, A Channel
Passage* and innumerable other poems. Even those
who professed themselves among his most fervid ad-
mirers exclaimed that they could not bear the introduction of words like " dirty " and " blear-eyed " into
the middle of poems otherwise beautiful. What such
people fail to realise is that in his search for beauty the
true poet must occasionally find himself confronted by
ugliness ; he refuses to shut his eyes to it ; he knows
it to be monstrous, unreasonable and yet almost a
commonplace to less sensitive, saner minds who can
accustom themselves to the monstrous and gradually
become blind to it, in direct proportion as they become
blind to the beauty all around them ; fearlessly he sets

out to correlate it with his other vision, and the result is to alienate men and women of weaker stomachs who imagine that he dabbles in uncleanness because he likes it.

In the first, and in some ways the greatest, poem in this volume,[1] *King Lear's Wife*, Gordon Bottomley has given such critics ground for complaint, which they have not been slow to take.

What right, they ask, has a poet to deduce that Lear in his earlier life was wanton, callous and neglectful of his wife, making mistresses of her maidens ?

They declare that this is a play of great beauty, spoilt by hideous touches, notably by lyrics about lice, which have nothing to do with the great Shakespearean tragedy.   In point of fact, anyone who has for years been troubled by the earlier play will recognise at once how much the new one clears up the ground.   It is impossible to reread *King Lear* after finishing *King Lear's Wife* without noticing again and again points that used to puzzle the imagination, now made perfectly plain.   Why did the old King, in his madness, burst forth into that frenzied speech about adultery ? There was method in his madness ; there always is in Shakespeare's madness.   " This is not altogether fool, my Lord."   His mind casts back to some episode in his earlier days, to Gormflaith :

" Open your window when the moon is dead,
   And I will come again.
   The men say everywhere that you are faithless,
   The women say your face is a false face
   And your eyes shifty eyes.   Ah, but I love you,
      Gormflaith."

[1] *Georgian Poetry, 1913–1915.*   Edited by E. M.   Poetry Book Shop. 1915.

The following passage sheds an entirely new light on the relationship existing between Cordelia and her much older sisters :—

> " Because a woman gives herself for ever,
> Cordeil the useless had to be conceived
> To keep her father from another woman."

Does it not help us in our differentiation between Goneril and Regan that Goneril is here shown firm, wary, swift and secret, the virgin huntress, harsh in her purity, one lustful to kill but one who would kill cleanly, full of contempt for her sister :

> " Does Regan worship anywhere at dawn ?
> The sweaty, half-clad cook-maids render lard
> Out in the scullery, after pig-killing,
> And Regan sidles among their greasy skirts,
> Smeary and hot as they, for craps to suck. . . ."

She kills her father's mistress and so obtains an ascendancy over him which she never after loses. " I thought she had been broken long ago," says Lear in his last speech. " She must be wedded and broken ; I cannot do it." What a blaze of sudden light this throws on Goneril as we have known her only in her later days. We gained some insight into Mr Gordon Bottomley's poetic vision in the earlier volume, but in *King Lear's Wife* he may be said to have arrived. Mr Marsh is not wrong when he speaks of the honour which the author has done to the book by allowing his play to be published for the first time there. All readers at once feel impatient on coming to the end that they cannot at once rush out and see it acted.

The quiet sadness of the neglected dying queen, the savagery of Lear, the freshness of the cold Goneril, the

tragedy of Cordeil, the lullaby with which Hygd is
hushed to sleep :

" The owlets in roof holes   Can sing for themselves ;
    Thesmallest brown squirrel Both scampers and delves;
    But a baby does nothing—She never knows how—
    She must hark to her mother   Who sings to her now " ;

the love-making of Gormflaith :

" It is a lonely thing to love a king,
    Life holds no more than this for me : this is my hour " ;

her singing in the garden, her premonition of approach-
ing disaster all go to prove that Mr Bottomley has a
sense of beauty and a sense of the dramatic.

No one would deny that there are ugly things here
and there, just as there are ugly things in life, but
certainly beauty predominates.   Goneril's worship on
the hills at dawn, raising up her " shining hand in cold
stern adoration Even as the first great gleam went up
the sky," her lament over the body of her mother :

" This is not death : death could not be like this. . . .
    I did not know death could come all at once.
    Come back : come back ; the things I have not done
    Beat in upon my brain from every side . . .
    If I could have you now I could act well . . .
    My inward life, deeds that you have not known,
    I burn to tell you in a sudden dread
    That now your ghost discovers them in me."

All these are beautiful, beautiful not with an exotic
richness that hides its meaning under a magic rhythm,
but beautiful with the inevitable simplicity of the
Anglo-Saxon, monosyllabic yet haunting. It is their
very directness, their terse, uncompromising, actual,
everyday speech that first attracts us in all these new

writers. Mr Bottomley does not strive to heighten his effect by the introduction of the quaint or the remote ; he is almost Blake-like in his choice of phrases. The result is that he has written a play which will long remain in the memory in spite of the weak machinery of the laying-out women which we could well have spared. It is a fine achievement, not the least fine part of its great attraction lying in that direct, straightforward simplicity which is the keynote to the whole volume.

Rupert Brooke occupies the second place of honour, and we are here given valuable glimpses of his later development.

In *Tiare Tahiti* we find him rebelling once more against the Paradise of the Wise ; he is so much in love with material beauty, " Miri's laugh, Teipo's feet, and the hands of Matua, Mamua, your lovelier head . . . " that he cannot reconcile himself to the idea that in another life there might be richness of life without matter and the individuality of matter :

" How shall we wind these wreaths of ours,
    Where there are neither heads nor flowers ? "

" There's little comfort in the wise," he concludes. To accentuate this point further there is also included *The Great Lover*, in which the poet shows us his over-powering passion for the beauty of the ordinary things of life :

"White plates and cups, clean-gleaming,
    Ringed with blue lines . . . new-peeled sticks
    And shining pools on grass."

His great regret is that they cannot accompany him into the life hereafter. His wit is shown by the inclusion of *Heaven*, in which the poet frames a religion and a view of the Beyond for fish ; a poem compact of bitter, caustic irony relieved by humour. One war sonnet and two more on the subject of the afterlife complete the extracts from one of the greatest poets of our time ; they are certainly representative and ought to drive anyone who has not yet read all Brooke's work (if any such exist) to remedy this deficiency. He who has given expression to all the insatiable yearnings of his age deserves its gratitude.

W. H. Davies is still the simple singer of the hedgerows :

> " And I'll be dreaming of green lanes,
>   Where little things with beating hearts
>   Hold shining eyes between the leaves,
>   Till men with horses pass, and carts."

Charming, naïve and clear-sighted, he stands quite alone to-day as an interpreter of nature.

Walter de la Mare is still master of that fairy language that captivated us so surely in the previous volume. None of us has forgotten the charm of

> "' Is there anybody there ? ' said the Traveller,
>   Knocking on the moonlit door."

It is not likely that we shall soon forget *The Mocking Fairy* of the new volume :

> "'Won't you look out of your window, Mrs Gill ? '
>   Quoth the Fairy, nidding, nodding, in the garden " ;

nor the delicate, fantastic joy in *Off the Ground* :

> " Three jolly Farmers
>   Once bet a pound
>   Each dance the others would
>   Off the ground.

> One—Two—Three !
>   And away they go,
> Not too fast,
>   And not too slow " ;

of their progress through

> "Withy—Wellover—
>   Wassop—Wo . . ."

until at last they reach the great green sea, whereupon
Farmer Turvey joins the mermaids and wins the bet.
De la Mare seems to make poetry for the pure delight
of rhyming, for the sheer ecstasy of hearing words
bubble like a mountain burn : the irresponsibility of
childhood, infants' happy laughter—these are the
things that his poetry brings back to us ; we forget
the scheme and order of life, its myriad perplexities ;
we are content simply to sit spellbound and listen ;
here, at least, is happiness of a sort.

John Drinkwater is a poet of very brilliant calibre.
He has certainly never before risen to the height that
he reaches in *The Carver in Stone* of this volume ; here
one may read exactly what is the impelling force that
guides the young genius of to-day ; this Carver with
eyes

> " Grey, like the drift of twitch-fires blown in June,
>   That, without fearing, searched if any wrong
>   Might threaten from your heart

is " Every-poet " of the Georgian age ; he is talking of
himself :

> " Slowly out of the dark confusion, spread
>   By life's innumerable venturings
>   Over his brain, he would triumph into the light

Of one clear mood, unblemished of the blind
Legions of errant thought that cried about
His rapt seclusion. . . ."

Here we find ourselves again in the atmosphere of
Rupert Brooke ; the sense of adventure, the sense of
an eternal yearning after self-expression, the brave
attempt to leave something behind us which will last
long enough to show those who shall come after that
in spite of multitudinous futilities there is much fine
stuff intermingled with the dross of the world if we
could only see it and translate it into real metal ; but
the Carver cannot bear the travesties which pass for
sound workmanship with the crowd :

" Figures of habit driven on the stone
    By chisels governed by no heat of the brain,
    But drudges of hand that moved by easy rule.
    Proudly recorded mood was none, no thought
    Plucked from the dark battalions of the mind
    And throned in everlasting sight."

Worst of all are the critics, wise

" With words, weary of custom and eyes askew
    That watched their neighbour's face for any news
    Of the best way of judgment, till, each sure
    None would determine with authority,
    All spoke in prudent praise."

Sickened by the inanity of the judges, when he is
bidden to reshape his chosen god along the walls of the
temple together with all his fellow-craftsmen, he seizes
on the idea of carving a queer, puff-bellied toad, with
eyes that always stared sidelong at heaven and saw no
heaven there. This toad seemed to him to stand for

an emblem of his kings and priests ; he loathed the
false work of his colleagues that passed for true and
so determined that his truth should not be doomed to
march among this falsehood to the ages.   So he chose
a secluded spot and there fashioned his toad, and round
it his people's gods, tigers, bats and owls " . . . all
signs of sightless thought adventuring the host that
is mere spirit " ; his leopard became " fear in flight
before accusing faith," his bull bore " the burden of
the patient of the earth."

> " And other than the gods he made . . . the stalks
>   Of bluebells heavy with the news of spring, . . .
>   All were deftly ordered, duly set . . .
>   Till on the wall, out of the sullen stone,
>   A glory blazed, his vision manifest,
>   His wonder captive.   And he was content."

In this poem we are made to feel all the wild, unsatisfied longings of the would-be creator, the ecstatic
joy of him who builds for eternity, the pæan of triumph
of the man who has risen superior to all the little
empty world of critics and out of the crucible of his
mind has formed and perfected solid, substantial,
lasting beauty.   It stands as the victorious anthem
of the poet of our era whose hand has found at last
something worthy to do and is doing it with all his
power.

No more shall we hear the cry of the restless spirit
of Brooke, no more will the sweet, exotic flavour
of Flecker's Eastern poems lull our senses in these
volumes ; of these two we take our farewell here, and
deep indeed is our regret.   Widely differing as these
poets were, they both attracted much the same lovers.
Who could resist the metre of *Yasmin* ?

" But when the silver dove descends I find the little
   flower of friends
   Whose very name that sweetly ends I say when I
   have said, Yasmin."

We hear it again in *The Gates of Damascus* :

" The dragon-green, the luminous, the dark, the
   serpent-haunted sea,
   The snow-besprinkled wine of earth, the white and
   blue flower foaming sea."

Unlike most of his school, Flecker relies for effect on
strange words and Oriental names ; there is more of
Keats in his beauty than in most of his younger
contemporaries. As a master of metre and lyrical
expression he stood high among his companions, as
can be seen in *The Dying Patriot* :

" Noon strikes on England, noon on Oxford town,
   —Beauty she was statue cold—there's blood upon
      her gown.
      Noon of my dreams, O noon !
   Proud and goodly kings had built her, long ago,
   With her towers and tombs and statues all arow,
   With her fair and floral air and the love that
      lingers there,
      And the streets where the great men go ! "

No more beautiful poem has been written since the
war began. And now he can sing to us no more. One
more apostle of beauty is lost to us just when we needed
him most.

No one who had read *The Hare* of Wilfrid Gibson in
1912 doubted that he had a rare gift of dramatic,
musical self-expression, but in *Hoops* he has outgrown

any puerilities of which he might then have been justifiably accused. Here again we have the passionate
love of beauty, this time beauty of form, as desired by
a mis-stitched, gnarled, crooked stableman and odd-
job man attached to a travelling circus :

" I've always worshipped the body, all my life—
    The body, quick with the perfect health which is
        beauty,
    Lively, lissom, alert . . .
    The living God made manifest in man."

Wilfrid Gibson seems to owe something of his easy,
colloquial style in verse to Masefield's longer narrative
poems ; he seems—alone in this book—to be carrying
on that tradition which threatened to become an obsession amongst our poetasters before the war. But
Wilfrid Gibson has something to say ; he does " see
beauty in all its forms and manifestations " ; he
certainly does, more almost than all the others, " feel
ugliness like a pain " ; though he does not shut his
eyes to it, as all those who have read his short volume
of war poems know.

Ralph Hodgson is a new-comer, and all true lovers
of poetry will welcome him with open arms, for he has
come to stay. *Time, you old Gypsy Man*, we regret to
see, is not included in this volume ; but that, after all,
is obtainable in *Poems of To-day*. We certainly could
not spare either of the two of his poems which are
included. Many people prefer *The Bull* to anything in
the book. It is a wonderful piece of realism ; the
beauty and horror of the jungle permeate every line ;
the whole poem is throbbing with life ; it reads almost,
as someone has said, as if it were written by one bull
about another ; we seem actually to see one tortured
animal

" Standing with his head hung down
In a stupor, dreaming things :
Green savannas, jungles brown,
Battlefields and bellowings,
Bulls undone and lions dead
And vultures flapping overhead.
Dreaming things : of days he spent
With his mother gaunt and lean
In the valley warm and green,
Full of baby wonderment
Blinking out of silly eyes
At a hundred mysteries."

. . . and now he is deserted, dying . . . and

" From his visionary herds
And his splendid yesterday,
Turns to meet the loathly birds
Flocking round him from the skies,
Waiting for the flesh that dies."

Ralph Hodgson more than fulfils Lord Dunsany's
definition of a poet, for he does more than know
mankind as others know single men ; he seems
to know the world of beasts better than most of us
know single men.

But there are sure to be some to whom this poem
will come as a *tour de force* ; they will acknowledge its
beauty of finish, the perfect workmanship that went to
the making of it, but they will deny that such a subject
is the end and aim of poetry.   Let such readers turn to
The Song of Honour ; there will they find a universal
hymn of thankfulness from all the world that should be
sung on the hill-tops by every lover of Nature ; it is the
hosanna of all created things :

" The song of each and all who gaze
    On Beauty in her naked blaze,
        Or see her dimly in a haze.
    The song of all not wholly dark,
    Not wholly sunk in stupor stark
        Too deep for groping Heaven."

All the songs that ever man sang are grouped together here and poured out in one glorious medley, the song of every singing bird, of poets, painters, wise men, beggars, of men who face a hopeless hill with sparkling and delight, of sailors, fighters, lovers, of men whose love of motherland is like a dog's for one dear hand, sole, selfless, boundless, blind :

" The song of men all sorts and kinds,
    As many tempers, moods and minds
        As leaves are on a tree."

It places Mr Hodgson among those rare singers who uplift us and put new courage in our hearts by reason of their sublime joyfulness ; we forget the real genius of his lyricism in the sheer unreasoning abandon of his theme. He makes us, too, want to cry out with thankfulness for being alive.

Mr D. H. Lawrence is a poet of rigidity ; some years ago he wrote some beautiful verses on *A Schoolmaster* ; since then he has been cursed with an obsession of sex which has threatened to destroy his equipoise ; he still achieves beauty at intervals, but there is an undercurrent of morbidity which disturbs the whole true current of his art. You see it most plainly here in *Cruelty and Love* ; somehow he always leaves us with a sense that lust is at the back of both his cruelty and his love ; it is too fleshly altogether : " He caresses my mouth with his fingers, smelling grim Of the rabbit's fur." The girl talks of her lover " nosing like a stoat Who sniffs with joy before he drinks the blood."

Mr Francis Ledwidge is the other new-comer; he sings sweetly, cleanly and surely on *A Rainy Day in April*. He is the singer of the open fields and may (we hope he will) carry on the tradition of W. H. Davies.

The only selection from Mr Masefield is not really typical of the last two years' work done by him, but it was the only one at the disposal of the editor. Probably all of us would have preferred *August 1914* to *The Wanderer*. Still, in some sense, the poem only goes to prove more conclusively than ever how radically wrong are those critics who imagine that these realist poets of ours are not just as desperately serious in their search for beauty as the most romantic amongst us.

The theme of the poem is the same as that which runs through nearly all Mr Masefield's poetry—the power of beauty, the blindness of fate :

" Blind pieces in a mighty game we swing :
Life's battle is a conquest for the strong ;
The meaning shows in the defeated thing."

There is the same true workmanship and perfect execution that characterise most of his work, but in some ways he seems outside the scope of this book ; probably it is because we were reading his *Ballads and Poems* twelve years ago, and all these other men are more or less new to us. One of the few precious cameos of a trifling nature which this book contains is called *Milk for the Cat*, by Harold Monro ; it is certainly a miracle of description, but it is, after all, a fantastic trifle. On the other hand, the theme of *Children of Love* (the infant Christ and the child Cupid) is most delicately handled, and is one of the many beautifully conceived ideas in the volume.

The volume ends, as it begins, with a play: Mr Lascelles Abercrombie's *The End of the World*.

The plot of *The End of the World* is quite simple. The scene is an ale-house kitchen; a stranger comes in full of news to the assembled drinkers, news which they attempt to drag from him by various means.   He tries to convey to them his state of mind :

" I wonder, did you ever hate to feel
   The earth so splendid and so fine ? "

They come to the conclusion that he is mad :

" Yes, I was mad and crying mad, to see
   The earth so fine, fine all for nothing " ;

he then opens the door and shows them a comet in the sky ; he says that that means the end of the world ; they are about to be burnt up :

" Time shall brush the fields as visibly
   As a rough hand brushes against the nap
   Of gleaming cloth—killing the season's colour . . .
   And sailors panting on their warping decks
   Will watch the sea steam like broth about them."

The publican wishes he had his old wife with him :

            " This would have suited her.
   ' I do like things to happen ! ' she would say,
   Never shindy enough for her ; and now
   She's gone and can't be seeing that."

Each man takes the news differently and calls down the derision of the dowser on their original scepticism :

" Ay, you begin to feel it now, I think ;
                        But Life,
  Life with her skill of a million years' perfection,
  Of sunlight, and of clouds about the moon,
  Spring lighting her daffodils . . .
  And mountains sitting in their purple clothes . . .
  O life I am thinking of, life the wonder,
  All blotcht out by a brutal thrust of fire
  Like a midge that a clumsy thumb squashes and
    smears."

Huff the farmer seizes the occasion to gloat over the faithlessness of his wife; now at least he will see vengeance. The man with whom his wife ran away comes in and Huff attempts to make him cower, but to no purpose, and the curtain rings down on Act I., leaving the dowser alone bemoaning the intolerable waste of beauty that all this scorching of the world will bring about.

On the rise of the curtain for the second and last act we see Sollers, the wainwright, wrecking the ale-house room in a frenzy of apprehension ; the publican comes in weeping, " I've seen the moon; it has nigh broke my heart . . . I never before so noted her." Beauty at last is beginning to mean something to him now that it is all about to be smashed up and ruined. Merrick the smith, begins to achieve a philosophy ; he begins to find a meaning in the life which is just slipping past him :

" You know, this is much more than being happy.
  'Tis hunger of some power in you, that lives
  On your heart's welcome for all sorts of luck,
  But always looks beyond you for its meaning.

The world was always looking to use its life
In some great handsome way at last.   And now—
We are just fooled. . . . I've had my turn.
The world may be for the sake of naught at last,
But it has been for my sake : I've had that."

Huff comes in, moody, unable to find comfort in the
vengeance he thought to obtain from the panic-stricken
evil-doers ; his good, straight life has been like that of
a crawling caterpillar . . . he thinks of a long day past
in Droitwich where he saw women half-naked cooking
brine . . . he could have been daring once but missed
his chance.   Suddenly Shale, his wife's lover, comes in
and implores Huff to take his wife back ; Warp, the
molecatcher, enters during the scene that follows and
tells them that there is nothing to fear ; the comet
is going away from them ; Huff's ricks are alight,
certainly, but there is to be no end of the world—yet.
Mrs Huff turns both from her lover and her husband :

" They thinking I'ld be near one or the other
    After this night."

We are left with Vine moaning :

" But is it certain there'll be nothing smasht ?
Not even a house knockt roaring down in crumbles ?
—And I did think, I'ld open my wife's mouth
With envy of the dreadful things I'd seen ! "

There is no doubt about the fascination of the play ;
it holds the attention ; there is not a false note from
beginning to end.   It contains all the philosophy of the
younger school ; the unending search after beauty, the
refusal to shut the eye to ugliness and dirt, the endeavour to find a meaning in life, the determination to

live life to the full and to enjoy.   At all costs they strive
to avoid sentimentality ; these country folk in *The
End of the World* really live ; they may be coarse ;
they certainly have their tragedies, but they are human.
We seem to know them through and through ; we
certainly sympathise with their trials and resent their
wrongs as bitterly as we do our own.

This volume is intensely typical of the age ; everything is tentative, experimental ; we are no longer
satisfied with the old gods, the old ideals ; we set out
to prove all things and get most horribly hurt in doing
it ; but life becomes much more of an adventure ; we
are at least brave enough to cut ourselves adrift from
the old, safe, enclosed harbourage ; we make many
and gross mistakes, but we do achieve something ; we
begin to learn for ourselves what life really means and
are not content to let our elders tell us what they think
it ought to mean.

It means beauty to start with, and that is an almost
new thought ; at any rate beauty has to be found by
each individual soul at the cost of much sorrow of heart
and much unfortunate experience with the ugly ; it
means love, which is not so easily to be found as our
forefathers seem to have thought ; we are not to be
put off with shams . . . it means courage, and courage
is not to be cultivated in safety, in an arm-chair ; we
have to cut adrift, away from convention and laws
made for a milk-livered generation. *Georgian Poetry
1913-1915* is a brave book.

IV

SOME MORE MODERN POETS

IT is commonly said that the only true critics of poetry are the masters in the same craft, and if the case of Swinburne may be taken as typical, I agree. We think of Francis Thompson's tribute to Shelley and Masefield's contribution to our completer understanding of Shakespeare, and shudder at the thought of a mere prose-writer daring to penetrate the sanctuary and lay his rude hands on the beauty he can never hope to explain. Suddenly we think of Hazlitt and take comfort. To what critic do we turn so often, and why ?

Because he acts as half-way house in the ascent of Parnassus ; he is the intermediary between the gods and ourselves, because he does what the poets themselves never find time to do, and that is to translate for us exactly what they are at as he understands it. The poets are so busy doing things that they never stop to explain and we are left labouring far in the rear, panting, dispirited . . . and sometimes even sympathise with our intellectually moribund, materially minded acquaintances or relatives who start at the word " poetry " as if they had been shot, and exclaim : " What's the use of it, anyway ? What useful purpose does it serve ? " as if they expected it to be a dynamo in the physical as well as the spiritual world.

Those of us who have no poetry in our composition and yet delight in it as the cleanser and purifier of life, who regard poets as the unacknowledged legislators of the world, in some way are perhaps best fitted to bring a realisation of it home to the businesses and bosoms of men ; we pay less heed to the technique (in so doing, of course, we miss some of the beauties) and more to the matter. For it seems to me of the first importance that a poet should have something to say. I don't exactly mean a message to bear, but a song that will ease the heart, cause æsthetic delight, help us to face life with a cheerier spirit, fuller of determination not only to see it through, but to make the most of it.

Poetry makes the deaf to hear, the blind to see, the maimed and halt to walk . . . if it doesn't do this, it isn't poetry. Hence it follows that sincerity and nobility of purpose are as essential to our poet as sweetness and music ; in fact, these follow from it, for there is no sweetness where there is no light and no music where there is no motive. Facile versifiers abound ; you pick up their stuff in all the daily and weekly papers ; they are not to be despised any more than an undergraduate is to be despised for dishing up second-hand opinions to his tutor and calling it an essay ; it is popularly known as an education. It may be ; you and I are not professors, we are not paid to read or give academic exercises—we needn't waste our time over what appears in ephemeral journals.

In times of intense emotional crises, face to face with the eternal realities of birth and love and death, man will sing ; he cannot help it. Consequently we seem to be at present a nation of soldier-poets and poet-soldiers. All I can do is to make a haphazard selection and try to show how the mosaic fits, how far they cohere and where they cut themselves adrift from the tendencies of their time.

It is a mistake to suppose that we owe this sudden renaissance in poetry solely to the war, for much of the work now appearing was written before or regardless of it.

Flecker, for instance, was doomed before ever its shadow came.   In some degree he is the most modern of them all, for he returned to that tradition against which the Georgians set themselves.   He reacted consciously against that reaction from the tradition of material beauty, which is so marked a feature of all the twentieth-century poets.   He rebelled against the idea that there should be any message in poetry, and set out, sharpening his tools at the best forge, that of continuous energy, with the sole idea of creating beauty.   " It is not," he says, " the poet's business to save man's soul, but to make it worth saving."   Consequently in all his mature work we get a riot of colour and sensuous beauty, names and men and relics made romantic and bizarre.

When he was in England he longed for the East, but when he attained his wish he wished to be in England once again.   Like all of us, he was happiest in the place where he was not.

Unlike most poets he did not try to transform the common into the miraculous, but rather pressed on at once into the virgin region of fantasy, and so we get the exquisite *Golden Journey to Samarkand*, on which, in the mind of the general reader, Flecker's fame will rest.   Has ever poet hit upon a more haunting melody than that of *Yasmin* and *The Gates of Damascus* ?

But it must not be imagined that because he dwelt so persistently on beauty that he has left us no idea of his own theory of the riddle of the universe.   " We poets crave no heaven but what is ours," he says, and his heaven is this familiar world refashioned without man's and Nature's pain . . .

> " Grant me earth's treats in Paradise to find,
>   Nor listen to that island-bound St John,
>   Who'd have no Sea in Heaven, no Sea to sail upon ! "

thereby linking himself up with both Kipling and Brooke.

So insistent is his love for the sea and the beauty of ships that I doubt whether I could find any poem more typical of Flecker's work than *The Old Ships*. We have in it that delicious honey of Hymettus, admixture of colour and sensuous beauty that have made his name famous to-day and will cause a place to be reserved for him eternally in the Temple of Parnassus.

THE OLD SHIPS

I HAVE seen old ships sail like swans asleep
Beyond the village which men still call Tyre,
With leaden age o'ercargoed, dipping deep
For Famagusta and the hidden sun
That rings black Cyprus with a lake of fire ;
And all those ships were certainly so old—
Who knows how oft with squat and noisy gun,
Questing brown slaves or Syrian oranges,
The pirate Genoese
Hell-raked them till they rolled
Blood, water, fruit and corpses up the hold.
But now through friendly seas they softly run,
Painted the mid-sea blue or shore-sea green,
Still patterned with the vines and grapes in gold.
But I have seen

Pointing her shapely shadows from the dawn
And image tumbled on a rose-swept bay
A drowsy ship of some yet older day ;
And, wonder's breath indrawn,
Thought I—who knows—who knows—but in that
  same
(Fished up beyond Aeaea, patched up new
—Stern painted brighter blue—)
That talkative, bald-headed seaman came
(Twelve patient comrades sweating at the oar)
From Troy's doom-crimson shore,
And with great lies about his wooden horse
Set the crew laughing, and forgot his course.
It was so old a ship—who knows, who knows ?
—And yet so beautiful, I watched in vain
To see the mast burst open with a rose,
And the whole deck put on its leaves again.

This and *Brumana* seem to me to mark the high-water mark of Flecker's genius.

But I want to leave the well-known men and talk almost at random about one or two of the hundreds who are writing poetry in partial obscurity, to see how far they carry on the tradition of their masters.   There was recently published a slim volume called *Fragments*, by a subaltern in the Welsh Guards, Evan Morgan, out of which I will quote one sonnet.

LABURNUM

Lo ! from thy verdant arms drooping and pensile,
Molten gold falls in summer-scented cones ;
Clinging with quivering tongue, thirsty, prehensile,
Into thy lips thy velvet lover drones.

Subtle thy raiment, shading thy umber arms,
Falls like to sun-bars, or maiden's aureole tresses ;
Piercing thy emerald cloak, naked thy charms,
Lie for passion'd June's untuned caresses.
One early rose-kissed cloud of morning's love
Saw through thy tapestries a naked nymph
Amidst thy sinuous arms more sinuous move
And slip into the lily-painted lymph.
Her God-like lover with a silvery net
Drew back his prize all glistening and all wet.

There is much in this sonnet which will cause grave searchings of heart among the older school of poets, but it has freshness, it is original if slightly bizarre in tone and rather too intellectual. The influence of Rupert Brooke is immediately manifest. Morgan is an obvious disciple both of Flecker and Brooke, though he necessarily lags far behind. Like so many of these young poets, he is careless about rhyme schemes ; he rhymes " ore " with " floor," " amber " with " unbar " and even " castle " with " battle." His publisher allows such ridiculous solecisms as

" The clouds are shook out in their play."
" Thou shouldst lift up your hands, dear, and nestle me
    over your heart."

We forgive all the touches of cœnobitic loons and ocelliferous leaves (even Cowper never descended so low as that !) when we come across the perfect simplicity of *Song in Valediction* and the sensuous loveliness of *Laburnum*. He plays with realism in an odious sonnet to a drift of seaweed, and dwells too frequently on anatomical perfection ; it is all very young, but certainly worth doing . . . as he says, and he is his own best critic, " Here is Love, Joy, Sorrow, Reflection, a cosmopolitan piece, ill-shapen, sincere." The ill-shape may be grown out of; sincerity is too rare and too valuable to be sneered at. We welcome him among the Georgians.

My next example is Egbert T. Stanford. His influences are William Blake and Francis Thompson, as will be seen in *Great in their Littleness*. His one object is to take the common things of life and weave them into song. He is the apostle of light and happiness. " Life looms with laughter: God fills our world with gladness to the brim," he sings again and again, trilling like a lark for the pleasure that is in him. After treading the fire-strewn floors of hell he emerges strengthened, joyful and endowed with the gift of pure lyrical song, and, like all true poets, has something to say which strikes an entirely new chord. I seem to remember a text in the Bible which runs somehow like this: " Blessed are the barren; for they shall bear children "—the kind of paradoxical phrase I could not understand. To Mr Sandford as to Blake such things are pellucidly clear, and in *The Voice* he translates so that we purblind people can realise the glory and the truth of that prophecy. His is the gospel of song, and strife and love and life.

GREAT IN THEIR LITTLENESS

THE faintest star in darkest night
Adds light unto the realms of light.

The smallest wave that breasts the sea
Helps with the ocean's melody.

The frailest flower that decks earth's sod
Lends lustre to the feet of God.

THE VOICE

DEEP from a day, as sunless as 'twas lone,
There came a voice,
Saying to her : " Rejoice !
Not every child is formed of flesh and bone.

" So, when his eyes are bruised and stained with tears,
Do thou bring forth sweet Laughter.   When wild fears
Assail his soul, then let thy little one
Be Joy ; and bid thy children run—
Run straight to him.—Ah ! Dost thou know—
Thine offspring shall wax strong
And thou, thyself, shalt go
From strength to strength, with them.   E'en though
Thou couldst not be the mother of his son,
Thou still mayst be the Mother of his Song."

"Live ! Live ! Live !" he writes. "They only
die who never try to live."

How exactly he echoes the thoughts of every woman
in the land in *Her Prayer—For Him*.

HER PRAYER—FOR HIM

I DO not ask that he may never yield
When fighting on the foam or on the field,
Since this I know :—
Where'er his country calls my man will go.
I only pray
That while he is away
You guard and guide him day by day !

And give me strength to tend his little ones
Until he comes.
On land or sea,—
Wherever he may be,
God, kiss my man for me !

In the last two poems which I have time to quote of
his, as in the one I have just quoted, we find the same
universality : in each he crystallises a point of view
that all of us have kept in the secret recesses of our
hearts and not been able, for want of adequate
expression, to give voice to.

IF I SHOULD DIE

IF I should die
Before you, dear,
God knows that I
Would be so lonely in that other Land ;
Yet, I am sure that He would understand,
And have permission given
That I might wander in and out of Heaven
To meet you, here.
Love, shall I tell you where to look for me
In that dim day ?—
Not in the silent grave-yard way,
Through which grim ghosts of sorrow stray,
I shall not tarry there—
Come to a sunlit bush or tree,
To wind-swept moor, to storm-lashed sea ;
By brook, or bank, or flower, or star,
And, where the stained-with-struggle are—
Look for me there ! look for me there !

IN WAR

SHE spread the cloth for two
And placed his chair.
Then cried : " How silly !
Why, I thought that he was here."

At length there came a letter,
Saying : " Dear,
Did you find me yesterday ? . . .
. . . How I did pray
That I might meet you
In our wee home-way." . . .
Ah, then she knew
Why she had placed his chair,
And plate, and cup and saucer . . .
He was there.

Mr Theodore Maynard, my next choice, may be
known to you. I certainly hope so, for if not
you have missed a real poet. His slim volume,
called *Laughs and Whifts of Songs*, is a real delight.
He is one of those enthusiasts who have shirked
no battle for the stricken earth against its tyrants'
spears and arbalests with courage and with mirth.
Yes—that is the word—mirth. He has something
of the large, fat, good-humoured touch of Gilbert
Chesterton, whose disciple he obviously is ; a mystic,
like Sandford, yet he is poles removed from him in his
sense of colour, which pervades every poem. He is
simple, sincere, direct, whimsical and withal humorous.
He is the poet of that serene cheerfulness which is the
peculiar gift of the happy warrior. We see that at once
in *When I Ride into the Town. The English Spring* is

just typical of the age in which we live, now that we have grown to recognise at last how lovely is our own land.   In *Apocalypse* we get that same hankering after material beauty hereafter which Brooke so exquisitely described in *Tiare Tahiti*.   *To a Good Atheist* and *To a Bad Atheist* show us the distance we have travelled in overcoming our ancient prejudices and at last arrived at a sane judgment.

APOCALYPSE

SHALL summer wood where we have laughed our fill ;
　　Shall all your grass so good to walk upon ;
Each field which we have loved, each little hill,
　　Be burnt like paper—as hath said Saint John ?
Then not alone they die !   For God hath told
　　How all His plains of mingled fire and glass,
His walls of hyacinth, His streets of gold,
　　His aureoles of jewelled light shall pass,
That He may make us nobler things than these,
　　And in His royal robes of blazing red
Adorn His bride.   Yea, with what mysteries
　　And might and mirth shall she be diamonded !
And what new secrets shall our God disclose ;
　　Or set what suns of burnished brass to flare ;
Or what empurpled blooms to oust the rose ;
　　Or what strange grass to glow like angels' hair !
What pinnacles of silver tracery,
　　What dizzy, rampired towers shall God devise
Of topaz, beryl and chalcedony
　　To make Heaven pleasant to His children's eyes !
And in what cataclysms of flame and foam
　　Shall the first Heaven sink—as red as sin—
When God hath cast aside His ancient home
　　As far too mean to house His children in !

TO A GOOD ATHEIST

THAT you can keep your crested courage high,
   And hopeless hope without a cause, and wage
Christ's warfare, lacking all the panoply
   Of Faith which shall endure the end of age,
You must be made of finely tempered stuff,
   And have a kinship with that Spanish saint,
Who wrote of his soul's night—it was enough
   That he should drag his footsteps tired and faint
Along his God-appointed pathway.   You
   Have stood against our day of bitter scorn,
When loudly its triumphant trumpets blew
   Contempt of all God's poor.   Had you been born
But in the time of Jeanne or Catherine,
   Whose charity was as a sword of flame,
With those who drank up martyrdom like wine
   Had stood your aureoled and ringing name.
Yet, when that secret day of God shall break
   With strange and splendid justice through the skies,
When first are last, then star-ward you shall take
   The praise and sorrow of your starry eyes.

TO A BAD ATHEIST

You do not love the shadows on the wall,
Or mists that flee before a blowing wind,
Or Gothic forests, or light aspen leaves,
Or skies that melt into a dreamy sea.
In the hot, glaring noontide of your mind
(I have your word for it) there is no room
For anything save sawdust, sun and sand.

No monkish flourishes will do for you ;
Your life must be set down in black and white.

The quiet half-light of the abbey close,
The cunning carving of a chantry tomb,
The leaden windows pricked with golden saints—
All these are nothing to your rag-time soul!
Yet, since you are a solemn little chap,
In spite of all your blasphemy and booze,
That dreadful sword of satire which you shake
Hurts no hide but your own,—you cannot use
A weapon which is bigger than yourself.

Yet some there were who rode all clad in mail,—
With crosses blazoned on their mighty shields,
Roland who blew his horn against the Moor,
Richard who charged for Christ at Ascalon,
Louis a pilgrim with his chivalry,
And blessed Jeanne who saved the crown of France—
Pah! You may keep your whining Super-man.

The Mystic and Free-Will carry on the same broad
sympathies and acute perception, and we take leave of
a real live poet in *Requiem*, which for sheer beauty is
worth its place in any anthology.

REQUIEM

WHEN my last song is sung and I am dead
    And laid away beneath the kindly clay,
Set a square stone above my dreamless head,
    And sign me with the cross and signing say:
" Here lieth one who loved the steadfast things
    Of his own land, its gladness and its grace,
The stubbled fields, the linnets' gleaming wings,
    The long, low gables of his native place,

Its gravelled paths, and the strong wind that sends
    The boughs about the house, the hearth's red glow,
The surly, slow good-fellowship of friends,
    The humour of the men he used to know,
And all their swinging choruses and mirth "—
    Then turn aside and leave my dust in earth.

Miss Eva Gore-Booth has already earned for herself
a name not lightly to be forgotten in *The Little Waves
of Breffny*, which is closely related to *The Lake Isle
of Innisfree*. She sings of the East, of mysticism, but
most of all of the sun and the wind and the April rain,
and the wild seas' shining plain, the ancient joy in the
world's young eyes, the blue hills' dim eternal range.

THE LITTLE WAVES OF BREFFNY

THE grand road from the mountain goes shining to the sea,
    And there is traffic on it, and many a horse and cart ;
But the little roads of Cloonagh are dearer far to me,
    And the little roads of Cloonagh go rambling through
        my heart.

A great storm from the ocean goes shouting o'er the hill.
    And there is glory in it and terror on the wind ;
But the haunted air of twilight is very strange and still,
    And the little winds of twilight are dearer to my mind.

The great waves of the Atlantic sweep storming on their
        way,
    Shining green and silver with the hidden herring
        shoal ;
But the little waves of Breffny have drenched my heart
        in spray,
    And the little waves of Breffny go stumbling through
        my soul.

You would not expect me to introduce a Guardsman to you with such a remark, but Captain Colwyn Philipps, devotee of Rudyard Kipling as he was, has in his best work so simple and sincere a feeling that he achieves almost unconsciously the poetic in his pity and love for all humanity.   There is no need for me to quote extracts from his work, for, like his fellow-captain, Charles Sorley, he is very widely read.   These two, whom we could ill spare as poets and still less as men, have both been killed, and England is the poorer—all the best men go—as if God were jealous of our too good fortune in having them.

I turn now from individual works to anthologies, and first I would very shortly commend to your notice *The Country Life Anthology of Verse*, which maintains a level of excellence which I can best typify by selecting just two poems, *Separation* and *Parliament Hill*.   Even the weekly papers contain poetry of a kind that is certainly far removed from mere verse.

SEPARATION

Though you have passed so very far away
Your life is mine, as mine is yours, to-day.
Time, space, are powerless and not as bars
Our groping thoughts to sever.
Dawns, faint and fair, and sunsets flaming wide
Still bring you to my side ;
And all high hopes that throb beneath the stars
Are yours and mine for ever.

But ah ! the little things for which I sigh,
As each day passes by :
The open book, the flower upon the floor,
The dainty disarray,

The sound of passing feet,
The distant door—
Alas, the little things of every day !
The silent eve, my sweet,
The lonely waking—
Alas, alas ! for little things my heart is breaking.

ISABEL BUTCHART.

PARLIAMENT HILL

HAVE you seen the lights of London, how they twinkle,
    twinkle, twinkle,
    Yellow lights, and silver lights, and crimson lights,
    and blue ?
And there among the other lights is Daddy's little
    lantern-light,
    Bending like a finger-tip and beckoning to you.

Never was so tall a hill for tiny feet to scramble up,
    Never was so strange a world to baffle little eyes,
Half of it as black as ink, with ghostly feet to fall on it,
    And half of it all crammed with lamps, and cheerful
        sounds and cries.

Lamps in golden palaces, and station-lamps, and
    steamer-lamps,
    Very nearly all the lamps that Mother ever knew,
And there among the other lamps is Daddy's little
    lantern-lamp,
    Bending like a finger-tip and beckoning to you.

H. H. BASHFORD.

A far more important volume is Sidgwick & Jackson's
brave venture, *Poems of To-day*, an anthology for

schools. Its significance is overwhelming. First of all
it means that we do realise our own greatness, we are
in no doubt as to what is poetry, and we recognise
the difference that it makes to the lives of the young,
who are of all people the most easily influenced by
imaginative work.

The selection has been made with infinite care,
and includes nothing that does not stand the test
which we apply to real poetry ; each poem contains
a theme musically expressed, a thought that could
not have been translated into words in any other
way.

It tells of the beauty of the country-side, of love of
women, of high and noble actions, of all that goes home
to the hearts of men. My quotations must necessarily
be short.

The selections are divided into three groups : of
History, of the Earth, " of England again and the
longing of the exile for home, of this and that familiar
country-side, of woodland and meadow and garden, of
the process of the season, of the open road and the wind
on the heath, of the city, its deprivations and its con-
solations," and finally of life itself, " of the moods in
which it may be faced, of religion, of man's excellent
virtues, of friendship and childhood, of passion, grief,
and comfort. All these poems mingle and interpene-
trate throughout, to the music of Pan's flute, and of
love's viol, and the bugle-call of Endeavour, and the
passing-bell of Death."

Almost every modern poet is represented, from
Stevenson, Meredith, Bridges, A. E. Yeats, Alice
Meynell and Francis Thompson, to Gerald Gould,
Chesterton, Lionel Johnson and John Davidson.

Here is one extract, chosen almost at random, from
John Davidson :

" As I went down to Dymchurch wall,
   I heard the South sing o'er the land ;
I saw the yellow sunlight fall
   On knolls where Norman churches stand.

And ringing shrilly, taut and lithe,
   Within the wind a core of sound,
The wire from Romney town to Hythe
   Alone its airy journey wound.

A veil of purple vapour flowed
   And trailed its fringe along the Straits ;
The upper air like sapphire glowed ;
   And roses filled Heaven's central gates.

Masts in the offing wagged their tops ;
   The swinging waves pealed on the shore ;
The saffron beach, all diamond drops
   And beads of surge, prolonged the roar.

As I came up from Dymchurch wall,
   I saw above the Down's low crest
The crimson brands of sunset fall,
   Flicker and fade from out the West.

Night sank : like flakes of silver fire
   The stars in one great shower came down ;
Shrill blew the wind ; and shrill the wire
   Rang out from Hythe to Romney town.

The darkly shining salt sea drops
   Streamed as the waves clashed on the shore,
The beach, with all its organ stops
   Pealing again, prolonged the roar."

Here are old favourites like Yeats' *Lake Isle of Innisfree* and Newbolt's stirring songs of the sea, Brooke's

Grantchester and Kipling's *Sussex*, Meredith's *Lark Ascending* and Thompson's *To a Snowflake*, Masefield's *Beauty* and the best of Alice Meynell.

But perhaps nothing remains more clearly in the mind than that vigorous, peerless pæan of praise of Chesterton, *The Praise of Dust* :

> " ' What of vile dust ? ' the preacher said.
>   Methought the whole world woke,
> The dead stone lived beneath my foot,
>   And my whole body spoke.
>
> ' You that play tyrant to the dust,
>   And stamp its wrinkled face,
> This patient star that flings you not
>   Far into homeless space.
>
> ' Come down out of your dusty shrine
>   The living dust to see,
> The flowers that at your sermon's end
>   Stand blazing silently,
>
> ' Rich white and blood-red blossom ; stones,
>   Lichens like fire encrust ;
> A gleam of blue, a glare of gold,
>   The vision of the dust.
>
> ' Pass them all by ; till, us you come
>   Where, at a city's edge,
> Under a tree—I know it well—
>   Under a lattice ledge,
>
> ' The sunshine falls on one brown head,
>   You, too, O cold of clay,
> Eater of stones, may haply hear
>   The trumpets of that day,

'When God to all His paladins
  By His own splendour swore
To make a fairer face than heaven,
  Of dust and nothing more.' "

The English Association has done more to implant
a love of literature in the young than any other body
in existence, but it has never done more for the younger
generation than by publishing this collection of the best
poems of the day. The book contains nothing which
does not make an instant appeal to the heart of youth,
and each of the one hundred and forty-seven selections
has the true ring of inspiration and stimulates the young
to imitate and excel ; it gives them a standard to live
up to and, at the same time, widens their sympathies
and opens up new vistas of romance and virgin lands as
yet unexplored.

Mr Erskine Macdonald has collected the work of
twenty-four soldier poets, ranging from Captain Julian
Grenfell's *Into Battle*, already a classic, to the outpour-
ings of Sergeant Streets.

Few of these brave singers, however, has so sure
a touch as Lieutenant E. F. Wilkinson, M.C., whose
two poems, *Dad o' Mine* and *To my People*, deserve
quotation in full.

" Midsummer-day, and the mad world a-fighting,
    Fighting in holes, Dad o' Mine.
  Nature's old spells are no longer delighting
    Passion-filled souls, Dad o' Mine.
  Vainly the birds in the branches are singing,
  Vainly the sunshine its message is bringing,
  Over the green-clad earth stark hate is flinging
    Shadow for shine, Dad o' Mine,
    Shadow for shine.

No one dare prophesy when comes an end to it,
End to the strife, Dad o' Mine.
When we can take joy and once again bend to it,
What's left of life, Dad o' Mine.
Yet for one day we'll let all slip behind us,
So that your birthday, Dad, still may remind us
How strong yet supple the bonds are that bind us
Through shade and shine, Dad o' Mine,
Through shade and shine.

Leagues lie between us, but leagues cannot sever
Links forged by love, Dad o' Mine,
Bonds of his binding are fast bound for ever,
Future will prove, Dad o' Mine.
Your strength was mine since I first lisped your name,
    Dad,
Your thoughts were my thoughts at lesson or game,
    Dad,
In childhood's griefs, it was ever the same, Dad,
Your hand round mine, Dad o' Mine,
Your hand round mine.

Strengthened by shadow and shine borne together,
Comrades and chums, Dad o' Mine,
We shall not falter through fair or foul weather,
Whatever comes, Dad o' Mine.
So in the years to be when you grow older,
Age puts his claim in and weakness grows bolder ;
We'll stand up and meet them, Dad, shoulder to
    shoulder,
Your arm in mine, Dad o' Mine,
Your arm in mine."

How far we have travelled from the sickly sentimentality of the nineteenth century here ! This is the

frank, fearless, outspoken affection of a boy, not afraid
to love his father and to express this love straightforwardly, purely and strongly.   It is simple, with the
simplicity of one who has faced the eternal reality of
death and has no further use for the reticence or the
" good form " which used to be the god of youth.

In the next poem he goes still further and puts into
poetry his convictions with regard to war, life, death
and the life after death :

" If then, amidst some millions more, this heart
    Should cease to beat,—
  Mourn not for me too sadly ; I have been,
  For months of an exalted life, a king ;
  Peer for these months of those whose graves grow green
  Where'er the borders of our empire fling
  Their mighty arms.   And if the crown is death,
  Death while I'm fighting for my home and king,
  Thank God the son who drew from you his breath
      To death could bring

  A not entirely worthless sacrifice,
  Because of those brief months when life meant more
  Than selfish pleasures.   Grudge not then the price,
  But say, ' Our country in the storm of war
  Has found him fit to fight and die for her,'
  And lift your heads in pride for evermore.
  But when the leaves the evening breezes stir
      Close not the door.

  For if there's any consciousness to follow
  The deep, deep slumber that we know as Death,
  If Death and Life are not all vain and hollow,
  If Life is more than so much indrawn breath,

Then in the hush of twilight I shall come—
One with immortal life, that knows not Death
But ever changes form—I shall come home ;
Although, beneath
A wooden cross the clay that once was I
Has ta'en its ancient earthy form anew.
But listen to the wind that hurries by,
To all the Song of Life for tunes you knew.
For in the voice of birds, the scent of flowers,
The evening silence and the falling dew,
Through every throbbing pulse of nature's powers—
I'll speak to you."

This is brave and it is new; moreover, and infinitely more important, it is true. It states a quite
definite fact, a fact as comforting and uplifting as it
is certain. It is also poetry, if poetry means the out-
pourings of a spirit that will not be denied, the expression and crystallisation of a thought that cannot be
expressed or crystallised in any other way.

This volume is likely to prove of invaluable service
as a factor in the new education. Now that Sir Arthur
Quiller-Couch would have all our young men compose
poems, not in order to be poets, but to perfect themselves in the expression of their ideas, it is as well that
they should have easy access to all that is best in the
work of the moderns.

So many beginners imagine that the composition of
poetry is a heaven-sent gift, that the lines just come
and you write them down ; here is a strong corrective
for such loose thinking. If every would-be poet were
set down to study the technique and intricate rhyme
schemes of half the poems in this book, they would
learn a much-needed lesson.

Most of us have an overpowering love for some

corner of England, which we would give a deal to be able to put into words. It will help us more than a little to study the way in which greater men have tackled the subject : by constant imitation and conscious plagiarism we shall attain originality. This is one of the great paradoxes of progress ; each man builds his edifice, not on a plan conceived in his brain alone, but out of a vast and wide experience, based on the efforts of his forbears. The nearer they are to him in point of time the more valuable they are, for youth, especially the youth of to-day, is out of sympathy with the Tennysonian era ; he can understand Brooke and Flecker ; they represent the pinnacle of genius to him . . . and after all, why not ?

We talk a good deal about inspiring the young with a sense of beauty ; we form societies to take them to the tops of hills in order that they shall see and rhapsodise . . . it is a far easier and more beneficial act to let them see what the clear-sighted visionaries of their own age have to say about Nature's bounty : they will then extend their own vocabularies and learn to keep their eyes on the object and not indulge in vague and misty panegyrics or conventional, insincere idioms.

No one pretends that the book is complete ; it is enough that there should be people possessed of sufficient courage to declare that contemporary poetry is worthy of the study of the youth of to-day, but I should like a place to have been found for Gilbert Thomas' sonnet, *Birds of Passage*.

" Like swallows in some grey cathedral square,
    Resting awhile, then mounting free again,
    So round the cloistered temple of the brain
    Flutter the flocks of thought upon the air ;

And now and then, perchance, they settle there,
But oh, we strive to capture them in vain ;
For never will the wingèd soul remain ;
They sweep into the sky, and vanish—where ?
Return, ye swift, shy visitants, return !
Where have ye fled ?   To what enchanted shore ?
If ye our closest fellowship must spurn,
Return, and bring us only, as before,
Some vague, sweet song that makes the spirit burn—
Some twilight whispering of faëry lore ! "

The Catholic Anthology, as we gather from its Cubist
cover, is a violent attempt to divert our attention from
what we technically recognise as poetry to a chaotic,
disordered, formless type of versifying, mainly trans-
atlantic.

There are well-known names here, Ezra Pound,
Edgar Lee Masters, Harold Monro and Orrick Johns,
but no one of them succeeds in doing more than mildly
amusing us, except **T. S. Eliot**, who, in *The Love Song
of J. Alfred Prufrock* and *Portrait of a Lady* convinces
us that a poet has the right to free himself from the
trammels of artistic construction on rare occasions.

" And would it have been worth it, after all,
   Would it have been worth while,
   After the sunsets and the dooryards and the
      sprinkled streets,
   After the novels, after the teacups, after the skirts
      that trail upon the floor—
   And this, and so much more ?—
   It is impossible to say just what I mean !
   But as if a magic lantern threw the nerves in
      patterns on a screen :
   Would it have been worth while

If one, settling a pillow or throwing off a shawl,
And turning toward the window, should say : ' That
   is not it at all,
That is not what I meant at all.'

.   .   .   .   .   .

I grow old . . . I grow old . . .
I shall wear the bottoms of my trousers rolled.
Shall I part my hair behind ? Do I dare to eat a
   peach ?
I shall wear white flannel trousers, and walk upon the
   beach.
I have heard the mermaids singing, each to each.
I do not think that they will sing to me.
I have seen them riding seaward in the waves,
Combing the white waves blown back
When the wind blows the water white and black.
We have lingered in the chambers of the sea
By sea girls wreathed with seaweed red strown
Till human voices wake us, and we drown."

These certainly are lines " that young men, tossing
on their beds, rhymed out in love's despair to flatter
beauty's ignorant ear," as Yeats says.

There is a depth of feeling and a striving to articulate
without which no poetry is worth anything. What we
feel on laying down this volume is a rather harsh but
quite accurate judgment.

Would it not be better for these young men to wait
until they really knew what they did want before they
put on paper their childish gropings after truth and
beauty ? They are as uncertain as autumn leaves,
driven hither and thither by every whimsical gust of
wind, inconsequent, purposeless.

Mr Eliot, for instance, has all the makings of a poet,
but in the day of his success his lovers will think of

Miss Helen Slingsby and shudder that he should ever, even in childhood, have sunk to such a depth of bathos or failed to cultivate a sense of humour. That is the main fault of all these Impressionists : they have no sense of humour ; they strain at sublimity and achieve the ridiculous ; they take themselves far too seriously.

Turn from this side of America to Alfred Noyes' *Collection of Undergraduate Verse*, written by his pupils at Princeton University. His guiding influence is everywhere evident and we see the young men developing their sense of the poetic in a lucid, orderly manner ; these men are not only captains of their own souls, but of their words also.

> " All lovely things I love,
> Whether of sky or sea ;
> Earth and the fruit thereof,
> And the starry company
> That wander through Heaven above,
> Singing unceasingly.
>
> I love all sweet-voiced things :
> The coil of falling streams,
> The honeyed murmurings
> Of bees in their noontide dreams,
> And the brush of Night's great wings,
> That a sweeter silence seems.
>
> I love all silent thought
> Prisoned in cadenced sound ;
> And many a jewel brought
> From hearted caves profound :
> And yet in all I've sought
> Something I have not found."

This is a far cry from T. S. Eliot, and it is worth while bearing in mind that it is by a younger mind.

We see at once the influence of the great masters of English literature translated by Noyes himself :

" As I begin to see beyond thy rhyme,
  And learn to place each pleasing sound aright,
  And view the steps by which thy verses climb
  Through strength to beauty, and on from height to
      height ;
  Then I begin to feel that eagle's lure
  Which turns his gaze toward a challenging sun,
  To leave behind the dull and level moor
  For those high crags where glorious colours run.
  So would I know with thee that steep ascent,
  That difficult way to prospects yet unknown,
  The winding paths, the chasms deeply rent,
  The whispering pines by winds of poesy blown,
  And face that sun of song whose radiance flows
  In sky-born colours through this earth's dark prose."

Here we see at once the truth of that law which all true geniuses realise, that the human spirit in the height of its ecstasy desires and obeys the strictest laws ; the greatest freedom is only to be attained by severe apprenticeship, a paradox which needs very much to be brought home to the young writers of to-day. Mr Noyes ought to be a proud man to think that it is owing to his inspiration that the younger generation have grasped this fact, and are not ungrateful to him.

" Three things would I bring to you,
    Bring as a man to his mother returning ;
    A heart that is young despite the years ;
    The same old unfulfillèd yearning ;
    And all in all, let be what would,
    The keen, swift faith that God is good.

For these things do I owe to you,
Taught me once when I was a boy ;
And only the poor in heart forget
In graver times what they knew in joy,
Or think since their own small world is sad,
That the heart of the world is aught but glad.

Love of towers I learnt from you,
Skyward held like hopes of men ;
Love of bells across the fields
Heard at dusk intoned—and then
Just the way a yellow light
Fell from a window in the night.

The world is a world of Truth, I know,
And man must live by the truth, or die ;
But truth is neither a poor, dried thing
Nor a strumpet, tawdry, gorgeous lie ;
But just the fact, that by doing and giving,
Young dreams come true while a man is living.

So I would bring three gifts to you,
Got from you by loving and learning ;
A heart that is young despite the years ;
The same old unfulfillèd yearning ;
And all in all, let be what would,
The keen, swift faith that God is good."

It is in such a poem as this I imagine that Mr Noyes
sees those seeds which he speaks of in such high terms.
"The splendid task of carrying on the torch of literature," he says in his preface, "may yet be reserved for
America." Few of us would have guessed that the
extracts I have quoted were written by any except our
own youthful poets. The older country has extended
a helping hand to its younger sons across the sea and

shown them that sweetness and light come not except
by arduous practice in the imitation of the great
masters. The undergraduates of Princeton have at
any rate learnt their lesson admirably, and, to judge
from this volume, are a nest of singing birds presaging
a glorious future for a nation that has striven hard to
give voice to its high aspirations in prose and poetry,
without any too generous recognition on this side of
the Atlantic.

In conclusion, I hope I may be pardoned if I introduce the work of three boys. I have known and
attempted to educate many youthful poets, but three
of these, each absolutely individual and as different as
possible from the others, stand out from the rest.

The first, J. R. Ackerley,[1] is a captain in the East
Surrey Regiment. At school he was an avowed
disciple of Masefield. When he left he was about to
go up to Magdalene College, Cambridge; the war
broke out and he did the obvious thing. The influence of Masefield can easily be traced in *The
Everlasting Terror*, which I give in full, because I
think it deserves it.

THE EVERLASTING TERROR

To Bobby

For fourteen years since I began
I learnt to be a gentleman,
I learnt that two and two made four
And all the other college lore,
That all that's good and right and fit
Was copied in the Holy Writ,

[1] In *The Best of the Year 1922* (Collins) a poem of Ackerley's
was included.

That rape was wrong and murder worse
Than stealing money from a purse,
That if your neighbour caused you pain
You turned the other cheek again,
And vaguely did I learn the rhyme
" Oh give us peace, Lord, in our time,
And grant us Peace in Heaven as well,
And save our souls from fire in Hell " ;
So since the day that I began
I learnt to be a gentleman.

But when I'd turned nineteen and more
I took my righteousness to War.
The one thing that I can't recall
Is why I went to war at all ;
I wasn't brave, nor coward quite,
But still I went, and I was right.

But now I'm nearly twenty-two
And hale as any one of you ;
I've killed more men than I can tell
And been through many forms of Hell,
And now I come to think of it
They tell you in the Holy Writ
That Hell's a place of misery
Where Laughter stands in pillory
And Vice and Hunger walk abroad
And breed contagion 'gainst the Lord.
Well, p'r'aps it is, but all the same,
It heals the halt, the blind, the lame,
It takes and tramples down your pride
And sin and vainness fall beside,
It turns you out a better fool
Than you were taught to be at school,
And, what the Bible does not tell,
It gives you gentleness as well.

Oh, God ! I've heard the screams of men
In suffering beyond our ken,
And shuddered at the thought that I
Might scream as well if I should die.
I've seen them crushed or torn to bits,—
Oh, iron tears you where it hits !
And when the flag of Dawn unfurls
They cry—not God's name, but their girls',
Whose shades, perhaps, like Night's cool
    breath,
Are present on that field of death,
And sit and weep and tend them there,
God's halo blazing round their hair.
" Thou shalt not kill."   But in the grime
Of smoke and blood and smell of lime
Which creeping men have scattered round
A blood-disfigured piece of ground,
When Time weighs on you like a ton,
And Terror makes your water run,
And earth and sky are red with flame,
And Death is standing there to claim
His toll among you, when the hour
Arrives when you must show your power
And take your little fighting chance,
Get up and out and so advance,
When crimson swims before your eyes
And in your mouth strange oaths arise,
Then something in you seems to break
And thoughts you never dreamt of wake
Upon your brain and drive you on,
So that you stab till life is gone,
So that you throttle, shoot or stick,
A shrinking man and don't feel sick
Nor feel one little jot of shame ;
My God, but it's a bloody game !

Oh yes, I've seen it all and more,
And felt the knocker on Death's door ;
I've been wherever Satan takes you,
And Hell is good, because it makes you.
As long as you're a man, I say,
The " gentle " part will find its way
And catch you up like all the rest—
For love I give the Tommy best !
No need to learn of Christ's Temptation
There's gentleness in all creation,
It's born in you like seeds in pears,
It ups and takes you unawares,
It's Christ again, the real Lover
And not the corpse we languish over.
It makes us see, our vision clearer ;
When Christ is in us He is dearer,
We love Him when we understand
That each of us may hold His hand,
May walk with Him by day or night
In meditation towards the light ;
It's better far than paying shillings
For paper books with rusty fillings
Which say eternal punishment
Is due to those men who've spent
Their lives in gambling, drinking, whoring,
As though there were some angel scoring
Black marks against you for your sins
And he who gets the least marks wins.
This was a word Christ never sent,
This talk of awful punishment ;
You're born into a world of sin
Which Jesus' touch will guide you in,
And when you die your soul returns
To Christ again, with all its burns,
In all its little nakedness,

In tears, in sorrow, to confess
That it has failed as those before
To walk quite straight from door to door :
And Christ will sigh instead of kiss,
And Hell and punishment are this.

And so through all my life and days,
In all my walks, through all my ways,
The lasting terror of the war
Will live with me for evermore.
Of all the pals whom I have missed.
There's one, I know, whom Christ has kissed,
And in his memory I'll find
The sweetness of the bitter rind—
Of lonely life in front of me
And terror's sleepless memory.

June 30th, 1916.

There are lines in this which Masefield himself would have been proud to acknowledge :

" As though there were some angel scoring
    Black marks against you for your sins
    And he who gets the least marks wins "

is in the best Masefield manner.

I like it for its honesty and nervous energy. It is certainly beyond the power of any mere versifier, because of its perfect crystallisation of a mood. He has written with his eye on the object and brings home to us as a consequence the precise feelings of an imaginative poet in action. I doubt if anyone has portrayed so accurately the exact state of mind of the poet-soldier. I've watched the progress of this young poet since he was fourteen. I have a drawer full of his work, which I am convinced will some day be required at my hands by a discerning public. I can only give you his latest and let you form your own conclusions. It is no good extracting portions of them ; you must have them in their entirety, because you will not be able to come at them elsewhere. They are here printed for the first time :

OCTOBER 23RD, 1916

I

THAT he is dead
Seems unbelievable,
False, inconceivable,
He was so young.
Can it be said
Life indispensable
Falling insensible
Leaves us unsung ?
Picture the sight,—
Clothes hanging muddily,
Soppingly, bloodily ;
Eyes staring wide !
One little fight
Stretching him rigidly,
Clammily, frigidly
On to his side !

II

Picture the death,—
Young and so beautiful,
Lovable, dutiful,

Borne to the grave
Quite out of breath ;
Flowers of maternity
Plunged in eternity
Clean and so brave !
What is the prize ?
England is unmolest,
Happy and unoppressed ?
England is Free ?
Oh, these are lies !
Let England's glory wane !
Give him back whole again,
Him whom I bore in pain,
Give him to me. . . .

IF

I

I WANT to go to Devonshire
To hide myself away,
And try to find the glory-sun
That never warmed my day ;
To sit awhile and think a bit
Of all that might have been
If I had only heard of love
When I was seventeen.

II

If only I had had a chance
When I was still a child,
Instead of having smutty friends,
Instead of running wild ;

Instead of spending all my nights
Along with Cunny Jane ;
I wouldn't do the things I done
If I might live again.

III

But everything's a' finished and
There ain't a second " try " ;
I'll have to go on aimlessly
Until I come to die ;
I never had a chance to live,
A God to call my own.
I took the road I stood upon
And walked it all alone.

IV

I started off with Ned and Alf
Before I'd learnt to think,
And Ned was hanged in '99
And Alf 'e died o' drink ;
And I kept up with Cunny Jane
Until she sickened me ;
So that's the way I started off
In eighteen ninety three.

V

And now I'm thirty-five or more
And come to looking back
On how I broke the law at eight
By lighting Farmer's stack ;
On how I nearly killed a cop
And spent ten years in quod,
Because I never had a chance
Of understanding God.

VI

And so I long for Devonshire
To hide myself away,
And try to find the glory-sun
That never warmed my day ;
To sit a while and think a bit
Of all that might have been,
If I had only heard of love
When I was seventeen.

THE PRODIGAL SON

I

I'LL not remain to waken thee ;
I'll not remain to strengthen thee ;
I'll be the man I want to be
    Before the day is done ;
I'll go the way I want to go ;
I told t' fulish parson so,
I made t' parson's ears glow
    An' then I run !

II

I'm tired o' living like a weed,
It's not the life I want to lead,
I don't intend to go to seed
    An' die a Farmer's lout !
I'm young, an' strong an' full o' grit ;
I don't intend to simply sit,
I've had about enough of it
    To last me out.

III

No matter what the Dad allows,
I'll leave the farm and fields and sows,
I'll take the road without the cows
 An' walk it all alone.
There's Henry gone an' Alfred too,
An' I stayed back because o' you,
But now I'm off to see it through
 Upon my own.

IV

I'll never turn me back again
An' seek the little sunken lane
That leads me back to yellow grain
 An' you an' shadow joy.
I know the way a maiden cries ;
I know the vainness in her eyes :
—It isn't hollow, twisted lies
 That kill a boy !

V

I'll be the man I want to be ;
I'll never take farewell of thee ;
I'll take the road towards the sea
 An' setting o' the sun.
It isn't love that matters here,
It isn't pain, nor joy, nor fear,
It's pluck that makes you persevere
 When all is done !

July 30*th*, 1915.

" Masefield," you say ; of course : a young man must
imitate his masters. It is but Byron over again in his
youth imitating Pope, or Tennyson modelling himself
on Keats. He has a sense of the dramatic which is all

his own ; he is clever enough to see this and his plays (of which there are many) have not been acted in London theatres solely because of the weird plots which he persists in using : a Cabinet minister throwing a Cornish labourer over a cliff in one instance, and a tobacconist with a Swiftean sense of humour frightening the life out of a lady customer in his shop by pretending to be mad.

He has a direct personal style which is rare indeed. He already gives promise of a great future ; the poems I have quoted are not without genius.

My second example is a cadet at Sandhurst, Alec R. Waugh, son of Arthur Waugh. As a boy he was impregnated with a passion for Wilde, Dowson, Rossetti, Swinburne and Byron. He wrote a sensuous and luscious play on Vashti, modelled on Stephen Phillips and Arthur Symons, which had germs of beauty, but he too has developed enormously since he left school.

The first poem I quote of his was written while still at school, and shows at once his debt to these men.

THE PAGAN'S DREAM

I WATCHED the stately cavalcade of Sulla's triumph passing by,
I saw the palace Herod made where Mariamne's beauties lie,
I heard once more the fevered groan of Cleopatra's poisoned slave,
And the long breaker's sullen moan beside great Pompey's shifting grave.
The pageant of the past swept by, the Pagan held his former sway,
And passionate gleamed the purple sky, with memories of yesterday.

From the dim tombs of ancient years, from Babylon
   and Nineveh,
Welled the great fount of human tears straining towards
   the shoreless sea.
Fantastic forms with swirl grotesque trailing their
   rainbow canopy,
Wove into wondrous arabesque a saffron-tinted
   tapestry.
Apollo with his golden hair, and Helen on her rose-
   white throne,
Proserpina, for earth too fair, and Hera's billowy
   tresses blown
Across the ruby-painted sun shone bright beyond the
   foam of time
Where all the things in life begun, the half-dreamed
   dream, the unsung rhyme,
The love that burnt itself to hate, the Lily-Beauty
   turned to dross,
The longing wild unsatiate, the yearning and the
   poignant loss,
Sleep on for ever in the arms of rest's eternal slumberland
As Merlin once to Vivian's charms in that far-off
   Broceliande.
On silver wings, on fairy feet, I tripped across that
   magic sea,
Called by that music bitter sweet, that haunting,
   clinging melody,
Of Pagan hopes and Pagan dreams, of spires clad in
   amethyst,
Of stars whose lustre faintly gleams out through a veil
   of shaded mist,
Of icy glaciers' snow-tipped peaks, of bright red wine
   and purple rose,
Of passionate red-tinted cheeks where the fresh bloom
   of beauty glows,

Of endless splendid pageantry where all the longing of
the years,

Knits into one great ecstasy, one note of laughter and
of tears.

And there sit the immortals throned in silent splendour :
all the while

Tired men forgetting how they groaned in the past
years, upon this isle

Hear the slow music of the waves, hear the long echoes
of dead days,

Wafted from where life's ocean laves the shores of
night that dawn betrays.

Here is the end of all life's cares, and here the end of
all our grief,

Here is the guerdon of our prayers, for sleep is long and
life is brief ;

For love is but an hour's unrest and hate is nought, and
sorrow mirth ;

And here we reach the last behest of all we yearned for
upon earth,

Here is the song and here the feast, for through the
crossing of that sea

From all our woes and pain released we laugh into eternity.

We hear the roll of myriad drums that herald Cæsar's
conquering host ;

And Byron in his triumph comes from his well-loved
Ægean coast,

While Nero in his glory quaffs the wine of passion and
of love,

And Voltaire, ever cynic, laughs at all that he cannot
disprove.

They lie who say that when the soul has left the weary
twitching limb

We all must pay a penance whole for every pleasure,
every whim.

It is enough we have endured enough of sorrow here below,
By hopes fantastic have been lured to pleasures melting
  as the snow
Beneath our passion's burning flame, and we have
  known too much of pain,
That we should feel the aching shame of all our
  penitence again.
No : for we all shall soon forget the numbing anguish
  and lament
The crying for some Juliet, the pity for some deed half
  meant.
For we shall sit in ivory halls and sate ourselves with
  wine and song
While music and love's heat enthralls the soul that
  suffered overlong.
And when the Pagan pleasures tire and when the wine
  of joy is drunk,
And comes the end of all desire, when leafless stands
  the withered trunk,
Then shall we sleep and know no more, our eyes un-
  dimmed shall gently close
In some dark-lighted cushioned floor, filled with the
  fragrance of the rose ;
For sweet the dancing and the song ; but sweeter far
  the poppies' bloom ;
And there where love can work no wrong, silence holds
  sway within the tomb.

He has a sure sense of lilt and sweet music ; he
is filled with a love of beauty, even if this beauty is
acquired at second hand from books and not from
experience. After all, what experience do you expect
from a schoolboy of sixteen ?

How immeasurably he has advanced since then may
be gauged from the following :—

THE SECRET OF LIFE

SAITH the sage : youth flieth by,
  Like the dawn before the day :
Soon the flagon must run dry,
  Soon the rainbow fade away.
Store your treasures for old age :
      Saith the sage.

Saith the rose : one thing is sure,
  Nothing is more sweet than laughter.
Who can tell what may endure,
  What man knows what follows after ?
Take what's certain ere it goes :
      Saith the rose.

Saith my heart : life's secret lies
  Not alone in age nor youth,
But to both the same voice cries,
  Colours change but not the truth.
Only love and never part :
      Saith my heart.

IMMUTABILITY

IN the long emptiness of days
Before I knew you, on this hill
I used to lie and watch the rays
Of the dying sunset quiver
Through the reeds beside the river,
And on the laughing stream, until
It lay a sheet of ruffled gold.
Long shadows crept along the wold,

Ghostly, majestic : through the haze
Shrouding the waters, glimmered faint
Tall lilies swaying. . . .

                    . . . Beautiful
And calm as some old martyred saint
The evening died. . . .

                . . . My heart was full
Of a wild glory : joy and praise
Supremely mingled : Beauty thrilled
My hungry senses : colour swept
Before my eyes : my spirit leapt
Knowing its vague dreams fulfilled,
Its yearnings satisfied. . . .

                      . . . But now
I gaze across these fields unmoved,
Across these fields that once I loved.
For I have found you fairer far
Than morning mist or evening star.
How should I praise the dawn, the skies,
Once having looked into your eyes,
That smoulder with the ardent glow
Of hidden fire ?   Even the breeze
That flutters through the swaying trees,
Is not as soft as your white hand.
And, Love, the very sun is cold
When set against the rebel gold
Of your swift hair. . . .

                  . . . And yet I know
That love will die ; and I shall stand
Some day alone and watch the sun
Burn out its heart, its passion done.
While the lilies sway, and night
Trembles in the wake of light.

And the same cool wind will blow
Through the reeds beside the river.
Yet I shall not weep for you,
Nor for the love that has grown cold.
For though now your warm lips quiver
Under mine, we shall grow old ;
Old and past desire, sweet,
Miss the passion and the heat,
Kiss for habit's sake . . . Oh then
We, who have been so brave and true,
Clear-eyed and fearless, shall we stay
To mock at love, day after day
With words and make-believing, when
The flame is out ?   Shall we pretend
That we love still, or make an end
Of folly nobly ? . . .

                     . . . Oh, I know
That you will turn aside and go,
Taking your separate path ; and I
Shall stand here as before : and gaze
Across the valley where the haze
Hovers above the reeds, and shadows
Steal across the sun-kissed meadows.

And, love, for all that we're apart,
I shall feel Beauty in my heart,
Watching the long day sink and die.

8th July 1916.

SONNET

THE contest does not last so very long
    That we should cringe before it.   For a while
    The proud, disdainful gods look down and smile
On us and on our efforts : right and wrong

To-day seem merged in one.   Yet, Heart, be brave !
　Fearless and proud against immortal power
　Let us stand firm.   It is but for an hour.
There is no need for fear this side the grave.

But if some dim eternity should rend
　The veil of silence, and no bound is set
　　To Time and its processional of pain ;
　　If we should wake to journey on again
　With hopeless eyes, unable to forget. . . .
There is the fear. . . . If Death were not the end.
6th August 1916.

NOCTURNE

THE smouldering glow of sunset shines
Faintly through the bending pines ;
Twilight silverfooted creeps
Down the dimming paths and peeps
Into glooms and dark recesses
Covering with her falling tresses
Gently as a maid her lover,
Foxglove, violet, and clover.
And soft scents that sleep by day
Wake and through the darkness stray.
Earth and night and trees and sky
Are harpstrings to the harmony
That built a city out of dreams
Beside Scamander's winter streams.

To-night the pulse of music thrills
No less than then : the wooded hills
Are bathed in beauty and the song
Of solitude is borne along
The wandering pathways of the breeze
Now soft, now passionate like the seas

That thunder round the Cyclades.
All lovely things beneath the sun
Blend in that music and are one.
Beauty of colour, tune and rhyme,
Odour of muskrose and wild thyme,
And your swift laughter.   Though your
    feet
Tread other paths and find them sweet,
Safe from the shame of lengthening days
In every mood that Beauty sways
You dwell untainted.   I can feel
The fragrance of your warm breath steal
Over my face.   The perfumed air
Bows with the weight of your rich hair,
And murmuring among the trees
Your voice plays truant with the breeze.

So Love in after days when Death
Has made you his, and with cold breath
Silenced your laughter, keen and free,
Unfettered by mortality,
The sense of you will linger still
In flower and wind and wooded hill,
And safe from the grave's nothingness
In undiminished loveliness
Your lambent spirit yet will brood
Above the darkling solitude
And hovering in the evening air
Make the fairest things more fair.
And I shall find you when dim night
In twilight's mantle kisses light.
My heart an altar for your sake
Will burn with vestal flames that take
Intenser radiance from the sense
Of your divine omniscience.

And in the corners of my brain
Your presence will awake again
The leaping fount of poetry
With knowledge that though roses die
Beauty imperishable still
Works out its self-appointed will.

O Love behind the darkness waits
We know not what : the jealous fates
Guard well their secrets ; but as long
As life in fire and gold leaps strong
Through pulsing veins, and the glad earth
Scatters its gifts of love and mirth,
Passion and Friendship, the bright flame
Of your quick soul unchanged, the same
That sings to-night, will kindle men,
Out of their agony and pain
To mould a heaven out of thought
And seek the star that changeth not.

16th September 1916.

THE SEARCHLIGHT

WEARIED by the lost battle of the day,
   And sick with knowledge that all fair things must
     pass
   Sometime into oblivion or decay,
Nightlong I lay upon the scented grass,
   Quiet, at peace : the soft wind on my eyes
     Resting its summer wings.
   And I was free from the fierce mysteries
     And hopeless questionings
      Of life and art and love.

And I watched far above
   The long clear stream of light,
   Flicker and fade : shine bright and die
Then shine again, piercing with keen relentless eye
   The secrets of the night ;
Seeking the dark mysterious thing
That hovered somewhere in the dim expanse
   Of high heaped mysteries.
   In its wild dance
   Through the dim skies
  Its brilliance for a moment turned
  A sable cloud lost in its wandering
  Into a flaming radiance that burned
   In transient eternity.

  The Beam passed on, still searching the wide sky,
   On to the last grey limit of its bound,
  For the dark mystery that it never found.

   I watched and watched until I saw
   My soul and not the searchlight move
  Its fiery beam, probing the dark of outworn law,
   Of dead tradition, useless love
  Searching for truth, for one thing truly wise
Across a sky dark with the secrets of long generations,
   Blank with the emptiness of hollow nations
  To see against a host of lies.
And as that wandering light, I found nothing but the
   night
  And the gloom of the night
   Except on moments when some mood
   That held a semblance of the eternal truth,
  Before me burst in light,
  And for an instant, flamed like youth,
And then like youth subsided and was still.

While my soul through the night's wild solitude,
Sought for the one, the real, the imperishable.

But as I watched that lambent flame
   Steadfast, immutable, the same
   Dauntless in failure and reverse
   Striving against an alien universe.
I knew that sometime, either to-morrow or after many
     days,
   That beam would find the thing it sought.
And then the very night would blaze
   The sky would totter as a weak thing wrought
Of flame and fire and by itself consumed :
  Colours would leap and fall where shadows had loomed,
    And a primrose glow, like a halo, would rest
     On a world long opprest.

   And I felt that I too, before death
    Had crept and with sensuous breath
   Kissed me to slumber, should find
Within some long-locked chamber of my mind
   The truth, the eternal truth, the secret of all
That should light the pathway of man, and lead him
     afar
    From his sloth, and riot and carnival
     To the one true star
   That, hid no longer by mist
  Shone silver and gold, scarlet and amethyst,
    Pure as the mystic rose, warm as the Cytherean,
A splendour, the mingled glory of Pagan and Galilean.
    And out of the old world's dust
  A new world would rise, clean, laughing and whole,
   Untouched by the trammels of lies and lust,
    With flaming heart and a flaming soul.

21st October 1916.

TO YOUR DAUGHTER

FOR DORIS AND PETRE MAIS

THE Thracians when a child was born
    In solemn vigil wept, because
Yet one more soul, adrift, forlorn
    Must know the weight of mortal laws.

But when one died, with revelry
    They bore the silent corpse to rest
Glad that at least one man was free . . .
    To them not to be born was best.

.   .   .   .

What shall be said of you, whose eyes
    Are full of infant questionings,
Child for whom all our mysteries,
    And doubts and fears are unknown things ?

Your father's hand, your mother's kiss
    Are to you now sufficient heaven,
Yet a world waits you beyond this
    Where men for centuries have striven

To find its meaning ; yet have found
    Only that certain things are lies
And others transient. . . . Now the ground
    Lies heavy on their sightless eyes.

Youth hot upon its flaming quest
    At length sinks sobbing into age,
And whimpers for the unpossessed
    Dim-eyed. . . . This is your heritage.

And yet not wholly so : despair,
   Doubt, disillusionment and death
Belong to all, in them you share
   With all mankind the gift of breath.

But you the grim immortals bless
   With something more.   For in your eyes
Shines soft your mother's tenderness,
   Flames fierce your father's hate of lies.

In you two dauntless spirits blend
   The love and force whose questioning
Found life a sham, yet strove to mend
   And not destroy the twisted thing.

One with the mother-love that cried
   To merge the weak in the ideal,
The other wild, unsatisfied,
   Breaking through false things to the real.

And both these souls are one in you.
   This is your heritage . . . the rest
Matters but little, though you too
   Some day will cry that it is best

Not to be born, since right and wrong
   Seem bound together and the same
And dust's the end of every song . . .
   But Happiness is not life's aim.

A soul of such material wrought
   Is armed sufficiently to brave
The teeming myrmidons of doubt.
   That is enough this side the grave.

Unflinching you will face the truth.
  And others not so nobly wise
Will lay before your feet, their youth,
  Their hopes, and their hearts' treasuries.

So though you deem the gift of life
  Better not had, those others torn
And bleeding in the throes of strife
  Will thank their God that you were born.

These all see the light of day for the first time now, and it is for you to judge their worth. It is hard to criticise the work of one's own pupils—one is apt to be prejudiced—but they certainly do express that continual search after beauty which is the poet's peculiar prerogative. All that I can say is that I am proud to have a daughter who has inspired such a poem as *To Your Daughter*, and whatever fate may be in store for her, she is lucky to have had so sweet a tribute paid to her as this.

My last example is from a boy, K. de B. Codrington, now at Quetta. He has no definite master ; he has read widely and deeply, and browsed in all sorts of obscure nooks in the fields of English literature.

Like so many youngsters of to-day, he has learnt to sing through suffering.

He sings of Nature and her appeal to the instinct of beauty. I said that he had no definite master, but there are obvious traces of Rupert Brooke here and there, and sometimes, though much less obviously, of Flecker.

LONDON FROM THE COUNTRY

  THE sparrows twitter in the hedge
  And flutter by the window-ledge,

And golden-red another day
Creeps slowly up and fades to grey.
Great gathering clouds go sailing by,
Cold and grey in the sodden sky,
And softly pattering the rain
Beats down and blurs the window-pane.
The poplars by the garden wall
Sway in the wind and dead leaves fall,
All brown and sodden in the rain
By the window, into the lane.
The willows whisper in the wind
And in the field, just close behind,
The wind beats through the wet clover
All murmuring : " The best is over.
Grow old and live and die with us,
Among the willows and the grass."
To-day I watch the misty down.
Yet yesterday I slept in town,
Four stories high above the square,
Above the noise and clatter there,
Lulled by the traffic's rumbling song
Amid the ever-passing throng,
Five days of happiness supreme,
And now I'm here and they're a dream.

.   .   .   .   .

The shops, the restaurants in Soho,
And everything I love and know,
Those matinées, just you and I,
Are memories, and here I lie,
Watching the dawn-mists move and rise,
Dim wisps of grey against the skies.
Last night the arcs were burning bright,
Throwing great golden rings of light,
Now flickering above the throng,
Low dancing to the traffic's song ;

And here ?—the stars gleamed dim and cold
And overhead the storm-clouds rolled !
Last night, that table by the palm,
With its old waiter, fat and calm ;
The music rising soft and low,
Faintly in gusts from down below,
The clinking sound of touching glass,
As the quick waiters come and pass,
And you beside me, sitting there
As if that night would last a year.

.   .   .   .   .

The hanging ivy moves and sighs,
And slow the rose-sprays dip and rise,
And the wind blows by the clover,
Still whispering :—" The best is over."

EVENING CLOUDS

FAIR tints of evening in the sky,
    Why haste away so soon ?—
The wind still whispers on the hill
    And lingers on the dune.

The daffodils still nod their heads
    And bend before the breeze,
And still the painted butterflies
    Hang by the apple-trees.

Above the swallows homeward fly
    And circle round the eaves,
Yet day still loiters in the lane
    And glimmers on the leaves.

Night falls, and thou art gone, too soon,
  Fair pledges of the day,
And as the stars come creeping out,
  Thy glories fade away.

SPRING, 1916

WINTER is gone and spring is here again
  All green with tender buds, and hung with dew,
Loud sing the birds in every hedge and lane,
  Sweet songs of love, such love I bore to you.

And by the trees all fresh with morning rain,
  Like stars at evening breaking forth anew,
So bright you'd think they never fade or wane,
  The gold-eyed primrose cast a lighter hue.

The dancing sunshine and the birds' refrain,
  In all I see or hear, dim thoughts of you
Come back, like stabs of long-dead pain,
  And every beauty stirs the wound anew.

Last year you felt the waking sun's warm kiss,
  And watched the buds break out,—last year, and this.

ALMA MATER

SIGHS the wind in the scented limes
Just as it did in olden times,
Singing songs of the dim to-be,
Days that were then but dreams to me ?

Do the bells still chime along
Each lingering quarter with their song,
From early hall to afternoon,
Chiming away the time too soon ?

Still do the dancing sunbeams fall,
Glinting down by the library wall,
Glinting down by the gargoyle's head,
Painting the tiles a golden red ?

Do they go where we used to go
And do the things we used to do—
Roll on the field at half-past three,
Bathing at six and back for tea ?

Rules all round, yet never so free,
Is it just as it used to be ?
Are there shadows still on the grass,
—And do the clouds still, laughing, pass ?

Others go where we used to walk
And linger where we used to talk,
Times have altered everywhere,
Now strange faces turn to stare :

Unknown faces turn to stare,
With eyes that no remembrance bear,
Time has flown and the day was short
When I too loitered through the court :

Only the same old heart-felt love,
Only the laughing clouds above,
Only the wind in the linden tree,
Sings the same old songs to me.

REQUIEM

FOLD thine arms upon thy breast,
Close thine eyes and take thy rest,
Sunset in the golden west,
Glorious, dies.

I will sing no dirge for thee,
For in every brake and tree
Birds sing out in melody,
To grey skies.

So, now thou hast gone from me,
I will sing my melody ;
Day grows old, to wane and die,
Yet to rise.

Still the wind stirs the roses,
Hung in great fragrant posies,
But your sunset ne'er loses,
Golden skies.

Golden-tinted clouds sail by,
Twilight creeps across the sky,
Shadows fall and lightly lie,
On the eyes.

Night falls gleaming in the west,
Thou who wast of all, the best,
Fold thy arms and take thy rest,
Close thy eyes.

As usual, I am afraid to criticise them, because they
are too near to me.   They were shown up as work . . .
and amid all the humdrum platitudes and inconsequent
nonsense that boys produce as " prep.," to come upon
one such poem as *Requiem* is like reading a play of
Goldsmith after Mrs Aphra Behn, or a criticism of
Dixon Scott after the literary editor's reviews in a
newspaper.

All I feel at the moment is a fierce pleasure that
Ackerley, Waugh and Codrington all came, at one

time or another, under my influence. To me as an
individual they owe less than nothing ; to the books I
put into their hands, more than they will ever acknowledge. I refuse to believe that their poems are any
whit inferior to the majority of those which I have
quoted elsewhere in this paper ; the only difference lies
in the fact that they still have to make their name, to
find a publisher and a public.

V

THE MODERN NOVEL

THE novel proper, as we now understand the term, is supposed to have started with Mr Wells, in *Love and Mr Lewisham*, some fifteen years ago, perhaps as a direct result of the shaking up which we received during the Boer War. After flourishing for this short period with an almost astounding brilliance, there are now not wanting critics who declare that as a branch of letters novel-writing is decadent and quickly dying; that the result of this war will bring in a new vehicle to express our thoughts and aspirations. What I think these critics mean to imply is that the form of art in question has been so travestied and degraded that the true artist will soon turn with loathing from this medium and discover a fresh method of imparting whatever message he has to deliver.

But their reasoning is not sound. Who to-day doubts, for instance, that the theatre of this country has a future before it of as yet unguessed-at possibilities? We had a glimpse in 1912 and 1913 in the rapid spread of repertory companies, in the genius of Stanley Houghton, Yeats, Synge, Chesterton, Shaw and Bennett; the stage was coming into its own at last. The war broke out, domestic problems had to be shelved and gay recreation for us all became the cry, with the result that the only sort of theatre we care to visit these days is that in which we can indulge in cheery laughter and forget for the space of three hours

the darkness and horror of our time.   This is the day
of " Revue," and it shows sheer ingratitude on our part
if we join with those biased judges who would do away
with lightness, frivolity and jocund dance on the ground
that it undermines our morals and destroys our intellect.   It does nothing of the sort ; it revives us, it
tends to make us cheerful, it helps us to carry-on and
not give way to ghoulish fears and despair.   But the
day of the revue is not for ever ; with the coming of
peace the stage will become in the end what we intend
it to become, the platform from which we can thrash
out the problems that beset us with regard to life and
love and death.[1]

On the other hand, the trashy, noxious, prurient,
bastard novel increases and multiplies and is as strong
as mongrels usually are.   It is not with this that I am
concerned to-day ; it is with the score or so of great-
hearted men and women who keep their heads above
the water and write, not for the business man's leisure
hours, nor in order to fill up the evenings of the lonely,
stupid vicar's daughter, but (for the only reason that
justifies men in writing anything at all) because they
must . . . because their own lives are so complicated
that they must advise others not so experienced how
to extricate themselves from the labyrinth by which
they are encompassed.

It follows, then, that the first point to be noticed
about the present-day novelists is their sense of psychology ; they are introspective—and in that they
are unlike their fathers in art.   We look in vain to-day
for the simple, full-blooded, narrative style of Fielding,
the quietude of Jane Austen, the sentimentality of
Dickens, the dogmatic baldness of George Eliot, the

---

[1] I let this stand, to teach me not to prophesy comfortable things
in future.

historic sense of Scott, the uncleanness of Sterne, or the intellectual obscurity of Meredith.

The novelists of to-day have broken free from all tradition, not because, as their elders so often think, that they like shocking people, tilting at existing conventions or descending to the sordid, but solely because they are intent upon one thing alone, the search after truth. Like the great scientists and all true reformers, they are content to take nothing upon trust; they must prove all things and hold fast to that which they find to be good. Now, to be accurate, this definition of their aims necessarily makes us adjust our point of view about the date of the beginning of these traits. It is not *Love and Mr Lewisham* but *The Way of All Flesh* that holds the place of honour as the pioneer of this movement.

In that book, which might have been produced this season, so modern (in my present sense of the word) it is, we see a boy brought up in the deadening atmosphere of a country parsonage, exceedingly religious, bent on taking Orders, until he finds that he cannot honestly conform to the accepted belief in the efficacy of infant baptism. It is strictly autobiographical, and gives us, with a wealth of detail, all the doubts that assail the mind of youth with regard to the myriad beliefs which his elders hold quite complacently, but, according to his point of view, quite unreasoningly and therefore immorally.

And this brings me to my first great rock on which so many writers split, the relation of life to art. How far has the novelist the right to transcribe from life? How far ought he to aim at the objective and the impersonal?

If we listen to one who was himself both a consummate artist and able critic, R. L. Stevenson, we should conclude that no art ever dares, in Henry James's phrase, to compete with life. Life is monstrous, infinite, illogical, abrupt and poignant; art is neat, finite, self-contained, rational, flowing and emasculate.

A man settling down to write a novel, just like his brother artist, the musician or the painter, definitely decides upon a theme, which he harps upon, ruthlessly pruning away all irrelevancies until he has finished his artistic conception, which is orderly, consecutive and intelligible. Now life is seldom, if ever, intelligible, never consecutive and most certainly not orderly; your true artist half shuts his eyes to the dazzle and confusion of reality and flees the challenge of life, pursuing instead an independent and creative aim: he does not pretend to give a true picture of life; rather does he make, so far as he is able, his story typical, which accounts, of course, for Sam Weller, Mr Micawber and Mrs Gamp. Hence follow, to the artist's horror on the publication of each fresh work, a whole series of misunderstandings, each one of the small circle of his acquaintances endeavouring to " place " themselves and other of his friends in the book—whereas, of course, no man deliberately paints any man as he sees him, but, taking a trait here and a trait there, presents a composite portrait of the creature of his imagination.

Lest I tire you with these general hypotheses, as if I were here to prove a proposition in geometry, let me descend to the particular score or so of writers whom I have in mind as representative of the art of novel-writing at its best to-day, and I will try to be as modern as I possibly can be.

But before I can do this I must call your attention to an astonishing similarity in the writers of our era. Their theme is nearly always the same: they take a child and work out, with miraculous accuracy and meticulous care, his or her attitude to life from its earliest infancy. It is nearly always an only child, and hence imaginative, queer and lonely.

He does not fit into the curriculum anywhere, least of all into the rarefied atmosphere of a Public School (we have to go to E. F. Benson, beloved of dowagers and bookstall agents, for that); Oxford days (all heroes go to Oxford nowadays) are merely an occasion for scorching his wings, owing to the sudden liberty; he disappears in a chastened frame of mind to an East End Settlement or Bohemian Chelsea, or Paris—and there he meets with further chastisement from a world which deals harshly with those who have little respect for its canons and refuse to play for safety. We leave the protagonist fighting, having not so much worked out his salvation as cut away a few of the fungus growths that impeded his development.

What are we to make of writers who always take this line? Two things about them stand out clear: they are not lacking in courage, and they are broad-minded. I wonder if it has ever struck the opponents of the new school that there is an intense amount of sorrow in the lives of all these big present-day writers. A man does not lightly give up old comfortable beliefs and scandalise his mother, alienate his best friends and cut himself adrift from all those who would help him if only he kept in the groove of the Victorians without a very real sense of dread and misgiving.

After all, he may be wrong. All his elders tell him that he is; he is held up as a scapegoat; respectability shuns him and conventional morality labels him as abandoned. All he has to hold on to is the fiery white burning flame within, which is the manifestation of the divine as he sees it, the Holy Ghost of honesty; it needs more than a little courage to follow the Grail

which your father tells you is a will o'-the-wisp; it
hurts such a man to be told, as he is on every occasion,
that this much-vaunted open-mindedness and breadth
is only a euphemism for lack of depth and shallowness.
There may be lack of depth in the new writer before he
has found his feet; the very shallows are sometimes
mistaken by the passionate spirit for the deep waters,
but he soon learns to profit by his mistakes. No—it
is not the spirit that is lacking; the impulse is all right
—publishers will tell you that they are sometimes
surprised by the amount of good stuff which is sent
to them daily. What is wrong is the absence of any
technique; so anxious are these firebrands to give
voice to their disquietude, so keen to be gospellers, that
they forget that he who practises an art must obey
the laws that govern that art. They think that it is
enough to have something to say and say it, which
would be strictly true were novel-writing a sort of
photography, a literal transcription from life.

It is something very different from this even if we
agree that novels are now a chemical analysis of life.
In the scientific sense this is not quite true; it is impossible to put down on paper, with precise verisimili-
tude, what you have evolved as a result of your tests
with alkalis and acids; the compound of emotions,
impressions and volitions are not so easy to disinte-
grate, the human factor looms too large; it is men's
souls that you are striving to analyse and the process
brings tears of shame and pity; sympathy of a very
acute kind is essential in the analyst, which is obviously
not a feature that enters into the calculation of the
chemist. To put it even more plainly, there is no ease
in these new novels: they are uncomfortable, and
designedly so; they do not make for happy, restful
evenings; they are purgative pills for the soul, tearing

it up by the roots lest it should die for want of exercise or become sluggish through inaction.

And here I am constrained against my wish to have to talk on a theme that apparently causes quite a number of hostile critics to prejudge these feverish reformers and banish their work summarily at sight. The theme is realism. The fact that stoats slaughter rabbits in a bestially cruel manner, that Nature is harsh, ugly and unsympathetic, that man, in Meredith's phrase, has not yet rounded Cape Turk in his attitude to women, that mud and dirt exist, terrifies these writers : they are honest, so they refuse to blind themselves to the truth ; they are searching for beauty and meet ugliness, so they must needs write down the impression it makes on them. Hence follows the croak of the conventional about indecent and revolting details. The coward trick of employing asterisks is the resort of all the hucksters and the popularity hunters, while the band of twenty stalwarts goes its way, heedless of the cries of " Shame," and in the end out of the sordid they evolve splendour, out of the grotesque, beauty, out of the shams and lies, truth. So realism comes to mean reaction against the comfortable, dull, cowardly attitude to life which was so characteristic of the eighteen-nineties. It does not mean, and never has meant, playing in the mire for love of mud. I refuse to dwell on the point further. Let me come to the individual members of my score.

I will take the women first. It is a curious thing that whereas the sexes have never conflicted in the world of poetry (where are Christina Rossetti and Mrs Browning when set up against Keats, Milton, Shelley and the rest of our English singers ?) as novelists, women hold their own easily. There have been many ready to acclaim Jane Austen as worthy of a place nearer the Shakespearean throne than any other of our writers, and she is not, like Jael, alone. So to-day we have at least eight places among my score taken by women—Ivy Low, Viola Meynell, Ethel Sidgwick, Rose Macaulay, Dorothy Richardson, Miss E. H. Young, Sheila Kaye-Smith and May Sinclair. I will content myself with five. It is no argument—perhaps you are thinking of it—to suggest that our worst writers are also women. Each of these, in her individual way, fans the flame of revolt and drives home the crudity of life, the inexplicability of it all, the need for courage to test, to experience, to venture all in the cause of beauty and truth.

Ethel Sidgwick is no mean disciple of Meredith and James. *The Accolade* would have been welcomed by either ; she represents the intellectual, aristocratic side of the quarrel. Certainly impersonal, she yet lives again in her characters, who are living men and women, full of human frailty and human passions and of infinite charm, even when they fall short, as all the heroes and heroines in the novels under discussion do fall short, of the high calling whereto they were called.

She recognises, as do the others, how amazingly swift the transition is between the sublime and the ridiculous, how in a second of time a coward may become brave, a good man turn villain ; in other words, she refuses to believe in the old conventional theory, which is all right on the boards of the Lyceum (*The Morning Post* would say that it was the only safe guide in life), that men can be divided into sheep and goats ; if they could there would be no need for our age at all; there would be no problem ; it is the question of shadows and half lights and tricky optical illusions of the soul that so worries us. If all were either white or black this paper would be meaningless and so would the writing of novels.

Ivy Low and Viola Meynell have much in common and can be grouped together. They follow what their enemies call the convention of their school, the convention of unconventionality, and depict heroes who have nothing in them of the heroic; feckless, vacillating creatures who achieve nothing though they pass through indescribable tortures in their endeavour to make something of their lives. Now, your brusque business man gives little shrift to the weak and takes but a small interest in their puny efforts to make good. That really is typical of us as a people; we admire strong, successful people. What we need to cultivate far more is a feeling of sympathy with the weak, not maudlin, sentimental claptrap towards the poor and needy (that is our everlasting shame as a country, not as individuals, and organisation, not Dickens' system, is the only cure), but a tolerant attitude towards those who are less well endowed with any of this or the next world's good attributes, towards the uneducated tub-thumper who, behind all his low cunning and unreasoning hatred for what he calls the " aristocrats," has something fine in him; towards the stunted, the malformations that crowd everywhere, the miserable, unprepossessing nursery governess with the capacity for deep passion. It is the unsuspected depths in everybody that we want to get at. Men do low, black-guardly acts and yet are lovable; girls have neither brains, nor looks, nor strength, and yet—there lurks beneath the forbidding exterior an attraction—and that is what Viola Meynell and the rest of them want to find out and want us to find out in the lives of those near to us who are miserable and neglected as of no account. It is hard to group these writers together, but I think the guiding principle that is common to all of them is the avoidance at all costs of snobbery—snobbery of any kind. These accidental pronunciations, these tricks of eating, these vulgar colloquialisms, these dowdy clothes, these astonishing limitations all make us so deuced superior. I know little about pictures, but by a very happy accident I really do like the work that is supposed, by the only artists whom I know, to be the best we've got. I mean, of course, Augustus John, Mark Gertler, Nevinson, Rothenstein and so on. The sight of a Blair Leighton, a Marcus Stone, a Landseer or a Dicksee serves to keep me in remembrance of the time when I bowed to popular opinion and gave my own judgment no chance. And yet my novelist friends, men of taste and judgment, don't laugh at me—they are not snobs; they don't even laugh at me behind my back. . . .

Now, it's these people who have given me a soul: they haven't laughed; they have tried to find where my limitations extend. Other people don't: other people are snobs. These women writers are full of the milk of human kindness and extend their love to those who seem least of all deserving of it. The only people they cannot stomach are the safe, self-complacent men and women who have been nurtured from their earliest youth in the established tradition and done all the right things in the right way, even to marrying and being buried.

Of my dozen or so male writers I propose to take Conrad first, not necessarily because he is greater than any of the others, but because he stands rather outside the group. We ought to have been reading him thirty years ago, only, being led by the critics, we never recognised his genius until almost too late. One point he has in common with the younger school—in psychological analysis lies his greatness; his difference lies in the fact that whereas Bennett and the rest don't care about narrative, he revels in the telling of a tale. He is a born raconteur; he tells a story in the best possible way; he looks at it from every point of view; he has taken a valuable leaf out of Browning's book—I often wonder quite how much Conrad owes to *The Ring and the Book*. I again often wonder whether a finer analysis of a boy's life has ever been made than Conrad made of that excessively romantic son of the parsonage, inscrutable of heart, tearing himself out of the arms of a jealous love at the sign, at the call of his exalted egoism. He leaves a living woman to celebrate a pitiless wedding with a shadowy ideal of conduct. Everyone has at last read *Lord Jim*; alone among modern books we have here a hero who is quite certain of himself, realises quite definitely that errors are irretrievable and works out his scheme of expiation to perfection.

Wells, too, in some degree stands a little aloof from the moderns; the best thing about him which he holds in common with Arnold Bennett is his conviction of the sacredness of his calling as novelist. Not once nor twice but a hundred times Wells reiterates his gospel in the clear notes of the clarion; nothing is so sacred as work, nothing matters in comparison with getting your mind clear; life is wasted on every side; only the novelist really lives at all; only he has the true vision. Having cut away the frippery and foolishnesses of the myriad things which pass for living, he alone can point the way to where true happiness and contentment lie —in the cultivation of the scientific spirit, in passionate love and immense sympathy. To him has fallen the privilege of being able to reveal the soul of England during the past two years in *Mr Britling Sees It Through*, by far the ablest novel written since 1914. That is Mr Wells' triumph—he is the supreme clarifier and crystalliser. He writes not as Romain Rolland, with the detachment of a calm observer on a Swiss peak, but with the passionate resentment of a father who has lost his only son, who was to remould the world after his father's death—it is introspective and subjective to an extraordinary extent ; through it all we see the old Wells we had so learnt to love and reverence sadly chastened by a crime which was so exactly to fulfil his age-old prophecies and put back the progress of the country for countless years.

Wells had many detractors in the past, but no one could dare to deny that as a master in handling the English language and making it mean quite clearly and consistently exactly what he wishes to convey he stands alone ; his sincerity and honesty perhaps frightened those who were afraid of the lengths to which sincerity and honesty could lead men in their search for truth. But Wells has proved his large-heartedness long ago in his splendid sense of fun ; his sympathy with man, in spite of his narrowness and refusal to take the advantages of education, is over-whelmingly strong and gives us an insight into his capacity for love.

Freedom is his continual cry, freedom from all this absurd restraint that curtails our energies, damps our ardour and would deprive us of half the light and joy of living. " Come out," he cries, " into the market-place and test life ; better to fall over your own accord in the endeavour to learn to walk than to be carried about all your life hedged about with wet-nurses."

Arnold Bennett has many points in common with Wells : his humour and his not less fervent sense of the greatness of his calling. That he should have selected the very commonplace people of the ugliest district in

England is typical of modern art.   I refer you again to
Augustus John.   By the aid of countless details carefully correlated he gives you a never-to-be-forgotten
picture of the effect of two or more principal characters
on one another ; every trivial domestic incident is
painted in with a truth that almost staggers you.
After reading Arnold Bennett you feel as if you had
lived with his people all your life ; they are neither
intellectually brilliant, nor pretty, nor anything else
except commonplace—but they have their passions
as much as the Lady Barbaras of Galsworthy or the
Othellos of Shakespeare—and it is their passion that
makes them interesting.   But it is neither with Conrad,
nor with Bennett, nor with Wells, nor with the women
that I am principally concerned.   I am now getting
nearer to the heart of my subject, the younger school of
novelists, and I have such a galaxy of talent in my
mind's eye that I scarcely know with whom to start.
J. D. Beresford perhaps is the best, as he is an avowed
disciple of Shaw.   In his great trilogy dealing with the
life history of Jacob Stahl we see again the Wellsian
theory of subjectivity.   All Jacob's early struggle for
fame, his successive stages in the conflict of life to
secure real, lasting love, are told with an honesty of
purpose that almost scares you.   Beresford deliberately
sets out to dissect and reveal his inner being--there is
no plot, no climax ; there rarely is in the modern novel.
There is no heightening effect to secure a romantic
atmosphere ; it is all realistic, bald and cold—and yet
cold not with a moral frigidity, but cold as a perfectly
executed marble statue hewn out by genius at fever
heat from the formless block.   At the end of three
volumes Jacob has at last found happiness with Betty
and her babies, but even so he is still unsatisfied, he
is still a candidate for truth.   " Virtue lies only," he

writes, " in the continued renewal of effort ; the boast of success is an admission of failure." Jacob Stahl could never rest content with any such attainment as was provided by the comfort of his wife's love, by the fine, unselfish joy he finds in the care of his three children, or, least of all, by such satisfactions as come to him from his modern achievements in the world of letters. He is ever at the beginning of life, reaching out towards those eternal values that are ever beyond his grasp. He is handicapped in many ways and must continually regret his own ignorances and intellectual limitations, but he has not been threatened by that decay of mind which slowly petrifies and kills those who fall into the habit of fixed opinions.

"Truly he who marries and has children," says Bacon, " gives hostages for fortune," but our generation is giving the lie to this seemingly profound assertion. The point that matters is to preserve an unbiased mind—" the fight's the thing." Browning dimly recognised it in the unlit lamp and the ungirt loins, though he spoilt his ideal by that dreadful line immediately following, but this is ethical and I am here to discuss the artistic, so far as they can be differentiated.

Beresford is typical of his school ; he is what we call, in our ordinary language, " absolutely straight," and fearless ; the world is an unweeded garden, things rank and gross possess it merely. Instead of acquiescing in this quite true Shakespearean remark, instead of shutting its eyes to it as uncomfortable and shocking, the new generation forges straight ahead, intent only on solution. Now in the first place it is quite likely (though I don't believe this) that there isn't a solution ; it doesn't seem to me to matter if there isn't ; everything is relative, but the joy lies in the search if the end be but a chimera. Secondly, such a search makes for discontent and unhappiness—acute unhappiness, atoned for, we think, by moments of sheer ecstasy undreamt of by the rest of the world.

It is this sense of directness of aim, in spite of causing misery, that attracts us, in the first place, to perhaps the best known and most widely read of this school, Compton Mackenzie. I want, so far as possible, to avoid comparison, because I firmly feel that out of my score or so of great writers ten at least stand right out from their generation and deserve to live so long as English literature is read. Mackenzie may or may not be one of these ten—he is certainly not the leader.

It is difficult to speak in cold, critical terms of a book which all the reviewers (once given a lead) hailed as one of the masterpieces of our language.

It is his sense of beauty that captivates us : not the pseudo-romantic, bizarre sort of beauty with which some people credit him, owing to his unfortunate love of archaic forms, but the passionate love of precise, pellucid phrases, and it is this sense of beauty which enables us to probe into the secrets of youth and see a picture of a Public School boy's life, which is not merely so much wasted paper, but then, of course, it is unfair to take a school like St Paul's, situated right in the heart of London ; the influences that acted on Michael's life were mainly from without the school. At Oxford he tries to give an impression of the callow life of the undergraduate, forgetful of the fact that there is no typical Oxford or typical Cambridge. All that you can say of either is that poems might be written of the feet of the young men who pass so very quickly, of the amazing lack of sympathy they receive with any of the emotional crises they pass through—in other words, that to each individual soul the university means something quite different from what it means to everybody else. And Compton Mackenzie falls into the same error which lesser men naturally do, of thinking that " bonners " and " brekkers " and theatre " rags " and " bumpers " matter in the least.

No ; the secret of Compton Mackenzie's claim to greatness lies in this one sentence :

" Soon will come a great war and everybody will discover it has come either because people are Christians or because they are not Christians. Nobody will think it is because each man wants to interfere with the conduct of his neighbour."

That is where Mackenzie comes into line with my argument. In spite of all his delving in the depths— and I am afraid I hold with that time-honoured adage that we must all eat our peck of dirt before we die—he has a clear, sane vision : excess of vice, like excess of virtue, is a crime : in either case comes the interference with the conduct of one's neighbour : interference not emanating from sympathy, but proceeding from that police-like vigilance which is so prominent a feature of the idle and the obtuse.

Sinister Street is not satisfactory because it is not typical in its Public School picture nor can it be by the nature of things in its view of Oxford, and is too obviously out to paint extremes in the rest of the book. Nobody but a bishop would believe that such men as Meats exist in such quantities as to warrant inclusion in a work of art.

The counter-argument, that the heroes of the modern novelists are not typical, is quite untrue ; there are vast numbers of people now growing up who are dissatisfied with everything, full of doubts with regard to all the things which the last generation held as sacred.

There looms before them an abyss of unfathomable depth, full of horrors unless they are helped by pictures of others in like case with themselves. We are discovering that life isn't in the least what we thought it was going to be ; everybody fails us when we turn for support except this band of writers who are themselves suffering and experiencing.

But I don't want to leave Compton Mackenzie on the result of one and that his worst book.

In *Carnival* he showed us the life of a typical modern girl. Has it ever struck you how many country solicitors' daughters, and others who had been hedged in and barred off from any sane view of life as a whole, have been suddenly thrown into violent contact with the crudity of it—of late in munition factories and elsewhere ? They too are learning from experience, the sternest but only true school of life. To whom can they turn for support in an emergency with any hope of a rational answer to their questions except to men of the calibre I am quoting ? It isn't at all a question of resisting temptation ; it's solely a question of how to fulfil your destiny and thereby attain true nobility of character. The fugitive and cloistered virtue no longer exists ; ignorance is immoral, unforgivable, just in proportion as it is senseless and needless.

Jenny had to learn her hard lesson in the school of life, than which no lesson can be harder, to differentiate between love and passion, to uproot the animalism that still lurks, cloven-footed, in primitive human nature, and replace it by that divine fervour which anybody can attain once he gives up the canting, old-fashioned, effete theories about sex. Mackenzie's high-water mark is reached in *Guy and Pauline*, which is simply *The Statue and the Bust* rewritten.

" Where is the use of the lips' red charm,
  The heaven of hair, the pride of the brow
  And the blood that blues the inside arm—
  Unless we turn, as the soul knows how,
  The earthly gift to an end divine ? "

That is the secret of everything. Here we have an idyllic picture set in an exquisitely beautiful setting of two charming people madly in love with each other, and watch, with agony in our hearts, the gradual diminution of passion, the gradual realisation on the part of each of them that they were insufficient for each other—a book that might have saved many unions. It is the epic of mistaken ideals.

I take Hugh Walpole next because he is in some degree akin to Mackenzie, not, I mean, in the accidental fact that they both, like so many of the younger school, always go to Cornwall for their setting, but because of that far more important feature, their unanimity in their outlook on life. The whole of Mr Walpole's text lies on the first and last pages of *Fortitude* : " 'Tisn't life that matters—'tis the courage you bring to it."

Peter Westcott, imaginative, crude, potentially a genius, possessed of all the splendours and terrors which that word implies, suffers abominably, unjustly, at the hands of a girl brought up just in the way that all these men so deprecate, the way of ignorance and fear, of convention and second-hand opinions. Peter thinks that in her he will find that illimitable affection that is so necessary for him. She fails him, and he is utterly broken temporarily. We leave him on the Cornish moor listening to the new beatitudes which are so pure, so fine, so intensely typical of the new and glorious England which is now in its birth throes : " Blessed be pain and torment and every torture of the body.

Blessed be plague and pestilence and the illness of nations. Blessed be all loss and failure of friends and sacrifice of love. Blessed be the destruction of all possessions, the ruin of all property, fine cities and great palaces. Blessed be the disappointment of all ambitions. Blessed be all failure and the ruin of every earthly hope. Blessed be all sorrows, torments, hardships, endurances that demand courage. Blessed be these things—for of these things cometh the making of a man."

You see how they all hang together in their splendid creed—not home comforts but homeless discomforts, not safety but danger, not ignorance but experience, not self-complacency but hideous doubts, not the pretence of love but the eternal search after the unattainable: this is the gospel of to-day. The secret lies in dissatisfaction, strife and energy, the glorious buffeting and training of the soul.

Gilbert Cannan, intellectually superior to most of the school, yet comes to the same conclusion. "If ever you find yourself faced with a risk, take it," concludes old Mole, after a life of torture and the disillusionment of experience. There is a thing called yesterday, but that is only the dust-bin at the door, into which we cast our refuse, our failures, our worn-out souls. There is a thing called to-morrow, bursting with far better things than those which we have discarded. But into to-day the whole passionate force of the universe is poured—and therefore to-day is marvellous.

There are few men and women born without the kernel of passion, but what do they do with it? Passion is looked upon by our elders, who have outlived it, crushed it, controlled it so well that it has vanished, as something indecent, whereas passion is only the prelude, the necessary prelude, to idealism (so

laughed at in England), to the belief that there is a
wisdom greater than the wisdom of men.   In its place
we have bowed the knee to the Baal of hypocrisy, so
that every man's home becomes a theatre—a carefully
kept up pretence, everything stunted : soul, affections,
human passions.   Now we come to an age tired of this
amazing puppet show in the home, and what happens ?
What happens to the Chinese woman's feet when
unbound ?   They cause her agonies of suffering, so
that she cannot walk ; so it has been with us.   That
is the theme of *Old Mole*—described by one leading
reviewer as a " diverting study."   About as diverting
as Othello.   That is what the English reading public
want—diversion.   That is what I ought to be writing
a paper on—" The Modern English Novel—Some
Agencies of Diversion, with Illustrative Readings from
the works of Mrs Humphry Ward, Jeffery Farnol,
John Buchan, Ian Hay, Marjorie Bowen, Lucas Malet,
Beatrice Harraden, Jessie Pope, E. V. Lucas, E. F.
Benson, Gilbert Parker and Agnes and Egerton Castle."
It is just because, according to my theory, the modern
novel is not a diversion at all, but a new religion, an
essential factor in education, a complete guide to the
art of living, that I trouble to write a paper on it at all
—after which outburst, let me get on with my job.

Mr E. C. Booth has two novels to his credit, *The Cliff
End*, now ten years old, and *Fondie*, quite recent.

Fondie is slightly divergent from the school which I
am trying to depict, and owes nothing, so far as I can
see, to any of them, and yet, in spite of its glaring differ-
ences, it has this in common : its main object is analysis,
analysis of the soul of the flighty, lonely daughter of a
country parson and of her steadfast wheelwright lover,
Fondie.   Her dreadful vulgarity and odious rural limitations have the effect, which no doubt Mr Booth intends

them to have, of making us refuse to rest content until we have smashed for ever a state of things which permits of a beautiful flower like this being besmirched and trodden under—wasted, in a word. The love of Fondie is beautiful, the face and form of Blanche are beautiful, and yet both these things are wantonly destroyed—for want of what ? Experience. . . . By reason of that path of ignorance on which I have been harping.   Blanche is driven to drown herself ; we feel that it was the only way ; with things as they are, such ridiculous waste was the only solution . . . but whose the fault ?   Most clearly does the stern answer come : Mine—yours—everyone's. " I didn't know—I didn't know," she cries.

Now at any rate she can never grow old, age haunt her with no terrors, respectability never claim her as her rightful prey, writing upon her face the careworn lines and characters with which she signalises her elect. God's justice is greater than man's justice, God's wisdom than man's wisdom, God's love than man's love, and God's forgiveness than man's.   Yet Fondie, in spite of all, forgave all, loving her so much. We may leave it with the Infinite to love and forgive more than man, with all his limitations and narrow codes.   So runs the indictment ; the story is commonplace, to be read every day in the news columns and in the serial columns of every paper.

It is the attitude with which the author regards the story, the beauty of his nature expressed in the beauty of his language that makes us include him in the list of those who matter.   Such things are, such things ought not to be.   In common with the rest of his contemporaries, he does not write merely to interest by narrative, as the eighteenth-century novelists did, but to drive a message home.   These novels are

all lay sermons—and why not ?   I refuse to submit to
the dictum that art is self-sufficing and serves no useful
purpose—all that nonsense about " beating beautiful
ineffectual wings," and so on.

Mr St John Lucas brings us back to the main body
again : we can leave Mr Booth safely guarding our
flank. In *The First Round*, published seven years
ago, and its sequel, *April Folly*, we reach, perhaps, the
high-water mark of the school.

In the first place, though this is partially irrelevant,
The First Round contains the finest picture of Public
School life as it really is that has ever been printed.
I know that Mr Walpole, in *Mr Perrin and Mr Traill*,
did for a certain sort of school what Compton Mackenzie did for a certain sort of man—both these things
may have been necessary. Personally, I think Mr
Walpole's novel was necessary, but the true artist gives
us the typical, and the school depicted in *The First
Round* might equally well be Sherborne, Winchester,
Wellington, Uppingham or Shrewsbury. It is the life
story of a boy with the æsthetic faculties well developed ;
he has the makings of a great musician. Now there
are more of these types—types that are supranormal
—than are commonly allowed for, and they suffer indescribable torture wherever they are. Denis Yorke's
first round in the battle of life is an extremely severe
one, and he comes out of it just as Peter Westcott in
Mr Walpole's book—cleaner, saner, truer to the ideal.
Sympathy and forgetfulness of self—this was the
answer to the riddle of life, the magic talisman that
made existence beautiful in the darkest places, the
great compensation for all the poverty and suffering
and injustice in the world. The path was now plain.
A belief in others—this was the true path, not coldly
isolated, as he had thought, but full of hosts of other

pilgrims, on a journey where Love himself forbade that even the vilest should fall by the wayside for lack of succour from his comrades. In the sequel we see where this theory lands him. One of his pupils (he becomes a teacher of music) falls madly in love with him, and he is at present deceived into thinking that he loves her. . . . When he finds out, nothing will alter him from his determination to carry it through, but she finds out and leaves him. They meet years afterwards —an anticlimax, of course, like everything in life—a miserable conversation follows, and they separate again. An old man who has watched the meeting accosts the hero, and leaves him with this advice : " I've seen the world," he said. " I know life. Take an old man's advice and never do that — never hurt a woman. Women, women give us everything, love and adoration and pity, and then we don't know how to treat them, and they go away crying. They lay their hearts in the road and we trample on them. Never do that, young sir, never do that."

The irony of it—the same old lesson—the same causes, the same effect, misunderstanding, misery, neglect all through the one agency—ignorance. " He didn't know—he didn't know."

You must think that I have been unnecessarily serious, that after all, as the philosopher says, " Nothing matters half so much as we think it does." On the other hand, though, I grant you that at once it is equally true that everything matters a great deal more than we think it does.

There is light-hearted, full-blooded humour in every single one of these novels (with the exception, perhaps, of Conrad's) : without it half the philosophy would be lost. These young men do not take themselves quite so seriously as I have perhaps led you to think, but I

have only just time to touch upon the really salient
features. I dare not pretend to offer you anything
like a complete picture of (for instance) the sympathy
with which they draw the very people who are the prime
movers of all the evil—the parents, the schoolmasters,
the parochial-minded advisers of their youth. They
are all treated with courtesy, their good points given
full play; and they have, of course, any number of
good qualities. They have their awful tragedies too;
the only thing is that they are mercifully saved by
their very blindness from ever realising them to the
full extent.

I would press home the need for reading the humor-
ists, the inimitable Mr Munro, Stephen Leacock, E. V.
Lucas, James Stephens, G. K. Chesterton (who has, of
course, as much of a serious axe to grind as any of them),
and so on : they are as essential to our complete diges-
tion and æsthetic enjoyment as *hors d'œuvre*, or sweets
or succulent entrée, but they do not contain the body
of the meal. I am constrained to dwell only on the
soul-satisfying meat course—and your objection, every
man's objection, to meat is that it contains blood.
Vegetarians and other anæmic people (I am striving
not to be unfair) hate the thought of thinking of what
I must, for hurry's sake, call the realistic, naturalistic
school of meat. I am concluding on a general note.

The realists, I reiterate, do not dwell on the sordid
side of life out of a love of the sordid, nor on the ugly
because they prefer ugliness to the beautiful. " We
do not," in George Moore's words, " always choose
what you call unpleasant subjects, but we do try to get
at the roots of things : and the basis of life being
material, the analyst sooner or later finds himself invariably handling what this sentimental age calls coarse
. . . the novel if it be anything is contemporary history

[I refer you to *Dead Yesterday* and *Mr Britling* for confirmation of this], an exact and complete reproduction of the social surroundings of the age we live in.

"Seen from afar all things in nature are of equal worth and the meanest things when viewed with the eyes of God are raised to heights of tragic awe which conventionality would limit to the deaths of kings and patriots."

It is rubbish to suppose that the Realists adopted the idea of unhappy endings because they loved them ; like Shakespeare, they observed that certain causes produce certain effects, and they refused to shut their eyes to a fact which the whole world already knows. Conversely, or rather hence, neutral endings predominate in this school of writing because they also—notoriously—predominate in real life. But all this talk of unhappiness does not detract from beauty ; such an argument is only an illustration of the terrible way in which our minds get confused. Rather have the Realists discovered a new beauty in things, the loveliness that lies in obscure places, the splendour of sordidness, humility and pain. They have taught us that beauty, like the Holy Spirit, blows where it lists—no true Realist but is an Idealist too.

VI

MODERN DRAMA

TWO totally different factors have led me to try
to elucidate exactly whither we are tending
in our stagecraft at the present time : (1) the
hubbub caused by certain generals and bishops who
see in " revue " nothing but " suggestiveness " and a
vicious lure ; and (2) the brilliant critical work of the
late Mr Dixon Scott, published under the title of *Men
of Letters*.

With regard to the theatre of to-day the most obvious
criticism to make is that out of all the thirty or so plays
now running in London, every one of which draws a
full house every night, only two are by men of recognised standing in the dramatic world, and one of these
is a revival. And yet only three years ago our most
enlightened and unbiased historians were stating quite
definitely that the novel had had its day and was
immediately to be supplanted by a literary revival
in drama which should astonish the world. The
machine-made plays of Sardou had been ousted by
the freer, more naturalistic school of Ibsen. The stage
had become a platform for the discussion of all the
intricate problems of modern life, the emancipation of
women, the crime of poverty, false romanticism, Home
Rule, the struggle between labour and capital, the evils
that arose from all forms of stereotyped conventions,
and so on. Most of the leading writers of our time had
contributed their quota to these polemical discourses,

161

nearly always with brilliance, if not with an altogether satisfactory knowledge of craftsmanship and technique. There were also meteoric flights of poetic geniuses who neither followed nor founded any school, but flashed brilliantly for an hour and then swept by.

Then the war came, and with it the cessation of all serious drama. All domestic problems vanished before the one great, overwhelming one of coping with the enemy, and this was scarcely one to brook being discussed on the boards. Moreover, there was no argument; the maximum output of energy directed into its best channels was the only theme of the ardent patriots. The nerves of the nation became tense, its muscles taut; we all went into training. The result was that we temporarily lost sight of art or its uses. Relaxation we understood to be necessary for all of us, else why should soldiers ever be granted leave? The point was: What sort of relaxation was best for the fighter and worker? We were not long left in doubt. America stepped into the breach left by the legitimate drama's decease and charmed us with "revue." Musical comedy maintained a rather precarious hold on its conservative lovers, comedy and tragedy proper died, the music halls, in order to save their lives, were compelled to abandon isolated "turns" for this new craze, and as a result we have now the choice between "revue" and . . . nothing.

Men back from the front were supplied with the dishes for which their souls ached: lightness, prettiness, merriment, catchy songs, colour, youth, and, in moderation (because of its exceeding rarity), beauty. They found it possible to forget all the mud and blood, the horror of separation and death; for three hours they could laugh whole-heartedly, lose themselves in delight and carry away impressions of gaiety which would buoy them up in dark moments which threatened their future.

Suddenly a warning voice sounded : the voice of a man whom all Englishmen respect ; a second followed ; a third . . . and half the nation began to repeat the admonition. "These 'revues' are vulgar, naughty, even vicious ; they lead men on to active evil ; they affect our morals ; we are becoming as a result loose, decadent, foul-minded." It was an astonishing thought. Most of us in our heart of hearts had deplored the decay of all serious plays, but it was easy to understand that a man back from the front would not wish to be wearied with the domestic problems of Poor Law and housing abuses ; on the other hand, we had heard so much of the renaissance of a poetic spirit in the trenches that we thought that some genius might have produced a literary drama to satisfy the craving for beauty which we all confess to. But it had never struck us that these gossamer-like, inconsequent, jovial " revues " were active agents of the devil : we had taken them as narcotics. That they were frequently dull, rarely as witty as we could have wished, with no definite point, we knew ; so were many sermons, but we did not stigmatise sermons as immoral on that account ; that many of the girls were pretty and vivacious we hoped, but did not always find, but surely it was possible to like prettiness and youthful charm without debasing that liking into something worse. Frankly, we looked in vain for those demoralising features which were said to be the ruin of our manhood. The jokes, such as they were, seemed to be in much better taste than those current in the music halls and musical comedies of five years ago ; they were also a trifle less dull ; once or twice they almost approached the subtle . . . but you don't want subtlety in a narcotic.

You require no stimulus to the intellect, rather is the object to soothe it, to send your thinking powers to sleep. That object the creators of " revue " seem to me to have produced.

I am amazed at the hue and cry raised at present against these so necessary amusements, but it does indirectly raise the question of serious acting.

Surely there must by now be many people who are tired of an interminable round of " telephone scenes," of the effect (once so bizarre and delectable) of playing the " revue " backwards, of jingling, meaningless rhymes, and songs that drive you desperate with their thinness of melody and lack of originality in theme.

It is time a new dramatist arose to carry on the high traditions of 1913, to give us fresh ideas and nobler ideals, to amuse us, not by buffoonery, but by subtlety and charm, to ensnare us artistically. We do not want merely the revival of Shakespeare and Sheridan, we want a fresh impetus in the world of drama as we have in the sphere of poetry and painting, fiction and music. Why is it that the theatre alone has played us false in this crisis ? In the face of incredible difficulties, artists and musicians have kept the flame of beauty alive in our hearts; it is time beauty returned to the stage. At the present day most thinking men and women seek pleasure anywhere but in the theatre : the galleries are crowded, the concert halls better attended than ever before. The only reason why the " revues " are full is because everyone necessarily gravitates in war-time to London. The country is unbearable ; we tend to become introspective, which spells madness in these days. Being in London, we naturally attend its theatres . . . consequently money is pouring into the laps of the managers and proprietors.

But if only a little courage could be cultivated by these most conservative purveyors of amusement I think that they would find that Brighouse and Barrie are not the only serious playwrights who are able to command our attention. Where are Granville Barker, Shaw, Arnold Bennett, Masefield and Chesterton ?—to mention the most obvious quintette.

Do the theatre owners really think that we are unable to appreciate the artistry of such plays as *The Madras House*, *Nan*, *Magic*, *The Great Adventure*, or *How He Lied to Her Husband*? We are much more critical, much more alert than we used to be, as a natural consequence of our quadrupled energy. We do not want eternal narcotics as our refection; after a time they cease to take effect. A change of environment, not mere blankness, is the best refreshment for the body and brain, the jaded munitioner or the wounded warrior. It is just as much a national service for our great playwrights to exert their powers on our behalf as it is for those of us whose lot lies in more mundane duties to do what we best can for the cause to which we are pledged. Who then are the men we look to to come forward and " cleanse our stage," and what is it that we expect from them ?

It is at this point that I would introduce Mr Dixon Scott's critical essays to the notice of those unfortunates who are as yet unfamiliar with them.

Many critics, particularly Mr Chesterton, have written brilliant expositions of the work of Bernard Shaw, but no one has got so close to the heart of the matter as Mr Dixon Scott. To find out exactly what Shaw has done for the stage we have to go back some years, to the days, in fact, when he set out, Quixote-like, to make the theatre " a factory of thought, a prompter of conscience, an elucidator of conduct, an armoury against despair and dullness, and a temple of the Ascent of Man " . . . all this simply because he happened to be dramatic critic of *The Saturday Review*, for, as Mr Dixon Scott has pointed out, Shaw's besetting weakness is a certain stubborn pride of soul which cannot permit him to admit, even in a whisper to himself, that the cause he is engaged in is not crucial. As Rodin has said, susceptible to impressions like all artists and a philosopher at the same time Shaw cannot do otherwise than deceive himself. At any rate by 1898 he had deceived himself into thinking that the drama was his special mission. Now in the first place he lacked the prime essential of all dramatists, the quality of an imaginative sympathy : the quality of just watching with ever-growing delight the doings of every sort and size of people ; no one could be less fitted than he was to give the public the sort of play that they ought to have had. He was intolerant of his audience's stupidity and viciousness, " part of them nine-tenths chapel-goers by temperament, and the remainder ten-tenths blackguards." His early training in socialism had made him unsociable, and a moment's thought will convince us of the limitations of a playwright who wantonly narrows his range because of his misunderstanding of and contempt for the people.

Secondly, the very brilliance of his diction, terse, intellectually incisive, keen and crisp as it had become by years of practice, necessarily cut him adrift from more than nine-tenths of his fellow-men. He could only write definite dialogue, so all his characters have to be men and women of quite definite convictions. All the dramatis personæ seem to belong to one exclusive caste. Thirdly, this exclusiveness made him innocently accept what was then known as the " New Woman " (how grotesque and old-fashioned she seems to-day) as woman.

The amazing thing is that in spite of these limitations—
and it is imperative that we should grasp what they
mean—Shaw's plays do remain the most tonic of our
time.   Behind it all he is actuated by a passion for
purity, gentleness, truth, justice and beauty ; once you
realise this, and regard these plays with the sympathy
they doggedly deride, then you will receive the help
which they hunger to offer.   Such is Mr Dixon Scott's
solution of the vexed question of Shavian drama, and
it is, I think, a fairly conclusive one.   Is there no room
for these intellectual fireworks to-day ?   Surely there
must be thousands of tired men and women who would
revel in a revival of *Fanny's First Play* or *Candida* even
if Shaw could not be induced to write on some fresh
topic.   Shaw on Local Tribunals, on the American
Invasion of the Stage, on the New Army, the New
Woman, the Rich Munition Worker would be richly
humorous, delightfully irritating.   It is not necessary
to believe in Shaw's creed to enjoy his plays ; to take
them too seriously is to lose half the fun, but to allow
a whole winter season to run without giving him a
chance of standing on his head is to deprive ourselves
of one of the most mirth-provoking and intellectually
stimulating treats imaginable.

For those who refuse to see the amusing side of
Shaw's polemical discourses on strikes and morals I
would suggest that a revival of Oscar Wilde's artificial
comedies should be tried.   There at any rate will be
no talk of the poor man's rights, for the simple reason
that there are no poor in his world.   There is Jermyn
Street, Piccadilly, Half-Moon Street, just as there used
to be Bath and Vauxhall Gardens.   There are no problems of poverty any more than there are problems
of morals.   There is just artistry, delicacy and the
beauty of a hothouse plant, and with it silvery laughter,

quiet and self-complacent : not at all a bad recipe for those who wish to forget the pain and lies that await them outside the theatre. It is no question of holding the mirror up to nature either with Shaw or Wilde any more than it was with Congreve and his fellow Restoration dramatists. It is, we may say with R. L. Stevenson, with the object of escaping from life that we turn to books or the stage to-day. No one wants to see our actual conflict with the powers of evil depicted on the London stage. We want to be amused : why not permit society's licensed jesters of the last two decades to come and cut their capers before us once again ? Age cannot wither nor custom stale their artificial humour.

Again, what has happened to the Irish players ? Only a few years ago we were all agog with enthusiasm over the " Celtic Revival," with the sparkling, astringent, tonic qualities of Synge and his compatriots, Yeats, Lady Gregory, St John Ervine, Rutherford Mayne, Lennox Robinson and the rest of them.

Certainly we find a different school of thought catered for again here. There is no question of changing the world. Synge writes down in a musical, rhythmical prose that has never been equalled before nor since exactly what he heard and saw in those remote islands off the west of Ireland. Is there no room to-day for such a play as *The Well of the Saints*, with its central *motif* of the tragedy of fulfilled desire ; do we no longer care to witness artistic representations of world-truths ? To judge from letters and articles in the Press, we are only just beginning to be alive to them : why then banish them from the stage ? Do our theatrical managers really believe that a revival of *The Playboy of the Western World* would involve financial loss ? Why, there never was a time when men and women were so interested in the development of the soul within us. War has made many of us "likely gaffers in the end of all" who might otherwise have been content to crawl from cradle to grave feckless, blind, unambitious and useless as Christy Mahon was before Pegeen Mike (the prototype of war) awoke in him self-confidence and the thousand latent talents which were to make a man of him. There is no sermonising here, but only a vast imaginative sympathy, a telling sense of dramatic values and the haunting melody of a patois few of us had ever appreciated before. There was, moreover, acting of a kind we had never seen in England; these Irish players appeared merely to be living their ordinary lives and we privileged to look through the windows of their cottages as they went about their business, ignorant of our presence.

No wonder the best critics became optimistic and prophesied a brave future for the drama . . . but why have war's alarms driven them from our midst? We need them now more than ever we did.

Why did the repertory system make such headway in Dublin, Glasgow, Birmingham, Manchester and Bristol and fail ignominiously in London? There can be no doubt that salvation lies in this system and in this alone. . . . Such a play as Mr Chesterton's *Magic* has a perennial charm. It can no more grow stale than Max Beerbohm's cartoons or Henry James's novels can. It is for all time. That being so, there is no need to put it on for two hundred nights and then consign it to oblivion as is done with the majority of long-run plays, the machine-made melodrama, the treacly sentimental comedy, the vacuous musical farce or the pageant-play. In common with the works of other geniuses which deal with beauty and the eternal verities it ought to take its turn for a fortnight, say, sandwiched between *Strife* and *The Tragedy of Nan*, then be given a rest and produced again in three or four months. It is just such a fantasy as will whirl you away into a wonderland of pure mirth mingled with real pathos, where shrewdness and intellect are not blunted but rather exhilarated and sharpened. It leaves you thinking, as you come out, over the many suggestions, the flashes of insight into the meaning of life which encrust the play like so many rich jewels. It has the gift, which is almost the criterion of every good play, of not leaving you where it found you. You have advanced yet another rung on the difficult ladder of life.

All these men fulfil Synge's dictum that " on the stage one must have reality, and one must have joy." Mr Granville Barker, the pierrot on pilgrimage, is the next playwright on whom the critical genius of Mr Dixon Scott alights : of his plays he picks out *The Madras House* as the high-water mark of his genius. " Here we have," says Mr Scott, " a beautiful loyalty to life, an exquisitely natural unfurling and effoliation of character and motive, undeflected by an arbitrary concept or merely intellectual creed ; a deliciously fluent pose, balance, grace of construction and design ; beauty comes flying back to this play, a glittering invader, gloriously flushing and confirming all its action." In eighteen years Mr Barker has written only four plays, but each of these will outlast the generation for whom it was written ; for eighteen years he has been laboriously, slowly cutting letters out afresh, in order that he can see and use the virgin ore beneath our phrases, fighting down to something dense as metal, as enduring as a marble pavement underneath, economical as a cablegram and yet with a charm, grace and elegance, a silvery slenderness, a quivering " life " like the spring of a sword-blade ; by a magic of fusion, the incompatible qualities of curtness and charm are made one. Mr Dixon Scott calls *The Marrying of Ann Leete* our one genuine modern tragedy of manners. Mr Granville Barker has been frequently bracketed with Shaw by undiscerning critics, whereas the truth lies in the fact that they are totally opposed. Shaw, convinced that he has the truth in his pocket, flings it in our faces with contempt, while Mr Barker watches us ordinary mortals with a wistful wonder, like a wondering pierrot searching for the truth, prefacing every statement with a tentative, whimsical " perhaps."

Mr Barker sets his characters free in his mimic, magic world, whence all accidentals have been banished, where they can move and change and respond without any interference, and lets them evolve there as they will (none of Shaw's creatures ever evolve !), trusting the spark of vitality with which, as a creator, he has endowed them to guide them in accordance with the final laws of life ; as Philip says at the close of *The Madras House* : " Male and female created He them . . . and left us to do the rest. Men and women are a long time in the making, aren't they ? "

There is a quietness about Barker which is quite foreign to Shaw, a breadth of vision which we should welcome with open arms on the stage to-day if only we were permitted to witness it.

And what of Stanley Houghton ? I am not pretending that *The Younger Generation* and *Hindle Wakes* show us Houghton working in his true medium ; he died before he really found himself. Mr Dixon Scott is probably correct in his inference that another five years would have seen the dramatist as a successful writer of fiction. The immediate point at issue is that there was much in his plays which we deplore the want of to-day. He may have been imitative : we can detect the influence of Shaw, Wilde, Hankin, Bennett, and even Synge in most of his work, but he wrested from these a sense of witty and crisp dialogue which is altogether dead now.

In his plays he may, as Mr Brighouse asserts, have observed life from the comic writer's point of view, which is not the poet's. For his art, not the beauty of life, but the absurdities and hypocrisies of daily existence, were the targets of his aim. Even so we may be duly grateful for such a manifestation of the Comic Spirit, for she is woefully lacking in the theatre to-day. *Hindle Wakes* and *The Younger Generation* did at least bring reality back to the stage, and also joy : they woke us up to the fact that " even in the North " (so provincial are we Southrons !) things are moving ; the youth of the age was knocking at the door and demanding a right to live its own life in its own way. Mr Dixon Scott is hardly just to Houghton ; he is too keen to prove that he was a dramatist by force of circumstances, a novelist by instinct ; he forgets that even in the little that we possess of his dramatic work he shows an insight into character, a sense of " situation," and an amazing shrewdness which are just the qualities we most need on the stage at this juncture.

He does not moralise like Shaw ; he just stands aside, draws the curtain and lets his characters develop normally, shocking us by their crudity, pleasing us with their reality, tickling our minds with their " foreign " method of speech and code of manners.

The debt owed by the drama to Masefield, who succeeds in whatever form of literary composition he undertakes, is by no means inconsiderable. *Pompey the Great* no doubt owes its modern note to *Cæsar* and *Cleopatra*, but its poetry is all Masefield's own. *Nan* is an attempt to create a new form of drama in which beauty and the high things of the soul may pass from the stage to the mind, a result of that power of exultation which comes from a delighted brooding on excessive, terrible things. It is only by such a vision as is presented to us in plays of this calibre that the multitude can be brought to the passionate knowledge of things exulting and eternal.

The short, staccato sentences of Masefield, who always works with an economy of vocabulary little short of astounding, are like scintillating jewels. Like all his great contemporaries, he lets his puppets loose and watches them develop ; no one is ever the same at the end as he was at the beginning of the play, whether actor or audience ; it is nonsense to pretend that we are depressed by an artistic representation of the terrible ; it is only the exploitation of the sordid by the muck-merchants that revolts us ; there is an intellectual delight to be found in all real tragedy unlike any other sort of delight in the world . . . and yet we are told that because it is war-time we must not have serious plays : " They will make us brood." Nothing could be further from the truth.

The quarrel, as a matter of fact, goes deeper than that. It is a question of the unintelligence of the English stage as a whole. The public is given what the public wants ; there are hundreds of intelligent dramatists only too anxious to put intelligent dramas on to the boards, but they are kept out in the cold, solely because the managers will not risk taking on their shoulders the education of the public. Had this not been so we should not have Arnold Bennett lying fallow at this moment.

Cupid and Commonsense, What the Public Wants, Milestones and *The Great Adventure* may not be highly imaginative plays, but they are intelligent, they have humour, they did fill a most pronounced gap in the history of English drama; they left the audience pondering over various problems of modern life, with a determination to get more out of existence, to see, to move, to squeeze whatever juice they could from the inchoate, humdrum medley of contradictions which made up their days. Furthermore, they lent themselves to good acting and brought out the latent talent of all the cast.

None of these modern dramatists ever writes one-man plays. All the subsidiary characters have their own intrinsic importance; they are not mere puppets, who walk on and off, arousing no interest. We are keenly alive to the human side of all the dramatis personæ. Galsworthy, of course, like Shaw, uses the stage as a platform for the presentation of his theses on social problems. More than any contemporary artist he detaches himself from his characters, and gives both sides of a case with scrupulous fairness. In *Strife* we are compelled to admire both the conservative stolidity and courageous obstinacy of the capitalist, and the struggle of the men against their employers. Galsworthy will never show his hand. He has a superb sense of situation and of atmosphere, and presents both with beautiful, consummate artistry. In *The Silver Box* each character is delineated with a masterly insight and a tremendous sympathy made individualistic by the exact truth of the dialogue. No other dramatist has ever succeeded in giving the everyday talk of the artisan and charwoman with such artistic truth; his favourite maxim, that " character is destiny," gives the keynote to all his creatures, particularly to the poor, feckless hero of *Justice*; he is always quiet and relentlessly logical, and never makes a bid for our

tears, which may account for the extent to which our
emotions are always roused on witnessing one of his
plays.   He rouses us to fury by his carefully feigned
aloofness ; the truth is that he himself is passionately
alive to the anomalies of the law and the dire and
awful penalties that man incurs, unwitting, by taking
one false step.   His conception of tragedy is akin to
Shakespeare's : man sets the wheels of Fate in motion
and no power on earth can prevent them from
slowly crushing him and grinding round to their
inexorable end.   " The wheel is come full circle : I
am here " might well be taken for the text of all
his plays.

Yet just as the Elizabethan audience, in the intervals
of fighting, could and did revel in the tragedies of
Shakespeare, delighting therein, so surely would our
warriors of to-day find solace and comfort in witnessing these plays of Galsworthy with their artistic beauty
and philosophic quietude.   They supplied a craving of
the soul when they were first written, in the far-off
days of peace.   Surely our souls do not crave less for
inspiration now than they did then.

Barrie has made numbers of mistakes as Stevenson
foreshadowed as long ago as 1892 (" Stuff in that young
man ; but he must see and not be too funny ") ; he
wrote *Rosy Rapture*, which would have damned a
lesser man ; but he also wrote *An Admirable Crichton*
and *Peter Pan*, and he is immediately forgiven.   His
strength lies in his power to rouse our delight in a one-
act play, *Rosalind, The Will, The Twelve-pound Look*
and *The New Word*—he can quietly, whimsically yet
quite surely in half-an-hour make us run through
the whole gamut of human emotions ; he is a master
of quaint conceits, of bizarre touches and childlike in-
genuousness—and yet all the time, as Mr Dixon Scott

puts it, we are cognisant of two quite separate " egos " fighting for the mastery in this man's composition : one, the solemn aspirant, tremendously aware of the dignity of letters, worshipping portraits of great writers with all the grim ambitiousness of the Scot ; the other, an incurable lover of the pretty and the prankish. People are fond of saying that he has never grown up ; the truth is that he has grown dull and dwindled just when he longed most passionately to tower, and finds his feet perversely trotting off to the Round Pond to play with children, when all the time he was ordering them to mount the granite staircase that leads to lasting fame. " When he is neither humorous nor pathetic he is nothing," says Arnold Bennett ; " imagine a diet all salt and sugar "—and this is, in truth, the final word with regard to him. He is always touching us to laughter or tears ; no one living can move us more quickly to weep with laughter and then, within a moment, cause us to weep with grief, only to laugh hilariously again the next second. His diet is really all condiments : there is no " body " in it, no lasting nutriment, as there is in the work of Galsworthy and Barker—and yet there is artistry, there is a shimmery sort of beauty, opalescent, gossamer.

Few of our theatrical optimists, in 1913, would have dared to prophesy that by 1916 St John Hankin would be dead, but his name has crossed the lips of no playgoer since the war began. Surely we have not advanced so far that we can afford to neglect such supremely witty, clarifying, astringent work as *The Charity that Began at Home*, *The Cassilis Engagement* and *The Return of the Prodigal*. He has something of the aristocratic detachment of Galsworthy, the same limpid, musical prose style and acute perception of dialogue—all of which excellences are sadly to seek

in the stage to-day ; we might as well shut our eyes
to the beauty of Wilde. They have this much in
common : a shrewd sense of humour and a telling
sense of " situation." Hankin cared a good deal about
social problems, Wilde not at all. Both were devoted
to the cause of art, and gave of their best to make the
stage intelligent and literary. Perhaps no other man
is so well qualified to make us forget the miseries of our
own time as a genius of Wilde's temperament, with
his astonishing epigram and paradox, his remoteness
from actual workaday life and amoral attitude to
everything.

It is time some producer took his stand and re-
suscitated legitimate drama, revived Wilde, Hankin,
Bennett, Synge, Houghton, Arthur Symons, Stephen
Phillips, Chesterton, Masefield, Barker and Shaw, and
encouraged the young generation to follow in their
steps and perfect what they left undone. There is no
lack of native talent ; it is only waiting for an invitation
to come forward.

It is not immorality that we charge the stage with
nowadays : it is dullness, sheer blankness, a desperate,
stereotyped form of entertainment, without a spark of
originality, relying on age-old, threadbare jests, inane
dialogue, and an absence of any artistry. The acting
is all right. It is marvellous how much our leading
actors and actresses can get out of the wooden, lifeless
parts which are assigned to them.

We cannot too often repeat Synge's dictum that on
the stage one must have reality and joy ; as at present
constituted, there is a lamentable absence of both.
Nothing could well be further removed from either
than the plays which are commonly accounted successes ; a false, hysterical giggling has supplanted joy,
and an artificial convention, as remote from actuality

as the feuilleton in a newspaper, has taken the place of realism.

We never needed amusement more than we do now ; we do not want, as Shaw tried to delude himself into believing, the theatre turned into a sort of pulpit, but we do want it to appeal to our sense of the beautiful, and our intellectual senses. We do not want to be sent to sleep ; we want to be transported, as Shakespeare, Goldsmith and Sheridan transported our fathers, into a land of sheer delights ; we want to feel again the purgative joys of true tragedy, to revel in the rarefied atmosphere of pure comedy, to laugh at the manifestation of the Comic Spirit, not to cackle like buffoons at the antics of clowns and vulgar double entendres.

VII

SAMUEL BUTLER

i

TO the question, "What sort of man was the author of *Erewhon*?" I suppose the best and quickest answer would be: "He was the sort of man who preferred Handel above all other composers, Italy above all other countries, disliked Tennyson, Dickens and Thackeray, and was not afraid to say so, and, according to Shaw's own account, was the prime influence in the formation of that iconoclast's character."

That he is still but little known in educational quarters can be gauged by the fact that at one great Public School the librarian bought from Mr Fifield his complete works, under the impression that they were by the author of *Hudibras*. I know of no other big school where the complete works of our Samuel Butler are to be found. He was related neither to the Bishop nor to the Restoration poet. His grandfather was the headmaster of Shrewsbury; his father the vicar of Langar, near Nottingham, where Samuel himself was born on 4th December 1835. He naturally attended the school where his grandfather had been headmaster, and was there for six years. In 1854 he went up to St John's College, Cambridge, and took a first-class in the Classical Tripos in 1858. In the same year he went to London with the idea of working among the poor and eventually taking Holy Orders, but he now began to doubt the efficacy of infant baptism, which led to his abandoning this project, and he sailed to New Zealand and started sheep-farming instead.   His interest in Darwin's theory of Selection began to manifest itself in 1862, when he wrote to " the Press " on the subject in an article called *Darwin on the Origin of Species—A Dialogue.*   In 1864 he returned to England and settled down for the rest of his life at 15 Clifford's Inn, London, as a painter, exhibiting at the Royal Academy and else-where.   He had constantly been over to Italy since his early boyhood, and in 1870 he returned there to recover from a spell of overwork.   The same year he met Miss Eliza Mary Ann Savage, who so influenced the rest of his life, and whose character is so splendidly portrayed in Alethea in *The Way of All Flesh.*   In 1872 *Erewhon* was published, and the following year saw the publica-tion of *The Fair Haven,* an ironical work purporting to be " in defence of the miraculous element in our Lord's ministry upon earth, both as against rationalistic impugners and certain orthodox defenders," written under the pseudonym of John Pickard Owen, with a memoir of the supposed author by his brother, William Bickersteth Owen.

This book, to Butler's supreme joy, was taken seriously by certain Church papers and praised for its splendid defence of orthodox Christianity.

Between 1876 and 1886 he experienced serious financial difficulties, but he had the good fortune in the first of these years to make the acquaintance of Mr Henry Festing Jones, who has preserved for us so many of his conversations and given us Butler's greatest work in *The Notebooks,* wherein is contained all the cream of his philosophy and humour.

In 1877 was published *Life and Habit,* which gives in detail his views on Darwin's theory and his points of divergence from it. It was followed, in 1881, by *Alps and Sanctuaries*, one of his most interesting and perhaps the most charming of his works, as he wrote it in holiday mood and illustrated it throughout himself. In 1883 he began to compose music as nearly as he could in the style of Handel. Two years later Miss Savage died, and the year following the death of his father finally ended his financial distress.

In 1892 he gave his lecture on *The Humour of Homer*, in which we see, for the first time, his conception as to the authorship of the *Odyssey*, which he maintained was written by a woman and very probably by Nausicaa.

In 1897 he printed *The Authoress of the Odyssey*, to strengthen this view, and in 1899 he published a most valuable criticism on Shakespeare's Sonnets, in which he follows the autobiographical tradition very strongly. 1901 saw the publication of *Erewhon Revisited*, and on 18th June 1902 he died, leaving behind the MS. of his purely autobiographical novel, *The Way of All Flesh*, which was published by R. A. Streatfeild in 1903.

As everyone knows, Butler's fame in his lifetime was not great, but every year since his death has increased the circle of his readers. Gilbert Cannan's able book, followed by that of Mr John F. Harris, has done much to keep him before the public eye, and it is probable that as time goes on the thinking public will be attracted more and more to a man who could think so clearly, argue so convincingly, preserve so perfect a sense of humour and freshen and enliven the imagination and the intellect as Samuel Butler did. He is certainly safe for his " good average threescore years and ten of immortality " if ever man was.

ii

To anyone beginning to read Butler for the first time I should recommend *The Way of All Flesh*, *Alps and Sanctuaries*, *The Humour of Homer* (together with the other essays in that delightful book) and *The Note-books*—that is for a person constituted as I am, with no very definite leanings to biology and the laws of natural selection. *Erewhon* as a modern Utopia is a magnificent piece of writing and worked out with a skill that Swift would not have been ashamed of. To the majority of readers, however, Butler is just the author of *Erewhon* and nothing more ; everyone has read that. I need therefore scarcely waste time in describing what most people know.

" In the department of satire," as Bernard Shaw once most truly said, " Butler is the greatest English writer of the latter half of the nineteenth century." It is very much to be doubted whether irony has ever had a cleaner or more sparkling exponent in this country at all. There was so little bitterness in Butler : he was all compact of quaint, whimsical, jovial touches ; he was one who loved life even after being granted a view into the crystal, such as is given to but few.

The Way of All Flesh perhaps ought to be read first in order that the reader may gain an exact picture of the sort of man Butler was. Many modern readers find it fatiguing to be taken back over so many generations of the life of the Pontifex family, but what Butler had to unfold required a sense of leisure ; he recognised that to the making of a great book went years of labour, and he was content to draw on a big canvas so that we should get the proper perspective of his own life. We are shown the hideous, convention-ridden atmosphere

of a country parsonage in all its phases, and never has
this odious existence been more ruthlessly exposed or
with such wealth of detail. We are given the boy's life
at school, with the gradual dawning of his doubts as
to many of the things which the Victorians adhered to
like limpets as part and parcel of their creed, without
which the whole fabric of their lives would fall about
their ears.

His life in lodgings in London is so vividly done that
nothing could ever make us forget Mrs Jupp, who deserves to live as long as Mrs Gamp. His adventures
with his fellow-lodgers are ghastly, and yet inevitably
true . . . that is what so attracts us about the whole
book : it is real ; you don't feel at all that it was
written about an age long past which we abhor
beyond all others. It would be just as true were it
written about life to-day. Perhaps we care less about
these strange cavillings over orthodox beliefs. We are
also more emancipated in other ways, but we, too, have
just the same fight for the right to live our own lives
even if the hydras we oppose are slightly different from
those against which Samuel Butler so successfully tilted.
The romance of his life we can only guess at. We know
how much he cared for Miss Savage . . . we should
have known that from his picture of Alethea alone.
Why he never married her we do not know ; his affection for her may have been like Swift's for Stella ; it
certainly seems so to the casual reader.

Authors are notorious for the way they make a mess
of the best part of their lives ; their relations with their
womenfolk are best left alone ; it is hard to probe their
reasons and not altogether important.

The feeling that one has on finishing *The Way of All
Flesh* is that we must begin it all over again at once . . .
we then wish and wish that he had written not one but

twenty novels—so terse a style, so definite a point of view, so much sense, so little padding is not to be seen once in ten years in the novels of to-day.

iii

Alps and Sanctuaries was received with contemptuous silence from the critics, for the most part ; those who mentioned it treated it with open hostility. It is impossible to imagine either point of view to-day. It is an open-air, genial book packed with good things, not least among which are the amazing sketches from the pencil of Butler himself. It is simply an account of a walking tour through Italy taken by Butler in the company of his friend, Festing Jones. In it we find that overmastering love of Handel, which was one of Butler's most pronounced characteristics, coming out on every page : a chapel, a valley, a snow-clad peak, a village— any picturesque setting sets him off and he immediately puts it to music. He is reminded of a snatch from an oratorio of Handel, and puts it straight down in the book, and so insidious is his description that he makes you see the place more clearly than any other writer, solely because of his threefold power of attracting you by his music, his painting and his writing.

He tells us all sorts of interesting things about himself : of his dislike of Milton, of his habit of marking in red on the ordnance map the places he passes. He gives you exquisite hints for the avoidance of canting, hypocritical points of view.

Witness this test for liking a picture :

" Would you care to look at it alone ? "

and this for the appreciation of good music :

" Do you find your attention straying to the advertisements on the back of the programme ? "

His sense of the whimsical is almost Celtic, and reminds us of James Stephens. " The potato is a good-tempered, frivolous plant, easily aroused and easily bored ; and one, moreover, which, if bored, yawns horribly. . . ." " The spider is an ugly creature, but I suppose God likes it."

It is in *Alps and Sanctuaries* that there occurs that famous emendation : " There lives more doubt in honest faith, believe me, than in . . ."—which was corrected in the margin of the British Museum copy (a story that sounds too good to be true). How Butler would have loved to have seen that marginal correction.

Philosophy, too, abounds. " A bad sign for man's peace in his own convictions when he cannot stand turning the canvas of his life upside down." This might have been taken by G. K. Chesterton for his life motto, so exactly does it fit that robust Christian.

" Surtout point de zèle," he continues, " take a spiritual outing occasionally, try seasonarianism, people must go to church to be a little better, to the theatre to be a little naughtier, to the Royal Institution to be a little more scientific than they really are."

Is there not some healthy, breezy sort of feeling that comes over you as you read that ? No one but a definitely religious and devout man could have written it—one who had resolutely faced all the problems that worry humanity and forced an answer out of the infinite. Samuel Butler, most of all men, was delighted to wrestle with that same spirit whom Jacob met . . . but who nowadays, for some reason, leaves us alone to our flabby unfitness. (I am speaking here solely of moral fitness, of course.) His literary criticism is of a piece with his philosophical.

" Disraeli's novels are so much better than those

of Thackeray and Dickens because he was always growing."

Then comes the startling information that " any man who can write can draw to a not inconsiderable extent."

The only educational system that has any working value in his eyes is the apprenticeship system. "The principle is that a man should be doing something he is bent on doing and get a younger one to help him. The elder takes the work of the younger in payment."

Apropos examinations : "The most examination-ridden people in the world are the Chinese, and they are the least progressive."

With regard to worrying about the way to fame : "Doors are like the Kingdom of Heaven, they come not by observation, least of all do they come by forcing ; let them just go on doing what comes nearest, attentively, and a great wide door will one day spring into existence." Optimist ! And this is the man whom short-sighted critics have called bitter.

He takes an apt simile from climbing in his advice to would-be artists and writers : "Nothing taxes so much as looking up, nothing encourages so much as looking down. It does a beginner positive harm to look at the masterpieces of Turner and Rembrandt. The secrets of success are affection for the pursuit chosen, a flat refusal to be hurried or to pass anything as understood which is not understood, and an obstinacy of character . . . together with a slight infusion of its direct opposite."

We close the book on a note ringing like a gale sweeping all our preconceived, second-hand theories away like a piece of paper on the rocks.

" Raffaelle, Plato, M. Aurelius, Dante, Goethe and two others (neither of them Englishmen) should be consigned to limbo as the Seven Humbugs of Christendom."

I said : " We close the book." I am wrong. The wise man will find infinite enjoyment in perusing the index, where he will be sent back to follow up such clues as are given by " Pantheism of Rhubarb," or " Rhinoceros grunts a fourth," and other delectable treasures. *Alps and Sanctuaries* deserves far more fame than has yet been accorded to it. It is a joyous, thoughtful book—a sort of *Alice in Wonderland* of a great scientist and philosopher. And it is a truism that the holiday moods of these world-thinkers are not lightly to be despised ; their lightning flashes of merry wit are all pregnant with illuminating, blinding shocks which electrify our system and cause us to delve deeper for ourselves into the world's mysteries and come away from our search enriched beyond all our wildest dreams.

iv

One of the many things we missed by being born about the time of Queen Victoria's jubilee was hearing Ruskin lecture ; another was William Morris. To this we now have to add Samuel Butler's scintillating gossip to working men on *The Humour of Homer*. How he must have shaken the dovecotes of Oxford and Cambridge, if they even so much as heard that a new prophet had arisen who knew not Homer but openly flaunted his belief in the woman authorship of the *Odyssey*. His translation is the only one we know which renders the pure spirit of the Greek into modern, up-to-date English prose.

Here, if anywhere, he has followed his own advice that a man should be clear of his meaning before he gives it any utterance ; having made up his mind what to say, he should say it briefly, pointedly and plainly.

It is in this book that we learn that the *Burmah*, on which he fully meant to sail for New Zealand, went down with all hands. " Surely there is a Providence that guides our ends." It is in *The Humour of Homer* that we also learn that Chapman & Hall refused the MS. of *Erewhon*, on the advice of no less gifted a critic than Meredith.

Butler conceived a theory, fantastic and half-humorous, that Wordsworth harboured a dark secret in his life, and in an amazingly humorous passage annotates the text of one of the " Lucy " poems to prove that he had done the poor girl to death. It would have puzzled him not a little to discover that he was nearer the truth than he thought, and that it remained for an American, in 1916, to reveal what had been successfully hidden from the world for over a century—namely, that Wordsworth, the revered apostle of orthodoxy, the stand-by of all who believe in regularity of living and rectitude of conduct, was the father of a natural child by a French girl whom he was unable to marry.

One piece of advice he gives us with regard to Homer which should be engraven on a text and distributed throughout every classroom in every classical school in the kingdom : " If we are to be at home with Homer there must be no sitting on the edge of one's chair, dazzled."

It is here that he makes his epigram with regard to the three Samuel Butlers of literary fame.

" If ' Erewhon ' were a horse I should say : ' Erewhon by Hudibras out of Analogy,' " in which there is a profundity of meaning uncommon in epigrammatic speech.

It delights the hearts of those of us who believe that

Shakespeare drew upon his acquaintances for his major
characters to find that Butler believed that Mrs Quickly
was found by the dramatist in real life and simply
photographed on to the stage. It needed courage to
say this in the eighties with impunity ; even in 1916
such a statement does not go unscathed.

There is a splendid paragraph in this book on " Titles
for Books I hope to Write."   One of the most inspiring
is " Half-Hours with the Worst Authors."   How many
of us could submit endless cuttings for that gallery
nowadays.

v

And now we are come to the book whereon we should
be content to let all Samuel Butler's fame rest, *The Notebooks*. In this volume are collected together all the
germs of all his work in tablet, portmanteau form.   To
read them is to copy them out ; to copy them out is to
learn them ; and to learn them is an education in itself.

Apparently Butler carried a notebook about with
him wherever he went, and copied into it whatever of
value he heard anyone say or whatever he said himself
that struck him as worthy of preservation.   His reason
for copying them was :

"One's thoughts fly so fast that one must shoot
them ; it is no use trying to put salt on their tails."

By the time that he came to die he had filled well
over five bound volumes, each one taking up over two
hundred pages of closely written sermon paper.   These
he wrote in copying ink, in order to keep a duplicate
of them, and we learn from them about his early life
at Langar, Handel, schooldays at Shrewsbury, Cambridge, Christianity, literature, New Zealand, sheep-
farming, philosophy, painting, money, evolution,
morality, Italy, speculation, photography, music,

natural history, archæology, botany, religion, book-keeping, psychology, metaphysics, the *Iliad*, the *Odyssey*, Sicily, architecture, ethics, the Sonnets of Shakespeare, and a thousand and one other things about life which interested him.

This we now have bound up in one volume of four hundred pages, owing to the indefatigable energy of Mr Festing Jones, who sifted and pruned and condensed and classified such as he found worthy of permanence, and, as I said, the result is that *The Notebooks* will remain for all time as the essence of all that is best in the work of this inspired humorist.

They are divided up into twenty-five sections, oddly titled in some cases, but in no case to be omitted by those who would learn more of life and morality as seen by the acutest man of his time. The first section is headed : " Lord, what is Man ? " and deals with mankind in general. The following note is perhaps typical of all : " A man is a passing mood coming up and going down in the mind of his country ; he is the twitching of a nerve, a smile, a frown, a thought of shame or honour, as it may happen."

We get here a glimpse of that theory which was so characteristic of Butler, that death was nothing, our immortality was the thought with which we enriched the world or that shameful deed which impoverished it. As to the art of living, he says : " A sense of humour keen enough to show a man his own absurdities, as well as those of other people, will keep him from the commission of all sins, or nearly all, save those that are worth committing." This little tang in the tail of his epigrams reminds us of Rupert Brooke and strikes a note which is commonly supposed to be much more modern than the Victorian age in which Butler lived. " Life is like music," he continues. " It must be

composed by ear, feeling and instinct, not by rule.
Nevertheless, one had better know the rules, for they
sometimes guide in doubtful cases—though not often."

It comes as a shock to the conventional, but how it
must have delighted the heart of the youthful G. B. S.
to hear his master say that all progress is based upon
a universal innate desire on the part of every organism
to live beyond its income . . . followed by the quaint
confession that he was glad that he had squandered a
good deal of his life. . . . "What a heap of rubbish
there would have been if I had not," he whimsically
concludes. Life beyond the grave to him means
seventy years of immortality, of fame after he is dead,
as a guide to the next generations of Englishmen who
shall come after him.

A delightful piece of philosophy is contained in one of
his earliest notes, to the effect that all things are either
of the nature of a piece of string or a knife. One makes
for " togetheriness," the other for " splitty-uppiness."
" In high philosophy one should never look at a piece
of string without considering it also as a knife, nor at
a knife without considering it as a piece of string."

The second section is on Elementary Morality, where
we find a code of right and wrong which acts like
ammonia on our dulled senses. " When the righteous
man turneth away from his righteousness that he hath
committed and doeth that which is neither quite lawful
nor quite right, he will generally be found to have gained
in amiability what he has lost in holiness. It is as immoral to be too good as to be too anything else. How
often do we not see children ruined through the virtues,
real or supposed, of their parents ? Truly he visiteth
the virtues of the fathers upon the children unto the
third and fourth generation. Vice is the awakening to
the knowledge of good and evil—without which there

is no life worthy of the name. There cannot be a ' Hold fast that which is good ' without a ' Prove all things ' going before it."

Here we see the reaction against the Nottingham-shire Rectory coming out with a vengeance. This is the result of the convention-ridden atmosphere of strict Sabbatarianism. Oh! that men might be made to see the agony they inflict on their children by a thought-less, rigid code of ethics, doled out without thought of temperament or changing times. Here is a text that should again be hung, not only all round the dormitories of Public Schools, but in every church and chapel in the British Isles.

It is also well that some of us should take to heart what our doctors so frequently tell us, that intellectual over-indulgence is the most gratuitous and disgraceful form which excess can take; for we pride ourselves hypocritically on the fact that half England does no work at all, while we slave for our daily bread night and day without rest throughout the livelong year . . . boasting about it as if it were a virtue; one might as well brag of drinking night and day.

The extremes of vice and virtue, Butler is never tired of pointing out, are alike detestable; absolute virtue is as sure to kill a man as absolute vice is, let alone the dullnesses of it and the pomposities of it.

It sends a disagreeable thrill through one's too comfortable mind to remember that, after all, morality is the custom of one's country and consequently that cannibalism is moral in a cannibal country. On every page of *The Notebooks* we see more and more how much Shaw owes to Butler; of course he has acknowledged the debt, but for some inexplicable reason no one has yet taken the trouble to believe him. Ignorant critics still hiss Nietzsche, and we are content to leave it at that.

Compare this statement, for instance, with countless passages in Shaw's plays : " I believe that more unhappiness comes from the attempt to prolong family connection unduly and to make people hang together artificially who would never naturally do so than from any other." Here is the whole Shavian bag of tricks, the very thing that has sent country parsons boiling over with rage in the pulpit, seething with righteous indignation about " sacred family ties " and all the rest of the jargon so popular among that type.

vi

I propose to pass over the notes that apply to such definitely technical theories as are contained in the Darwin controversy and the germs of *Erewhon* and *Life and Habit* because I am endeavouring here simply to show how necessary Butler is to all who think at all generally or care about the laws that govern our mode of life. Butler's contributions to evolution are, shortly :

(1) The identification of heredity and memory and the corollaries relating to sports, the reversion to remote ancestors, the phenomena of old age, the causes of the sterility of hybrids and the principles underlying longevity.

(2) The reintroduction of teleology into organic life.

(3) An explanation of the physics of memory.

(4) Vibrations—as a means of connection between the organic and inorganic.

With regard to vibrations he tells us that we shall never get straight till we leave off trying to separate mind and matter. Mind is not a thing, or if it be, we know nothing about it ; it is a function of matter.

Matter is not a thing, or if it be, we know nothing about it ; it is a function of mind.

He then proceeds to take an apt illustration from eating. Cooking, he says, is good because it makes matter easier by unsettling the meat's mind and preparing it for new ideas. So with thoughts ; they are more easily assimilated that have been already digested by other minds.

Sitting quiet after eating is akin to sitting still during divine service, so as not to disturb the congregation. We are catechising and converting our proselytes, and there should be no row.   As we get older we must digest more quietly still, our appetite is less, our gastric juices are no longer so eloquent ; they have lost that cogent fluency which carried away all that came in contact with it.   They have become sluggish and unconciliatory. This is what happens to any man when he suffers from an attack of indigestion.   The healthy stomach is nothing if not conservative.   Few radicals have good digestions.

Again, you notice the sting in the tail which increases the value of the whole epigram and opens up a whole new field of thought.

In this same section of notes on Mind and Matter we come across that note on Nightshirts and Babies which so pleased the heart of John Harris.

" On Hindhead, last Easter, we saw a family wash hung out to dry.   There were papa's two great nightshirts and mamma's two lesser nightgowns and then the children's smaller articles of clothing and mamma's drawers and the girls' drawers, all full swollen with a strong north-east wind.   But mamma's nightgown was not so well pinned on and, instead of being full of steady wind like the others, kept blowing up and down as though she were preaching wildly.   We stood and laughed for ten minutes. The housewife came to the window and wondered at us, but we could not resist the pleasure of watching the absurdly lifelike gestures which the nightgowns made. I should like a *Santa Famiglia* with clothes drying in the background."

vii

But it is on the subject of the making of music, pictures and books that Butler pleases the ordinary man of the world most. Here we get more clues than we can find in any other literary man's work that I can for the moment recollect, except, perhaps, Robert Louis Stevenson.

"What we should read," he says, "is not the words but the man whom we feel to be behind the words."

Again : "Words are like money : there is nothing so useless, unless when in actual use. Books are simple imprisoned souls until someone takes them down from the shelf and reads them."

He says that the same rule applies to the making of literature, music and pictures ; what is required is that the artist shall say or depict what he elects to say or depict discreetly ; that he shall be quick to see the gist of a matter and give it pithily without either prolixity or stint of words . . . the fewest words or touches, there lies the secret of the whole business.

Shortly after this we come upon a most illuminating piece of advice : "I have always found compressing, cutting out, and tersifying a passage suggest more than anything else does. Things pruned off in this way are like the heads of the hydra, two grow for every one that is lopped off. Brevity is not only the soul of wit, but the soul of making oneself agreeable and of getting on with people, and indeed of everything that makes life worth living."

To our surprise he tells us to let the main work slide when a number of small things remain to be done, just as we do with unpaid bills. If we attend continually and promptly to the little that we can do, we shall ere long be surprised to find how little remains that we cannot do. "The rule should be never to learn a thing till one is pretty sure one wants it," he says, apropos knowledge and power. "There are plenty of things that most boys would give their ears to know, these and these only are the proper things for them to sharpen their wits upon." If a boy is idle and does not want to learn anything at all, Butler would not have him flogged into learning things against the grain, but rather that he should never be made to learn anything till it is pretty obvious that he cannot get on without it.

In conclusion he tells us : " Don't learn to do, but learn in doing " [this is only the apprenticeship note amplified]. "Let your falls not be on a prepared ground, but let them be *bona fide* falls in the rough and tumble of the world ; only, of course, let them be on a small scale in the first instance till you feel your feet safe under you. Act more and rehearse less. Above all, work so slowly as never to get out of breath. Take it easy, in fact, until forced not to do so. Do not hunt for subjects, let them choose you, not you them. Only do that which insists upon being done and runs right up against you, hitting you in the eye until you do it. Till called in this way do nothing." This is invaluable advice to all young writers possessed of feverish energy who whip themselves into action, however flagging their spirit is.

One of Butler's great charms is this potent doctrine which compels you to act on his advice as if he were

some great Harley Street specialist. It is only what
we expect to find when we read that Butler is here
preaching after practising. He tells us that he never
made his books : they grew, insisting on being written ;
he confesses that he did not want to write *Erewhon*, he
wanted to go on with his painting ; only those books
live, he thinks, that have drained much of their author's
own life into them. The personality of the writer interests us far more than his work. Everything should
be read aloud as soon as it is written in order to detect
those weak places which when read to oneself are
passed over as all right.

Lastly, the audience to whom one should address
one's thoughts are mainly specialists and people
between twenty and thirty. After the age of thirty,
he shrewdly remarks, only a few men and women read
at all.

viii

The next note is on Handel and Music. From boyhood Butler had worshipped Handel. Even so, as is
so typical of Butler, he admires Handel as a man just
as he admires Shakespeare as a man, more than his
work ; behind all the art and the music he feels the
presence of the great, heroic soul. Perhaps the reason
for his placing him above Bach and Beethoven can be
more easily understood when we read that Handel is
so great and so simple that no one but a professional
musician is unable to understand him. The greatest
men do not go over the heads of the masses ; they take
them rather by the hand. Moreover, and this makes
a tremendous appeal to a man who detested shams,
Handel knew when to stop, and when he meant stop-
ping he stopped much as a horse stops, with little, if
any, peroration.

Add to this his capacity for bringing to mind a fine piece of scenery by a haunting strain and you have Handel's genius in a nutshell. It disgusted Butler beyond all expression to think that we buried Dickens in the next grave, cheek-by-jowl with Handel. Art, says Butler, and this applies equally to Handel's music and all great writing and painting, has no end in view save the emphasising and recording in the most effective way some strongly felt interest or affection. Everything else is sham art. We are to think of and look at our work as though it were done by our enemy. If we look at it to admire it we are lost. The only men who go on improving are those who are always *bona fide* dissatisfied with their work.

In the section headed "The Position of a Homo Unius Libri" we learn more interesting details of Butler's own life. He there tells us his aversion from the literary and scientific giants of his age. "If I was to get in with them I should hate them and they me. I should fritter away my time and my freedom without getting a *quid pro quo* ; as it is, I am free and I give the swells every now and then such a facer as they get from no one else ; I know that I don't go the right way to get on in a commercial sense, but I am going the right way to secure a lasting reputation and that is what I really care for. I have gone in for posthumous fame only, and that I believe I shall secure."

When he had written *Erewhon* people immediately implored him to set to work at once and write another book like it. Nothing, he says, is so cruel as to try and force a man beyond his natural power ; if he has got more stuff in him it will come out in its own time and in its own way. The more promise a young writer has given, the more his friends should urge him not to over-tax himself. He lost apparently over £750 on his

books, and gives as a reason the fact that he attacked
people who were at once unscrupulous and powerful
and made no alliances.   His own age would not tolerate
him because he attacked two powerful sets of vested
interests at once — the Church and Science.   It is
better, he concludes, to write fearlessly for posterity,
if you can afford to, than to write like George Eliot and
make a lot of money by it.   As to being adequately
paid, however, he says, who can say, when we realise
how much we inherit from past generations and all
that now makes life worth living, London, with its
sources of pleasure and amusement, good theatres,
concerts, picture galleries, the British Museum Reading
Room, newspapers, a comfortable dwelling, railways
and, above all, the society of friends we value.   In the
note which follows this on Cash and Credit we hear
more about the requirements of the true writer.   Emphasising again the need for brevity and clarity he proceeds to point out the necessity for honesty.   Whether
a book will personally do him good or harm should
never be allowed to weigh at all with a writer ; he only
is the genuine man of letters who lives in fear and
trembling lest he should fail in respect of keeping his
good name spotless among those whose opinion he
values, who never writes without thinking how he
shall best serve good causes and damage bad ones.
Such work is done as a bird sings—for the love of it—
it is persevered in as long as body and soul can be kept
together without thought or hope of pecuniary reward.
As soon as any art is pursued with a view to money,
then farewell all hope of genuine good work.   There is
a certain sort of person very commonly to be found
among those who despise all art, who asks, when he
sees a great picture, reads a fine poem, or hears a rich
sonata or oratorio : " Well, this is all very well, but

what useful purpose does it serve ? " And we are in nine cases out of ten hard put to it to answer in such a way as to make our opponent understand.

It is refreshing to listen to Butler on this vexed question : " When I look at those works which we all hold to be the crowning glories of the world, as, for example, the *Iliad*, the *Odyssey*, *Hamlet*, *The Messiah*, Rembrandt's portraits, or Holbein's, or Giovanni Bellini's, the connection between them and use is, to say the least of it, far from obvious. Music, indeed, can hardly be tortured into being useful at all, unless to drown the cries of the wounded in battle, or to enable people to talk more freely at evening parties. The uses of painting, materially speaking, are again very doubtful ; and literature may be useful until it reaches its highest point, but the highest cannot be put in harness to any but spiritual uses. So we conclude that it is fatal to the highest art that it should be done with a view to those uses that tend towards money."

As so many great writers have endeavoured to define that indefinable will-o'-the-wisp word Genius, we are all the more delighted to get still a different facet shown us by Butler. Everyone, he says, has more or less genius—that is to say, everyone has more or less madness and inspiration—but it is the small excess weight of it that carries a man over the border. It is, he says, exquisitely parodying Carlyle, the supreme capacity for getting its possessors into trouble of all kinds and keeping them therein so long as the genius remains. It is a mistake to suppose that men possessed of this spirit are always painstaking ; sometimes if they had been less so they would have been greater geniuses.

Pains can serve it or even mar it, but they cannot make it. Perhaps an even better definition would be that genius is the supreme capacity for saving other people from having to take pains, if the highest flights of genius did not seem to know nothing about pains one way or the other. Genius points to change, and change is a hankering after another world, so the old world suspects it as subversive of order, unsettling to our *mores* and hence immoral.

But you must be careful here to take Butler's connotation of morality. Absolute morality, it follows from the above, is absolute stagnation and death—hence immorality, in his sense, is not only necessary but beneficial—a synonym for all progress. And this in Butler's view is genius, the curious elusive faculty which so despises the world, of which the world is so permanently enamoured, and the more it flouts it the more the world worships it, when it has once well killed it in the flesh. As it cannot be bought with money so it still less can sell what it produces. The only price that we can pay for it is suffering, and this is the only wages it can receive.

Genius and common sense are like wife and husband, always quarrelling, and the latter always imagining himself to be master while in reality genius is by far the better half. Dullness is much stronger than genius because there is so much more of it—an Arctic volcano can do nothing against Arctic ice, as Butler beautifully expresses it. He sums up in a nutshell the difference between ephemeral and permanent success by the epigram that independence is essential for the latter but fatal to immediate prosperity.

ix

It would be hard to find so much wisdom in any other six volumes as is contained in the few notes, the essence of which I have tried to convey in the last section.   In section twelve we are brought near to the man himself, "The Enfant Terrible of Literature."   "If I cannot," he begins, " and I know I cannot, get the literary and scientific big-wigs to give me a shilling, I can, and I know I can, heave bricks into the middle of them." He immediately heaves a big one at the literary critics of his day.   "Talking it over, we agreed that Blake was no good because he learnt Italian at sixty in order to study Dante, and we knew Dante was no good because he was so fond of Virgil, and Virgil was no good because Tennyson ran him, and as for Tennyson—well, Tennyson goes without saying."

I should like to have been in the Athenæum Club with the bishops and headmasters and antique, well-groomed critics when that note was first published, and read it out loud to as large an audience as I could have gathered round me and then got Herkomer and Augustus John to paint their faces : another thing I have missed by being born too late.   For years we nourish within our own minds our secret dissatisfaction with poets who have been thrust down our throats as divine, never daring to contradict our elders, and here is a man old enough to be our great-grandfather who openly propagated his opinion fearlessly years before we were born.   What cowards we are !

He then goes on to throw bricks into the rose-garden of the Victorian prose-writers.   "Mr Walter Pater's style is to me like the face of some old woman who has had herself enamelled.   The bloom is nothing but powder and paint, and the odour is cherry-blossom. Matthew Arnold's odour is as the faint sickliness of hawthorn."   No one who reads that will ever be able to read either of these stylists without recalling these amazingly perfect similes.   What consternation they must have caused in the academic circles of his day : how good for the undergraduate bookworm of the day to have been compelled to write his essays from Butler's *Notebooks*.

It is at this point that Butler makes his general confession.

" I have left unsaid much that I am sorry I did not say, but I have said little that I am sorry for having said, and I am pretty well on the whole, thank you."

On the question of style we learn more in a paragraph of Butler's than from whole books of better-known men.

" I never knew a writer yet who took the smallest pains with his style and was at the same time readable. Plato's having had seventy shies at one sentence is quite enough to explain to me why I dislike him. A man may, and ought to take a great deal of pains to write clearly, tersely and euphemistically : he will write many a sentence three or four times over—to do much more than this is worse than not re-writing at all : he will be at great pains to see that he does not repeat himself, to arrange his matter in the way that shall best enable the reader to master it, or cut out superfluous words, and even more, to eschew irrelevant matter : but in each case he will be thinking not of his own style but of his reader's convenience. I do not know whether I have a style or not : What I believe and hope I have is just common, simple straightforwardness. More than this is a loss to yourself and your readers."

Incidentally it does seem to occur to him that he may have been begging the question, for after all is not this a definition of style—and a counsel of perfection at that ? Butler almost confesses so immediately after. In fact, he sums up his point of view and clinches the argument finally in another passage in an earlier portion of the book : " A man's style should be like his clothes, neat, well-cut and such as not to call any attention to him at all."

He returns immediately to his criticism of authors. He finds *The Pilgrim's Progress* an infamous libel on life and things, a blasphemy against the fundamental ideas of right and wrong ; its heaven is essentially infidel, a transformation scene at Drury Lane. " ' No crown, no cross for me ' is the bargaining, Jewish spirit that pervades it. There is no conception of the faith that a man should do his duty cheerfully, with all his might, though he will never be paid directly or indirectly. Still less is there any conception that unless a man has this faith he is not worth thinking about." No wonder Butler abandoned the thought of taking Holy Orders. Like nearly all other iconoclasts, like Shelley especially, he was angry at a world which refused to smash a half-and-half religion and demand for itself one nearer to its heart's best desire. " What a pity it is," he continues, " that Christian never met Mr Common-sense with his daughter Good-Humour, and her affianced husband, Mr Hate-Cant."

It is in this note that we learn of Butler's love for Swift, " a far more human and genuine person than he is generally represented," and, strangely enough, his dislike of Fielding.

Probably he was too much of a Puritan to relish the full-blooded canvas of the eighteenth-century novelist. He then generalises by pointing out what we have all of us thought, but no one, so far as I know, has ever yet expressed :

" The highest poetry is ineffable—it must be felt from one person to another, it cannot be articulated."

Apropos of versifying he says that the last thing a

great poet will do in these days is to write verses. He finds *Venus and Adonis* and *The Rape of Lucrece* fatiguing to read ; " They teem with good things, but they are got-up fine things." He considers that a sonnet is the utmost length to which any rhymed poem should extend. He certainly here, as everywhere else, practises what he preaches. I can for the moment recollect no genius so steadfastly consistent as Samuel Butler was, which is another proof of the likelihood of my theory that he was strictly a Puritan at heart : he had all the best qualities of that abused sect. Lest we should mistake his attitude to Bunyan from his foregoing remarks, he tells us that the Preface to *The Pilgrim's Progress* is verse but not poetry, while the body of the book is poetry but not verse.

On Homer we expect to find Butler at his best, knowing as we do his immense affection for the *Iliad* and the *Odyssey*. With regard to translation he says that if you wish to preserve the spirit of a dead author you must not skin him, stuff him and set him up in a case. You must eat him, digest him and let him live in you, with such life as you have, for better or worse. The difference between the Andrew Lang manner of translating the *Odyssey* and his own he compares to the difference between making a mummy and a baby. Lang tries to preserve a corpse, while Butler tries to originate a new life, one instinct with the spirit though not the form of the original. The only person who could ever really translate the poem adequately, he believes, would be some high-spirited English girl who had been brought up in Athens and therefore not been jaded by academic study of the language.

X

It is with a peculiar sense of anticipation that we turn to " Unprofessional Sermons " and read Butler's commentary on the superior ideals of the Greeks and Romans over the Jews. On the subject of Hebraic literature he is, as usual, fresh, satirical and vivid. He picks out The Song of Solomon and the Book of Esther as the most interesting in the Old Testament, but adds that these are the very ones that make the least pretensions to holiness and neither of them of transcendent merit. " They would stand no chance of being accepted by Messrs Cassell & Co. or by any Biblical publisher of the present day. Chatto & Windus might take The Song of Solomon but, with this exception, I doubt if there is a publisher in London who would give a guinea for the pair. Ecclesiastes contains some fine things but is strongly tinged with pessimism, cynicism and affectation; the Psalms generally are poor, and for the most part querulous, spiteful and introspective. Mudie would not take thirteen copies of the lot if they were to appear now for the first time, unless their royal authorship were to arouse an adventitious interest in them. As for the prophets, well, they will not hold their own against *The Pilgrim's Progress, Robinson Crusoe, Gulliver's Travels,* and *Tom Jones.* Whether there be prophecies, says the Apostle, they shall fail. On the whole I should say that Isaiah and Jeremiah must be held to have failed." To-day we can read this without a tremor. Nay, more, most of us can cordially agree, but think of the effect of such criticism, blasphemy they would have called it, on our fathers ! He finds the wisest text in the Bible in : " Be not righteous over much ; neither make thyself over wise : why shouldest thou destroy thyself ? Be not over much wicked, neither be thou foolish : why shouldest thou die before thy time ? " On the subject of knowing what gives us pleasure he quotes from his great namesake, not once nor twice : " Surely the pleasure is as great of being cheated as to cheat." So long as there is discomfort somewhere it is all right. Of prayer he says that prayers are to men as dolls are to children : it is not easy to take them very seriously. In the chapter labelled " Higgledy-Piggledy " we get a potpourri or hotchpotch of good things, none of them without value, many of them never to be forgotten once they are read. He writes of his notes here that they were nct meant for publication. The bad ones were to serve as bread for the jam of the good ones. Certainly there is little except jam at any rate in this part of the book. Witness such an excellent piece of advice as : " It does not matter much what a man hates so long as he hates something."

In an apology for the devil he tells us to remember that it must be remembered that we have only heard one side of the case. God has written all the books.

With regard to the time in which we now live it does us good to think that everything matters more than we think it does, and at the same time nothing matters so much as we think it does. The merest spark may set all Europe in a blaze, but though all Europe be set in a blaze twenty times over, the world will wag itself right again. It is important to those of us who want to gain a full picture of the man to realise that Nature not only meant to him mountain, rivers, clouds and undomesticated animals and plants but also—and much more—the works of man and man himself. Returning to the subject of Providence, he tells us that to put one's trust in God is only a longer way of saying that one will chance it, and as to Providence himself, if he could be seen at all, he would probably turn out to be a most disappointing person—a little wizened old gentleman with a cold in his head, wandering aimlessly about the streets, poking his way about and loitering continually at shop windows and second-hand book-stalls.

To understand a proposition thoroughly, in Butler's words, we must put it on its head and shake it like a purse, and we shall then be surprised to find how much comes out of it.

Often we find that Butler expresses something we have frequently thought but never been able to put into words. An illustration of this may be found in his note on that psalm in which David says that he has more understanding than his teachers. "If his teachers were anything like mine," says Butler, "this need not imply much understanding on David's part. And if his teachers did not know more than the Psalms . . . Heaven help them."

On the top of this comes one of the most poignantly truthful and wise remarks he ever penned: "To live is like to love—all reason is against it—all healthy instinct for it."

It is surprising to read immediately after this, from so stern an ascetic, that he had come to the conclusion that life is, *au fond*, sensual, say what we will. This utterance must have been forced out of him by that undeviating power to state at all costs the truth and nothing but the truth, but it must have been a harder saying to him than almost anything else he ever wrote. The courage of the rigid Puritan who refused to sell his eyes however much the truth hurt him is one of the finest things in all modern literature. The next note may, to a certain extent, explain this a little more clearly. It is called Women and Religion.

"It has been said that all sensible men are of the same religion and that no sensible man ever says what that religion is. So all sensible men are of the same opinion about women and no sensible man ever says what that opinion is."

He concludes the Higgledy-Piggledy section by a note which is never out of my mind when I stand on a platform saying good-bye to some loved friend who is leaving me alone and miserable : "I can generally bear the separation, but I don't like the leave-taking."

In the section on Titles and Subjects we get some glimmering idea of what we have missed owing to Butler's squanderings. What a book he would have made of *Tracts for Children, warning them against the Virtues of their Elders* or *The Elements of Immorality, for the Use of Earnest Schoolmasters.*

What we would not give to be able to read his novel about a freethinking father who has an illegitimate son, which he considers the proper thing; he finds this son takes to immoral ways — *e.g.* he turns Christian, becomes a clergyman, and insists on marrying.

How ably he would have edited the letters of people who have committed suicide together with those of people who only threaten to do so.

We get an insight into Butler's own mode of life from his simile of the cow : "A man, finding himself in the field of a profession should do as cows do when they are put into a field of grass. They do not like any field : they like the open prairie of their ancestors. They walk, however, all round their new abode, surveying the hedges and gates with much interest. If there is a gap in any hedge they will commonly go through it at once, otherwise they will resign themselves contentedly enough to the task of feeding."

It is with a discontented, wretched feeling that we

never have taken the trouble to explore our gaps that we close a volume of Butler : he at least was filled eternally with that divine *Wander-Lust* which is the germ of all progress and without which no great work can be done or immortal fame earned. Butler at least has this great advantage : he never leaves you where he found you ; he points the way to the gaps and gates which we had been too slack or too busy grazing to notice for ourselves, and few indeed ought to be those who, inspired by his example, fail to explore the country that lies beyond the calm, monotonous meadowland of our ordinary vocation.

xi

It is in the chapter on First Principles that he recounts for our benefit that inimitable story of the freethinker who exclaimed : " I am an atheist, thank God ! " which runs close to being the best short anecdote in the world.

With regard to his readers he says : " It is the manner of gods and prophets to begin : Thou shalt have none other god or prophet but me. If I were to start as a god or a prophet I think I should take the line : Thou shalt not believe in me. Thou shalt not have me for a god. Thou shalt worship any damned thing thou likest except me. This should be my first and great commandment and my second should be like unto it. If my readers must believe in anything, let them believe in the music of Handel, the painting of Giovanni Bellini, and in the thirteenth chapter of St Paul's First Epistle to the Corinthians.

" It is not the church in the village that is the source of mischief, but the rectory. I would not touch a church from one end of England to the other." It

almost recalls the Bacon-Shakespeare controversy to
read, apropos of theist and atheist, that the fight between them is as to whether God shall be called God or
shall have some other name.

This section on Rebelliousness is full of carping at
orthodox Christianity. " As there is a peace more
comfortable than any understanding, so there is an
understanding more covetable than any peace," which
is a point of view never before put into words, but no
less true in every whit than the more famous words of
the collect from which Butler found the origin of his
note.

When Butler gets on to the subject of cant and
hypocrisy we see more clearly than ever the legitimate
line between Swift and Shaw. " Gratitude like revenge," he opens, " is a mistake unless under certain
securities. We have organised a legitimate channel
for lust and revenge by the institution of marriage
and the law courts.

" So it is with the profession of religion and medicine.
You swindle a man as much when you sell him a drug
of whose action you are ignorant as when you give him
a bit of bread and assure him that it is the body of His
Lord and then send a plate round for a subscription."
This passage, unpalatable as it may be, is simply a
transcript from *A Tale of a Tub*, written even more
concisely and straightforwardly than Jonathan Swift
wrote. It is inevitable that a man who writes so fearlessly as Butler should be frequently misquoted by his
opponents, and on the subject of drunkenness it has
often been adduced against him that he advocated it.

What he actually said was that in spite of his hating
drunkenness he was convinced that the human intellect
owed its superiority over that of the lower animals to
the stimulus which alcohol gives to the imagination or

illusion, which is a quite different thing and undeniably true.

After having listened to innumerable persons hopelessly entangling themselves in their endeavour to explain the sin against the Holy Ghost, it is an immense relief to turn to a wise man like Butler and read his rendering of the meaning of this difficult passage.

"What Christ meant was that a man may be pardoned for being unable to believe in the Christian mythology, but that if he made light of that spirit which the common conscience of all men, whatever their particular creed, recognises as divine there was no hope for him. No more there is."

And yet, in spite of this note, there are men and women who maintain that Butler is an atheist, a blasphemer and a blackguard. What a crime it is in England to possess an organic mind and dare to follow St Paul's advice about proving all things before you accept any.

As he himself explains, he does not fall foul of Christians and their religion, but for what he held to be their want of religion, for the low views they take of God and of His glory and for the unworthiness with which they try to serve Him.

"When I was young," he continues, "I used to think that the only certain thing about life was that I should one day die. Now I think that the only certain thing about life is that there is no such thing as death." If this is not the utterance of a truly devout man, I have still to learn what devout means.

In " The Life of the World to Come," of all strange places, we hit upon another introspective, personal touch about himself, which is, after all, our main object of search. " I do not read much," he says. " I look, listen, think and write. I note what my friends say, think it over, adapt it and give it permanent form. They throw good things off as sparks ; I collect them and turn them into warmth."

Talking of fictional characters (quaintly enough, in the same note) he points out what Spender noticed in his comments of Bagshot, that bravery, wit and poetry abound in every village. " There is not a village of five hundred inhabitants in England but has its Mrs Quickly and Tom Jones. These good people never understand themselves, they go over their own heads, they speak in unknown tongues to those around them, and the interpreter is the rarer and more important person. The *vates sacer* is the middleman of mind." This section is a weird medley of inconsequent notes, but none the less invaluable on that account. It is here that we come upon that splendid note on " My Son," which no one but Butler could ever have imagined, much less written.

" I have often told my son that he must begin by finding me a wife to become his mother, who shall satisfy both himself and me. We should never have got on together : I should have had to cut him off with a shilling either for laughing at Homer, or for refusing to laugh at him, or both, or neither. So I settled the matter long ago by turning a deaf ear to his importunities and sticking to it that I would not get him at all. Yet his thin ghost visits me at times and though he knows that it is no use pestering me further, he looks at me so wistfully and reproachfully that I am half-inclined to turn tail, take my chance about his mother and ask him to let me get him after all. But I should show a clean pair of heels if I said ' Yes.' Besides, he would probably be a girl."

Now ask yourself candidly and honestly, is not this more satisfying, truer and more pregnant with pathos than Lamb's *Dream-Children*? Of course it is. It might also be made the touchstone on which you can test your appreciation of Butler. If this passage leaves you cold, go back to your Tennyson; Butler is not for you. If, however, you are among that quickly increasing colony of *Erewhon* lovers you will only read on feverishly—and as a result be brought up sharp by one of those astringent surprises which Butler delights to keep in store for some such moment as this by meeting a page of statistics about the sale of his works.

Apparently he lost money on every book he wrote except *Erewhon*, increasing his debit account from £350 to close on £800. On the opposite page to this interesting list of book-keeping we read : " If I deserve to be remembered, it will not be so much for anything I have written, or for any new way of looking at old facts as for having shown that a man of no special ability, with no literary connections, not particularly laborious, fairly, but not supremely, accurate as far as he goes, may yet, by being perfectly square, sticking to his point, not letting his temper run away with him, and biding his time, be a match for the most powerful literary and scientific coterie that England has ever known. I hope it may be said of me that I discomfited an unscrupulous, self-seeking clique, and set a more wholesome example myself. To have done this is the best of all discoveries.

" I am not one of those who have travelled along a set road towards an end that I have foreseen and desired to reach. I have made a succession of jaunts or pleasure trips from meadow to meadow. Nevertheless I have strayed into no field in which I have not found a flower that was worth the finding."

He then catalogues the seventeen different things that he has left for the world to judge him by, among the most important being the emphasising the analogies between crime and disease, the emphasising the analogies between the development of the organs of our bodies and those which are not incorporate with our bodies and which we call tools or machines, the clearing up the history of the events in connection with the crucifixion of Our Lord, the perception that personal identity cannot be denied between parents and offspring without denying it as between the different ages and moments in the life of the individual, the exposure of Charles Darwin and Wallace, the perception of the principle that led organic life to split up into animal and vegetable, the perception that if the Kinetic theory holds good, our thought of a thing is in reality an exceedingly weak dilution of the actual thing itself, the finding out that the *Odyssey* was written at Trapani by a woman, and the elucidation of Shakespeare's sonnets. Not a bad life-work for any man.

xii

It would be foolish to leave this fascinating subject without a word as to Butler's poems. *The Psalm of Montreal* is by far the most famous, on account of the glorious, breezy, unconventional finish to each stanza which everybody knows : "O God ! O Montreal ! "

The reason for this outburst is not so well known. The first stanza will explain :

"Stowed away in a Montreal lumber-room
  The Discobolus standeth and turneth his face to the
    wall ;
  Dusty, cobweb-covered, maimed and set at naught,
  Beauty crieth in an attic and no man regardeth :
               O God ! O Montreal ! "

" Beauty crieth in an attic and no man regardeth."
That was Butler's complaint against humanity, as it
has been the poets' despairing cry all through the ages.

In his next poem, *To Critics and Others*, he imitates
Walt Whitman with conspicuous success :

" O critics, cultured critics !
Who will praise me after I am dead,
Who will see in me both more and less than I intended,
But who will swear that whatever it was it was all
perfectly right :
You will think you are better than the people who,
when I was alive, swore that whatever I did was
wrong
And damned my books for me as fast as I could write
them ;
But you will not be better, you will be just the
same, neither better nor worse,
And you will go for some future Butler as your
fathers have gone for me.
Oh ! How I should have hated you ! "

I should very much like to quote more of this refreshing poem ; it is so exceedingly good for us to be
ridiculed in advance like this. Even after his death
he manages to sting, and he warns us not to thrust
him down the throats of the public of our or any other
age. " You, Nice People ! who will be sick of me because the critics thrust me down your throats, but who
would take me willingly enough if you were not bored
about me . . . neglect me, burlesque me, boil me down
[that's what I've done, being no critic], do whatever
you like with me, but do not think that, if I were
living, I should not aid and abet you. There is nothing
that even Shakespeare would enjoy more than a good
burlesque of Hamlet."

It would require an exceedingly able man to " rag,"
parody, or burlesque Butler, and he most certainly
knew it ; but he failed if he thought that by writing
this poem he would stop critics from writing about him.

It has been his good or ill fortune to have been the
subject of innumerable lectures and articles and even
books in recent years, and by a quaint irony he seems
to have had fewer bad ones than most men. Gilbert
Cannan and John Harris have each of them been
thoroughly imbued with the spirit of Butler, and have
certainly made the way easier for those who have failed
to find him hitherto. Anything which drives people
to read the man for themselves is so much to the
good, for the education of a well-read man may very
well be quite incomplete if he has missed the works
of the author of *Erewhon*. But Butler is nothing if not
unexpected.

Immediately following upon this nasty brick thrown
into the camp of the critics we find a translation into
Greek verse of Mrs Gamp's best remark about Mrs
Harris, which would delight the hearts of any but the
most conservative members of a Common Room.

To those who believe that Shakespeare's sonnets
were merely artificial I would recommend Butler's tremendous counterblast, purposely, with almost hideous
malignity, called *An Academic Exercise* :

" We were two lovers standing sadly by
  While our two loves lay dead upon the ground :
  Each love had striven not to be the first to die,
  But each was gashed with many a cruel wound.
  Said I : ' Your love was false while mine was true.'
  Aflood with tears he cried : ' It was not so,
  'Twas your false love my true love falsely slew—
  For 'twas your love that was the first to go.'

Thus did we stand and said no more for shame
Till I, seeing his cheek so wan and wet,
Sobbed thus : ' So be it : my love shall bear the blame :
Let us inter them honourably.'   And yet
I swear by all truth human and divine
'Twas his that in its death throes murdered mine.''

It would be hard to deny sincerity and passion to
this ; it would not disgrace the pages of any anthology
of English poetry that I know, and yet, so far as I can
recollect, it is included in none.

It is certainly very far removed from mere versifying
if it cannot be claimed as great poetry.

Once again we are reminded of Rupert Brooke's
poetry in the concluding couplet of the sonnet entitled
A Prayer, in which he asks that his open sins should be
forgiven and cleansed first, '' they being so gross,'' and
let the others wait :

" And cleanse not all even then, leave me a few,
    I would not be—not quite—so pure as you.''

I know of no one except some of the very youngest
poets of our time who have this power of leading up to
a daring climax and then turning the tables suddenly,
and so leave you with a point of view at once unexpected, startling, brilliant and yet true.

I have never heard it suggested that Brooke owed
anything to Butler, nor can I find any definite proof of
it, but in the light of the concluding lines of the above
and the next two sonnets I for one refuse to believe
that Brooke did not know his Butler.

In *Life After Death* the last couplet runs :

" Yet meet we shall, and part, and meet again,
    Where dead men meet, on lips of living men'' ;

and last of all in *Handel*, " best lov'd of all the dead
whom I love best," he finishes on a note of panegyric
that is rare indeed :

" Methinks the very worms will find some strain
Of yours still lingering in my wasted brain."

We are now at the end of our journey and I have
obeyed Butler's own advice in boiling him down rather
than criticising him, for the sole purpose of driving
those to whom he is still but a name to cull from the
vineyard whence I have just gathered a sample cluster
of grapes.

His great value to us of to-day is his exhilarating
irreverence, his amazing candour and entire absence of
self-consciousness. He washes us clear from all taint of
the dishonesty that clings round our stereotyped views
on Christianity, money and sex. He stands among the
masters of irony, Swift, Newman and Meredith, the
torch-bearer of that unique gift to a generation not at
all at home in its clear, rarefied atmosphere. His sense
of detachment enables him to become our greatest
commentator on life, by one who looks on. As Mr
Harris says : " In a sense he stands for civilisation
looking at itself and laughing in the realisation of how
funny it all is." This capacity for laughter on all
occasions is one of his most lovable traits, for whatever
else he was Samuel Butler was at all times lovable,
owing to his large-hearted humanity, his never-failing
kindness and undeviating sincerity. He preached in
what is the only possible palatable way nowadays, a
light-hearted, humorous vein. Everything made him
" chuckle "; every twist and turn in the world about him
left him immensely astonished and intensely amused.
He had, as Shakespeare had, the experiencing

mind; everything was grist to his mill; he forgot nothing, because he had the good sense to take notes whenever and wherever a thought or scene struck him as worth committing to paper.

This is an age of much writing and omnivorous reading, but as in art the process of selection is one of the hardest to attain, so in reading; if we choose this we must miss that. Woe to that man who wantonly and wilfully omits to make the acquaintance of Samuel Butler, for he will have lost a chance of making a life-long friend of one of the most penetrating, courageous and original men of letters which England has ever had the good fortune to produce.

We owe Bernard Shaw to him; our feeling on re-reading his works for the twelfth time is one of wonder that he has not left, not one foster-son only, but a score or more, each of them as much superior to Shaw as Butler was to him.

For all who wish to leave behind them some work which shall outlive their own lifetime, a careful study of Butler's works is not only a pleasure but a prime necessity. He will give them fresh ideas and renew their courage and shower on them hints about life and its meaning and how to transcribe its effect on them more abundantly than any other writer of his age.

VIII

RICHARD MIDDLETON

NOW that six years have elapsed since the untimely death of one of the most promising of the young geniuses of the century there seems some danger lest, in the storm and stress of the age in which we live, Richard Middleton should be neglected and forgotten by all save his few disciples and enthusiastic foster-children, which would be an incalculable loss to English letters, for there are few enough in these days who will dare to stand up and preach the gospel of the worship of the beautiful, and fewer still who are able to transport us, as Kenneth Grahame does, to the days when every tree was green, to our own golden age of infancy, to those dream-days of halcyon contents and immeasurably happy moments of early childhood.

Never has there been a time when we so acutely realised the worth of the priceless heritage which we have lost by growing up as now ; and anyone who will sing to us one of the songs of our own innocence, who will remind us of our own childish Arcadia, has a value far above rubies in a time of war.

Richard Middleton was that evanescent, shapeless thing, a meteor . . . he founded no school, he imitated no man, he carried on no tradition. I can recollect no one in the least like him ; he flashed into our ken suddenly, without warning, in 1910. In 1911, failing to make the world perceive that beauty and poetry were essential to man's welfare and recognising that

221

he himself had failed by too much dreaming and too little action, he determined to seek adventure in the unknown and committed suicide in Brussels at the age of twenty-nine.

He was educated at St Paul's School, and then went into an insurance office in the City, afterwards giving up " a large salary," to quote his own words, " in order to write poetry." He became a sub-editor under Mr Frank Harris, but his casual, cheerfully unpunctual nature hardly suited the profession he had now entered, so he threw it up in order to confine his attention wholly to poetry, all of which so pleased Mr Harris that he had no difficulty in getting it printed in the papers over which from time to time his editor had control. In *Contemporary Portraits* Mr Frank Harris gives us valuable first-hand impressions of a man who seems to have been known only to the few.

He had thick black hair, a furrowed forehead, shrewd, wistful, penetrating eyes (like Conrad), had never shaved in his life, and was devoted to, and beloved of, all children. He was deeply read in English, and possessed an astonishingly sure judgment of other men's work : of his own he had the self-criticism of the masters. His prose was always the prose of the singer—limpid, musical, rhythmic, almost too perfectly rounded. And yet in it there is the magic that makes words live ; all his thoughts pass through the testing crucible of artistic perception and come out changed, winged, eternal.

Whether it be that famous story of *The Ghost Ship*, where we seem really to see the fairy barque sailing away over the turnip field, through the windy stars, its port-holes and bay-windows blazing with lights to the accompaniment of singing and fiddling on deck on the part of all the village ghosts who have been inveigled away on it, or that incident in *The Brighton Road*, where the dead boy is eternally condemned to go on tramping—tramping . . . in all his stories there is an uncanny something which makes them take wing beyond the author's conception, that elusive quality which, for want of a better word, we call genius.

His stories are woven like delicate spiders' webs, besprinkled with dew; they are pure gossamer, unbelievably beautiful; but touch them and they fall to pieces in your hand. They must be read in their entirety to be appreciated: quotation in this case is like Dr Johnson's brick, no criterion whatever of the excellence of the building.

The effect is always heightened by a sure sense of humour which crops up in all sorts of unexpected places throughout his work.

What a quantity of wisdom is hidden in this paragraph on his own schooldays. "You're only here for a little spell," he said; "you'll be surprised how short it is. And don't be miserable just because you're different. I'm different; it's a jolly good thing to be different"—and then, after a pause—"All the same, I don't see why you should always have dirty nails. . . ." Or, again, in this story of the author, who, having finished his great book, "read it to his friends, who made suggestions that would have involved its re-writing from one end to the other; he read it to his enemies, who told him that it was nearly good enough to publish; he read it to his wife, who said that it was very nice, and that it was time to dress for dinner."

It is this faculty which must have so endeared him to children. Certainly no other man, Kenneth Grahame and Sir James Barrie alone excepted, ever entered so completely into the thoughts and ways of childhood.

No man has so faithfully transcribed the best moments and those hidden thoughts of our early days which we imagined were forgotten or a part of ourselves that was dead before we came across this book. How perfect and yet how characteristic is the sentence uttered almost unconsciously by the small boy in the wood. "All the wasted moonlight," he cried; "the grass is quite wet with it."

He brings back all the secret longings and untellable ecstasies of our early youth which we never breathed to the Olympians for fear of ridicule. Childhood's loves are strange loves but they are very real; uncanny to the adult mind, but so natural to the infant intelligence as scarcely to need comment. The majority of us are nowadays scarcely enamoured of the lawn-mower, but we have surely not forgotten the day when "the very appearance of the thing was cheery and companionable, with its hands outstretched to welcome mine and its coat of green more vivid than any lawn. To seize hold of its smooth handles was like shaking hands with an old friend, and as it rattled over the gravel path it chattered to me in the gruff tones of a jovial uncle. Once on the smooth lawn its voice thrilled to song tremulous and appealing and filled with the throbbings of great wings. And cheered by that song I might drive my chariot where I would. Not for me the stiff, brocaded pattern beloved of our gardener: I made curves, skirting the shadows of the tall poplars or cutting the lawn into islands and lagoons: with the cold inhumanity of youth I would marvel at the injudicious earthworms that tried to stay my progress and perished for their pains."

Surely that wakes a responsive chord in our minds of days when we burnt witches on the rubbish heap, when we coiled the garden hose round our legs, Laocoon-like, when we, too, launched our Argonauts, braving Farmer Bates' terrible wrath, by sailing past his forbidden meadow, when we too tramped through the woods in search of the magic pool by night.

There are only too few books that are able to transport us back to those golden hours when we played cricket (*real* cricket, when you were out if you hit the ball into the next garden, and stopped playing if you broke a window), owned pirate ships and magic carpets, and founded secret societies in the secrecy of the lumber-room.

Whenever we feel that nostalgia of childhood which overtakes each of us so often amid the worries and cares of life to-day, which causes us to batter vainly at fast-locked nursery doors, or to look sadly at the gaudy toy-shops, robbed by the cynical years of their fit halo, at such a time if we can find no children to play with and our hearts yearn for the fairy laughter of playing infants, to take down a volume of Richard Middleton's child fancies will do much to appease our longing and cause us to live over again those magic hours which we have now for ever lost. Everyone knows that the finest joys he experiences are just the most incommunicable : who can harness Pegasus to describe the sensation of a man who has just made a mighty, almost impossible tackle at "Rugger," brought off a long-practised shot of great difficulty at billiards, sung a song in such a way as to thrill his audience with a magnetism so great that they forget to applaud, climbed a hitherto inaccessible peak, written the last word of a play, novel or poem which he knows to be a living force, eternal, incorruptible : who, I repeat, can hope to express life's great moments even when we have reached years that perhaps have brought the power of self-expression ?

How much less can we hope to regain exactly or ever to reproduce in the minds of other people the days of our Golden Age : at the most absurd moments, while hurrying into school at the last moment, while catching a train, on a route march, in the middle of worrying out a mathematical problem, some insidious sound, a cock crowing, the scrunch of a wheelbarrow, the haycutter in the fields, the pack of hounds giving tongue, some wave of recollection sweeps over us and on the instant we are back in that old garden, chasing the guinea-fowl, penetrating the meadow brook to the forbidden haunts of the pixy-ridden mill and the deep trout pool, seated in the cleft of the blasted oak looking out over Westward Ho ! and Lundy for a sight of Amyas Leigh and Salvation Yeo, for John Silver and Captain Bartholomew Roberts ; some friends show us over their house, and having penetrated every recess, we say, to their complete mystification : " May I see the attic now, please ? " and coldly wondering at the lunatic they harbour as their guest they push us into the raftered room full of apples. In a moment we are thousands of miles away on a lonely sea, plying our raft, with rations given out and hope lost . . . when suddenly the cry goes up : " A sail ! a sail ! " and we are taken on board the friendly sloop and swear eternal vows of comradeship with the pirate chief, whose in-carnadined face, bandage-hidden, haunts our dreams a thousand nights. Such tricks do our senses play us, and how pitiable are those (if there exist any such, which I much doubt) who are never betrayed by the smell of leaves on a November night, by the sight of a Guy Fawkes bonfire, by the chestnut roasting on All-Hallows E'en, when they gaze into the fire and build again those gorgeous palaces which were once so real—so real . . . but I am lost myself. You see the effect of Middleton : he drives you back willy-nilly, and life becomes for a few precious moments all sunshine, laughter and innocence, and war and separation are no more.

But there is another side to Middleton which it is necessary to understand before we can pretend to have in our minds a picture of the complete man. He recurs to it again and again both in his prose and his poetry—and in its essence we might call this trait the lament of the writer, the tragedy of the artist ; an over-powering sense of the inadequacy of the word-maker and the dreamer in comparison with the man of action seems an ever-present topic in the mind of Middleton as it was in the mind of Robert Louis Stevenson.

" While ordinary efficient men and women are enjoying the promise of the morning, the fulfilment of the afternoon, the tranquillity of evening, we are still trying to discover a fitting epithet for the dew of dawn. For us Spring paves the woods with beautiful words rather than flowers, and when we look into the eyes of our mistress we see nothing but adjectives. Does a handful of love-songs really outweigh the smile of a pretty girl, or a hardly-written romance compensate the author for months of lost adventure ? We have only one life to live, and we spend the greater part of it writing the history of dead hours.

"Few of us are fortunate enough to accomplish anything that was in the least worth doing, so we fall back on the arid philosophy that it is effort alone that counts."

And then, in a passage pregnant with real introspection, he gives us a rare insight into his own character. It had been raining, he said, one morning, and while watching from his window he suddenly became conscious of a wet morning years before when he was eight

years old, a real wet, grey day, when he heard the rain
dripping from the fir-trees on to the scullery roof and
the wind every now and then drove the rain down on
the soaked lawn with a noise like breaking surf; he
remembered thinking how nice it would be if it rained
really hard and flooded the house so that they would
all have to starve for three weeks, and then be rescued
excitingly in boats . . . behind him in the room his
brothers were playing chess and his sister was patiently
beating a doll in a corner. The clock on the mantel-
piece ticked very slowly and he realised that an eternity
of those long seconds separated him from dinner-time.

He thought he would like to go out. The enterprise
presented certain difficulties and dangers, but none
that were insuperable. He would have to steal down
to the hall unobserved: he would have to open the
front door without making a noise and he would have
to run down the front drive under the eyes of many
windows. Once beyond the gate, however, he would
be safe.

In the wood near the house he might meet the
magician for whom he had looked so often in vain on
sunny days, for it was quite likely that he preferred
walking in bad weather when no one else was about.
Then he thought of the probable punishments that
would ensue, but they did not trouble him much, at
any rate in retrospect. And yet he did not go out:
he stayed dreaming until the golden moment for
action had passed and he was called back to a prosaic
world by the shrieks of the chess-players, who were
suddenly locked in battle. And this later morning,
as he stood at the window again watching the rain,
Richard Middleton indulges in the vain wish that he
had then set forth to seek adventure. He would have
met the enchanter in the wood and he would have

taught him to conquer worlds, and to leave the easy triumphs of dreams to madmen, philosophers and poets. He would have made him a man of action, a statesman, a soldier, a founder of cities or a digger of graves.

And then comes the crucial passage. He concludes the essay thus :

"It seems to me likely enough that that moment of hesitation before the schoolroom window determined a habit of mind that has kept me dreaming ever since. For all my life I have preferred thought to action : I have never run to the little wood : I have never met the enchanter. And so this morning, when Fate played me this trick and my dream was chilled for an instant by the icy breath of the past, I did not rush out into the streets of life and lay about me with a flaming sword. No : I picked up my pen and wrote some words on a piece of paper, and lulled my shocked senses with the tranquillity of the idlest dream of all.

"My life, my beautiful life all wasted :
    The gold days, the blue days to darkness sunk.
The bread was here, and I have not tasted :
    The wine was here, and I have not drunk."

I feel that in one sense this is the most tragically true, the most artistically great of all Middleton's writing.

It is absolutely impossible to read it without transferring the whole idea over to oneself. It is oneself who has failed, who has stood at the window, and through inertia, panic or for whatever cause, has let the golden moment go by, and instead of sallying forth sword in hand to rid the world of some abuse we have preferred the more comfortable fire and attempted to delude ourselves with the obvious lie that after all, perhaps, there was no wizard in the wood.

Sanity, we have been told, is simply a capacity for becoming accustomed to the monstrous; and Middleton's tragedy lies as much as anything in the fact that though he refuses to call ugliness beautiful, yet he is too much of a dreamer to sally forth sword in hand as the avenger of wrongs.

Most of us forget our early frantic anger at the needless horrors that abound on every side; we have our fight against it young, are thoroughly well cowed and are lucky if in the end we not only agree with and defend the existing chaos and mistake it for order, light and beauty, but quite definitely throw our whole weight on the side of ugliness and make a religion of it. Not so Richard Middleton:

"When a young man first awakens to a sense of the beauty and value of life, it is natural that he should be overwhelmed by the ugliness of the inheritance that his ancestors have forced upon him. He finds in the civilisation that he has had no place in devising a tyranny against which it appears almost impossible to make any resistance, a dogma which he is told everyone except a young fool must accept as a truth. . . . He may, for instance, think that it is better to grow and love roses in a cottage garden than to reign in an umbrella factory: but this briefest of the illusions of youth will be shattered forthwith by what appears to be the first law of civilised life: that a man can only earn his living by the manufacture of ugliness."

He then shows you the young man turning for comfort to latter-day prophets and philosophers, who spend their time, he finds (in Middleton's glorious phrase), in scheming little revolutions on a sound conservative basis : only in the poets can the young man find solace.

It is unnecessary, he goes on, to point out that the dangerous revolutionary spirit which worships lovely things is not encouraged in our national schools.

The children of the State are taught to cut up flowers and to call the fragments by cunning names, but they are not invited to love them for their beauty.

Their lips lisp dates and the dry husks of history, but they have no knowledge of the splendid pageant of bygone kingdoms and dead races.

The cheaper newspapers, which alone are read by the people, as a whole seek out and dilate on ugliness with passionate ingenuity . . . only in the poets, I repeat, can a young man find solace.

And would you know how to be a poet in Middleton's words ?

" Take something—I would say take anything—and love it, and thereafter, if he were a child of his century, I should have to tell him of love, the rude, uncivilised force that has inspired all the deeds worth doing, that has made all the things worth making. I should tell him that it was nonsense to speak of anything or anybody being worthy of his love, that the question was whether he could make his love worthy of any shadow of an idea that penetrates his education. I should tell him—to what end ? That he might see life as he would have made it, and weep his years away ; that he might find beauty and fail to win it ; that he might cry his scorn of ugliness on the hills and have never a hearer for his pains ? Pooh ! It were kinder to let him snore with the others. There are too many unhappy people already."

Yet Middleton himself, with his eyes open, chose the better way : it is as a poet that he lives for the majority of his readers, one who ever strove to keep the sun upon the western wall.

> " Roses and lilies blowing fair,
>   A sunny castle in old Spain,
>   A lock of my beloved's hair,
>   A tale that shall be told again,
>   Joy and sorrow, heaven and hell—
>   These are all the wares I sell."

As one of his critics has said, the visible world and the passions of men and women were all his care.

Mr Frank Harris declares that *The Bathing Boy* is finer than anything in Herrick.

His theory of poetry is to be found definitely, clearly and finally in that remarkable passage in *The Poet's Allegory* :

" So he pulled out his pipe and made a mournful song to himself of the dancing gnats and the bitter odour of the bonfires in the townsfolks' gardens. And the children drew near to hear him sing, for they thought his song was pretty, until their fathers drove them home, saying : ' That stuff has no educational value.'

" ' Why haven't you a message ? ' they asked the boy.

" ' I come to tell you that the grass is green beneath your feet and that the sky is blue over your heads.'

" ' Oh ! But we know all that ! ' they answered.

" ' Do you ! Do you ! ' screamed the boy. ' Do you think you could stop over your absurd labours if you knew how blue the sky is ? You would be out singing on the hills with me.'

" ' Then who would do our work ? ' they said, mocking him.

" ' Then who would want it done ? ' he retorted.

> " When I lived I sought no wings,
>   Schemed no heaven, planned no hell,
>   But, content with little things,
>   Made an earth, and it was well.
>   Song and laughter, food and wine,
>   Roses, roses red and white,
>   And a star or two to shine
>   On my dewy world at night.
>   Lord, what more could I desire ?
>   With my little heart of clay
>   I have lit no eternal fire
>   To burn my dreams on Judgment Day ! "

But we, the great British public, had no use for song and laughter, the sweet beauty of roses in those pre-war days : it is only now that poets can sell their wares and so continue to exist.

First John Davidson and then Richard Middleton—great singers both—had to leave a world grown old and cold and weary and plunge into the unknown, and in one last piteous cry Middleton takes his farewell of us :

> " So here's an end ; I ask forgetfulness
>   Now that my little store of hours is spent,   ·
>   And heart to laugh upon my punishment.
>   Dear God, what means a poet more or less ? "

IX

THE GENIUS OF JOHN MASEFIELD

THOSE of us who were at Oxford between 1905 and 1909 have good cause to be thankful for many things, but above all, for the fact that we were then waking to the reality that we were living in an age of Renaissance. On a certain gloomy November afternoon, long to be remembered, I went to the Corn Exchange to witness the production of some plays of Celtic origin, by W. B. Yeats, of whom we knew something, and of one, John Millington Synge, of whom we and the world about us knew practically nothing.

To have seen *The Playboy of the Western World* acted, with Miss Maire O'Neill as "Pegeen Mike," before anyone on this side of the Irish Sea knew of it, ranks us with the Elizabethan theatre-goers who first saw *Hamlet*, knowing not whether it was to be good or bad. Three or four years later it did not matter. Everyone recognised a master spirit in the Irish playwright, and an unfailing topic of conversation over any dinner-table was the ability of the Abbey Theatre Players to show us what acting really meant.

What mattered was that we were among the pioneers.

Much in the same way nothing can deprive us of the pride of having been one of the first to read and love John Masefield. In 1905 his name, it can safely be said, was absolutely unknown to the great majority of thinking men and women in this country, and yet there are among us several who are certain that he has written nothing so fine or lasting (except *August, 1914*, which is by far the best poem yet written on the war) since that time, and those who assert this are not carping critics. But I wish to expand that statement later.

Those of us who were lucky enough to come into the circle of Masefield-lovers while that circle was still one of small compass feel a thrill of joy and pleasure to think that we recognised the capabilities of the poet and came under his spell before the mass of readers had even heard his name.

The diversity of the man now is bewildering. First we knew him as a writer of lyrics and ballads, one or two of which are unlike anything else in the English language. Shortly after this we found him blossoming out into a novelist; *Captain Margaret, Multitude and Solitude* and *The Street of To-Day* are the novels of a poet, it is true, but they are still able to hold their own in that particular niche, a small one, which contains the novels we keep to read again. And *A Tarpaulin Muster*—a book of short stories—must not be forgotten.

No sooner had we recovered from the astonishment of this than we found him proffering us a second *Treasure Island*, beating Stevenson on his own ground. I know of many boys who prefer *Jim Davis* and *Lost Endeavour* to any other stories of buccaneers, pirates and adventure yet written.

Then those who have seen *Pompey the Great, Nan* and *Philip the King* acted declare that all other contemporary drama is insipid in comparison. He has the dramatist's true touch and absolute realisation of the exigencies of the stage.

But it is not to my purpose here to discuss Mr Masefield as a dramatist, as a novelist, or as a writer of boys' adventure stories.

It is his fate to have become the most popular poet of the age at a bound, and it is possible now, with the mass of material he has produced, to find reasons for this, and to come to some sort of conclusion as to whether it has benefited his art so to have been taken up as a craze.

In nearly every case it has been truly said of poets that their genuine success always varies inversely with their contemporary success. Martin Tupper, Byron and Longfellow are outstanding instances of versifiers who drew crowds to pay homage while they were alive, whereas Keats and Shelley were unrecognised by the great mass of readers of their age, and made little impression on their contemporaries.

As I have a thesis to propound, it will be better for my scheme not to take the poems in chronological order, but to arrange them in the best possible way for my argument.

In one of the lesser known, but most valuable, of Mr Masefield's works, *A Mainsail Haul*, published on the 1st June 1905, occur these verses :

" I yarned with ancient shipmen beside the galley range,
  And some were fond of women, but all were fond of change ;
  They sang their quivering chanties, all in a fo'c's'le drone,
  And I was finely suited, if I had only known.

  I rested in an ale-house that had a sanded floor,
  Where seamen sat a-drinking and chalking up the score ;
  They yarned of ships and mermaids, of topsail sheets and slings,
  But I was discontented ; I looked for better things.

I heard a drunken fiddler, in Billy Lee's Saloon,
I brooked an empty belly with thinking of the tune ;
I swung the doors disgusted as drunkards rose to dance,
And now I know the music was life and life's romance."

The poem gives a good sight into the mind of the author ; in all of his poems there is that insatiable hankering after the sea ; it is dragged in even at the end of *Daffodil Fields*, of all unlikely places.

The poem has practically nothing to do with the sea, but the author cannot resist the temptation to make the story a legend common among sailors ; hence you rise from reading this last stanza, as from all his other poems, with a strong taste of salt in the mouth.

But these introductory verses to *A Mainsail Haul* show us something more.   They explain his right to be considered *The Genius of the Ale-house*.   He must for ever confine his genius to that section of society whose vocabulary is nearly limited to " Hell," " By Crimes," " Bloody " and other even less savoury expletives.[1]

Imitators of Mr Masefield, and these have already been many, have based their forms of flattery nearly entirely upon this phase, forgetful of the fact that it is the lyrical beauty in the background of the poems that makes the poet what he is, and not the daring (it will soon cease to be that) innovation of employing bargee and bricklayer terms to heighten the sense of reality.

The language, customs, manners and traits of the drunkard and sottish are to him " life and life's romance."   He is " finely suited " in describing the ways of the doxy and the labourer's mistress.

---

[1] It is not because he likes it that he does this, but because his hypersensitive nature so abhors oaths that he is fascinated against his will, much in the same way as Anglo-Indian children are fascinated by the venomous beauty of snakes.

In a book published even earlier, *Salt-Water Ballads* (1902), we find this hymn of Consecration :

" Others may sing of the wine and the wealth and the mirth,
  The portly presence of potentates goodly in girth :
  Mine be the dirt and the dross, the dust and scum of the earth !

Theirs be the music, the colour, the glory, the gold ;
Mine be a handful of ashes, a mouthful of mould.
    Of the maimed, of the halt and the blind in the rain and the cold—
Of these shall my songs be fashioned, my tales be told."

What plainer statement of intention can man wish than that ? For eleven years did Mr Masefield cling to his ideal.

Bearing this in mind, I propose now to take in turn the larger portion of his recent output, most of which has appeared from time to time in *The English Review*.

The Everlasting Mercy came out in October, 1911. It tells the story of a young rip, Saul Kane, and starts in this promising fashion :

" From '41 to '51
  I was my folk's contrary son ;
  I bit my father's hand right through
  And broke my mother's heart in two.
  I sometimes go without my dinner
  Now that I know the times I've gi'n her."

It continues in the same easy strain to explain how he fought with a fellow-poacher, Billy Myers, on whose preserves he had been working.

" . . . we whom Jesus died to teach
   Fought round on round, three minutes each,"

By the fluke of his enemy spraining his thumb, Saul gained a totally unmerited victory.

All the company of spectators and victor then proceed to " The Lion " to celebrate the event. On the way up the dark stairs he accosts the barmaid, a mistress of his, and arranges an assignation.

A riotous scene ensued :

> " Jack chucked her chin, and Jim accost her
> With bits out of the ' Maid of Gloster.'
> And fifteen arms went round her waist.
> (And then men ask, Are Barmaids chaste ?)"

This last line reads more like the heading of a letter to a daily newspaper than a serious contribution to contemporary poetry.

After the company had drunk themselves silly, Saul drunkenly meditates on life.   At last

> " A madness took me then.   I felt
> I'd like to hit the world a belt.
> I felt that I could fly through air,
> A screaming star with blazing hair—"

Instead of that he " tore his clothes in shreds," flung his boots through the windows and dashed downstairs, smashing lamps on the way.   Then he rang the fire-bell.

Having roused the populace, he proceeds to harangue them, urging them to chase him, which they do. Owing to his fleetness of foot he easily escapes and manages to sleep till half-past two in the following afternoon.

Then a second frenzy takes him and he goes once more into the street.   By luck he meets the parson, and in a long socialistic speech denounces the universe.

The parson, one in a thousand, quietly argues for the present state :

> "You think the Church an outworn fetter ;
> Kane, keep it, till you've built a better. . . .
> To get the whole world out of bed
> And washed, and dressed, and warmed, and fed,
> To work, and back to bed again,
> Believe me, Saul, costs worlds of pain."

These last four lines are worth all the rest of the poem put together. It is the first time that that universal truth has been stated quite so boldly and yet with such unerring accuracy.[1]

Meanwhile (the parson continues),

> "my friend, 'twould be no sin
> To mix more water with your gin.
> We're neither saints nor Philip Sidneys,
> But mortal men with mortal kidneys."

It is a joy for once, by the way, to find a parson winning all along the line.

He finds himself a little later in the market-place, talking to a small boy who had lost his mother. Then follows a scene of real poetry and pure delight, gossamer-like in its flimsy flights, but having the true ring about it.

> "I told a tale, to Jim's delight,
> Of where the tom-cats go by night."

---

[1] It is really extraordinary how often Masefield reminds us of Pope. I have not space to expand this, but cf. *Biography* with Pope's best couplets ; it will bear the test.

But it is all too short and Mrs Jaggard comes hastily on
to the scene, and reviews Saul's and her own past life
in a whirl of words truly woeful.

> ". . . this old mother made me see
> The harm I done by being me. . . .
> So back to bar to get more drink . . ."

This time Miss Bourne, the friend, upbraids him : the
whole poem is a succession of sermons. But for the
first time we hit upon a mysticism that reminds us of
The Ancient Mariner :—

> "I got a glimpse of what it meant,
> How she and I had stood before
> In some old town by some old door
> Waiting intent while someone knocked
> Before the door for ever locked . . ."

Out into the darkness he speeds like Christy Mahon
to discover his own soul. In Nature's own wondrous
beauty he discovers peace : old Callow, the ploughman,
gives him the clue to salvation. So ends the poem that
made Mr Masefield famous as a poet.

Sufficient time has now passed for our judgments to
be cooled ; wherein lies the appeal of this strange novel
in verse ? It reads at times like a Salvation Army
tract, a Revivalist conversion hymn. The story is
graphic and real enough. Such things have happened,
do happen daily and are to be read in *The Christian
World* and *The Family Herald.*

There are traces of the passionate lyricism that
marked the young John Masefield, but we tremble for
what he is going to make of himself.

His carelessness in metre and rhyme is appalling. I

have already given several instances.   Here are some more :—

  " clock for you " is succeeded by " crock for you,"
  " fly 'un " by " Lion," " sons " by " once,"
  " merry all " by " burial," " black " by " back,"
  " floodin' " by " sudden," " is and was " by
" Caiaphas,"
  " mistakes "   by   " stakes,"   " bewild'rin' ' "   by
" children,"
  " knows his " by " disposes " and " here boy, or " by
" blubber for."

One could multiply these by ten and yet not exhaust the list.   He has taken a leaf out of Byron's book, and that not a good one.

In *The Widow in the Bye Street*, which followed close on the heels of *The Everlasting Mercy*, published in *The English Review* of February, 1912, he forsakes the octosyllabic couplet for a seven-line decasyllabic stanza, rhyming a b a b b c c ; a vastly improved vehicle for expressing a long story in verse.

It treats of the trials of a widow whose only son falls into a very obvious trap laid for him by a woman of no reputation, his passionate misplaced love for her, which results in his murder of her paramour, Shepherd Ern, and his consequent execution.

The whole treatment and finish are vastly superior to *The Everlasting Mercy* ; the tragedy is heightened and the verses are less diffuse and more carefully thought out.   The first part of the poem quickly gives you the barest facts of the lives of each of the principals, and ends thus :

  " So the four souls are ranged, the chess-board set,
   The dark, invisible hand of secret fate

Brought it to come to being that they met
After so many years of lying in wait.
While we least think it he prepares his Mate.
Mate, and the King's pawn played, it never ceases
Though all the earth is dust of taken pieces."

This verse, as a matter of fact, might equally well be placed at the head of all his longer poems.

There is something of Thomas Hardy's fatalism in all Mr Masefield's work.

Follows a description of the Fair where Jim Gurney, the hero, meets his Anna and the beginnings of his passion for her :

" Love is a flame to burn out human wills,
    Love is a flame to set the will on fire,
    Love is a flame to cheat men into mire,
    One of the three, we make love what we choose.
    He . . . swept out, repeating one sweet name,
    ' Anna, oh Anna,' to the evening star.
    Anna was sipping whisky in the bar."

Jim is led into deceiving his mother, and buying trinkets for his Anna, till at last there follows the inevitable scene, where his mother tries to make him see that he is throwing his love away on a light woman. The dialogue is dramatic, tense and real, and shows the enormous advance the poet has made in technique on his earlier work.   It's all no use.

" People in love cannot be won by kindness,
    And opposition makes them feel like martyrs."

It is in one of the soliloquies that follow that there occurs one of the imperishable thoughts that have never been so expressed before, and for which Mr

Masefield is bound to outlive this age. The poor old mother, finding her pleading of no avail, in bitter anguish cries :

" Life's a long headache in a noisy street."

Anna, meanwhile, is using Jimmy merely as a bait to bring back her former lover, Shepherd Ern, who had been errant during the fair, owing to the attractions of Gipsy Bessie ; she was entirely successful, and then immediately has no more use for Jim, who first suspects, then

" Raging, he hurried back to learn the truth."

He rushes in on the discovered pair, is knocked out by the Shepherd and makes off swearing revenge.

It reads like a play written for the cinematograph.

He runs down to the water, sensuous thoughts half killing him.

" All through the night the stream ran to the sea,
The different water always saying the same.
Cat-like and then a tinkle, never glee,
A lonely little child alone in shame.
Another snapped a thorn twig when he came,
It drifted down, it passed the Hazel Mill,
It passed the Springs : but Jimmy stayed there still."

It is in a stanza such as this that we realise the vein of truth and beauty, bursting to be expressed, that runs through Mr Masefield.

Whoever bettered that

" Lonely little child alone in shame ? "

Having stayed out all night, Jim goes to work, and ill, distraught, asks for the sack, gets it, drinks himself mad while his mother is searching for him, and would have found and saved him but for a cruel, malicious stroke of fate :

> "Whether she'd go to th'inn and find her son,
>   Or take the field and let the doom be done."

Of course she takes the field, while Jim rushes to his destiny.   He kills Ern with one blow of a " spudder " ; again we are irresistibly reminded of the *Playboy* ; and then at once he becomes sane again.

> "Man cannot call the brimming instant back :
>   Time's an affair of instants spun to days ;
>   If man must make an instant gold, or black,
>   Let him, he may, but Time must go his ways.
>   Life may be duller for an instant's blaze,
>   Life's an affair of instants spun to years ;
>   Instants are only cause of all these tears."

He is tried, convicted, converted and hanged.   Again it falls to the mother to utter one of Masefield's immortal lines :

> "God warms his hands at man's heart when he prays."

She is left comfortless, beaten, but alive :

> "Some of life's sad ones are too strong to die,"

and we are left on a note of pure poetry to watch the wandering witless ways of the old woman as she walks singing sad songs to remind her of Jim who is coming back to her soon.

> "The stars are placid on the evening's blue,
>   Burning like eyes so calm, so unafraid
>   Of all that God has given and man has made.

Burning they watch, and moth-like owls come out,
The redbreast warbles shrilly once and stops ;
The homing cowman gives his dog a shout,
The lamps are lighted in the village shops.
Silence : the last bird passes : in the copse
The hazels cross the moon, a night-jar spins,
Dew wets the grass, the nightingale begins."

No finer description than that can be found in any
poetry of our day, and he who denies that Mr Masefield
is a poet has to reckon not with a solitary instance like
this, but with stanza after stanza of a like beauty.

The whole poem shows an advance in every department of Mr Masefield's power. He has a better grip
of his subject, he digresses and moralises less, though
he still does so too much ; there is more real beauty,
less licence and carelessness, and greater cohesion
altogether than in *The Everlasting Mercy.*

In May, 1912, he published a little known poem,
entitled *Biography*, of inestimable value to all those
who would know something of the man behind the
artist. Of course, as we expect, there is the usual
panegyric on oceans :

"By many waters and on many ways
I have known golden instants and bright days.
The night alone near water when I heard
All the sea's spirit spoken by a bird."

There ought to be little danger of our forgetting, but
lest we should, he adds :

"When I am dust my penman may not know
Those water-trampling ships which make me glow,
But think my wonder mad and fail to find
Their glory, even dimly, from my mind,
And yet they made me."

His *Ballads and Poems*, if nothing else, would be sufficient to prove to any critic that his Coram Street days were not his happiest.

"London has been my prison : but my books,
　Hills and great waters, labouring men and brooks,
　Ships and deep friendships and remembered days
　Which even now set all my mind ablaze—
　—I felt the hillside thronged by souls unseen,
　Who knew the interest in me and were keen
　That man alive should understand man dead
　—And quickened with strange hush because his comer
　Sensed a strange soul alive behind the summer."

The whole poem is a revelation and leads one at last to what we had been expecting for so long : the epic of the sea, the prologue, *Ships*, appearing in July, 1912, and the poem itself, *Dauber*, in October of the same year.

The former is a catalogue of the great ships of yore that made the Mersey famous through the world :

"I cannot tell their wonder nor make known
　Magic that once thrilled through me to the bone,
　But all men praise some beauty, tell some tale,
　Vent a high mood which makes the rest seem pale,
　Pour their heart's blood to nourish one green leaf,
　Follow some Helen for her gift of grief
　And fail in what they mean, whate'er they do :
　You should have seen, men cannot tell to you
　The beauty of the ships of that my city."

Dauber is *The Ancient Mariner* of the twentieth century. Mr Masefield knows the sea as few poets have known it ; certainly as Coleridge never knew it.

The poem tells the story of a young farmer who refused to carry on the tradition of his fathers, but went to sea in order to paint it from the inside.

> " It's not been done, the sea, not yet been done,
> From the inside by one who really knows,
> I'd give up all if I could be the one,
> But art comes dear the way the money goes."

He had to work his way out in a vessel rounding Cape Horn, and in pursuing his art to encounter the gibes, and worse, of his mates, who with some of the Public School instinct towards what it cannot understand, did all in their power to harass and upset him.

Three reefers slashed his canvases to ribbons, as a result of which he made an ineffectual appeal to the captain and became the laughing-stock of the crew.

To one of the reefers, however, he communicates in a confidential mood his life story, how he had broken his father's heart for this whim, this passion, this insensate craving for painting and the sea :

> " That's what I loved, water, and time to read."

One day he got a job below the bridge, and then saw for the first time a clipper.

> " That altered life for me : I had never seen
> A ship before, for all my thought of ships :
> And there was this great clipper like a queen,
> With a white curl of bubbles at her lips,
> All made of beauty to the stern's ellipse,
> Her ensign ruffling red, her bunts in pile,
> Beauty and strength together, wonder, style.

I wasn't happy then : I felt too keenly
How hard it is to paint : but when I saw
Her masts across the river rising queenly,
Built out of so much chaos brought to law,
I learned the power of knowing how to draw,
Of beating thought into the perfect line,
I vowed to make that power of beauty mine."

Many storms were encountered before they reached
the Horn, all which tested Dauber's manhood and
stirred him on to high effort, so that by suffering pain
a little hour he might be able to draw that line of
sailors' faces sweating the sail, their passionate play
and change, their might, their misery, their tragic power
in order that men the world over should understand
their feeling through his power of portrayal.

Then follows that fifth canto, telling of the rounding
of the Horn, in which the poet rises to heights he never
reached before, and which alone would suffice to give
him a reputation above all living writers had he written
nothing else.   No description of a storm at sea has ever
approached this one ; the words pour out, wild, passionate, pell-mell, pregnant with reality, comparable only
with passages in *The Inferno* : it is far too long to quote :
I can only implore anyone who has not yet read it to
buy, borrow or steal a copy to-day.

Scenes of horror are ushered in by this superb
couplet :

> "then from the sea
> Came a cold sudden breath that made the hair
> Stiff in the neck as though Death whispered there."

The reader feels the ghastly dizziness that assails the
neophyte when he finds himself for the first time in the

rigging in a gale : the frozen hands, the cold sweat of fear, and all the tortures of the damned that Dauber had to undergo. Somehow he survived, but with a peculiar irony as dear to Mr Masefield's heart as to Thomas Hardy's, he escapes only to fall from the fore-topgallant yard weather arm shortly afterwards in the last gale before Valparaiso : he just breathed : " It will go on," not knowing his meaning rightly, but he spoke

> " With the intenseness of a fading soul
>   Whose share of Nature's fire turns to smoke,
>   Whose hand on Nature's wheel loses control.
>   ' It will go on,' he cried aloud, and passed."

Altogether this is the most powerful poem that Mr Masefield has written, because his whole heart and soul were in his work : he has the passion to paint for us in words what Dauber would have painted on canvas, the lives and ways of those who go down to the sea in ships and occupy their business in great waters.

Yet with it all, as in the later work of Shakespeare, there is an incredible carelessness as if he could not restrain his flow of words but had written the whole poem at a sitting. Unnecessary alliterations, stupid repetitions of words like " multitudinous," extraordinary and gross tamperings with the metre, all serve to weaken the general effect and give the reader the impression that it is the result of one gigantic effort inspired nearly throughout, but so good as not to be retouched again. " By God ; it is good, take it or leave it," he might say with Ben Jonson, and leave it we must at that.

The Daffodil Fields followed in February, 1913, not in February, 1912, as Mr Masefield says in his reprinted edition, published in October, 1913. This, like all his later work, is in the seven-lined stanza of *The Widow in the Bye Street.*

It is in epitome *Enoch Arden* retold and incidentally very much better. It starts with the dying request of Nicholas Gray that his two friends, Occleve and Keir, should look after his wayward son, Michael, after his death, and if possible see that he married Keir's daughter Mary, who was passionately devoted to him. They give their promise ; the old man dies—Michael comes home, but not for long.

> " I want to go
> Somewhere where man has never used a plough,
> Nor ever read a book ; where clean winds blow,
> And passionate blood is not its owner's foe,
> And land is for the asking for it."

He decides to go to the Plate, but in a scene of superb beauty makes love to Mary and secures her promise to wait three years for him.

Mr Masefield has seldom written more exquisite poetry than that in which he describes the night of their leave-taking.

> " Still as high June, the very water's noise
> Seemed but a breathing of the earth : the flowers
> Stood in the dim like souls without a voice.
> The wood's conspiracy of occult powers
> Drew all about them, and for hours on hours
> No murmur shook the oaks, the stars did house
> Their lights like lamps upon these never-moving
>   boughs.
>
> .   .   .   .
>
> June's very breast was bare this night of nights.
> Moths blundered up against them, grays and whites

Moved on the darkness where the moths were out,
Nosing for sticky sweet with trembling uncurled
snout."

The whole scene is worthy to rank with Richard
Feverel's immortal meeting with Lucy. It is all too
short : in a few stanzas

" The flag waved, the engine snorted, then
Slowly the couplings tautened, and the train
Moved, bearing off from her her man of men ;
She looked towards its going, blind with pain."

He soon forgets her, however, in the new country and
lives with a Spanish beauty, not even answering his
first love's letters. By a rather strained peetic licence
Mary's ardent but earthy, steadfast, disappointed
lover at home, Lion Occleve, has bred a wonderful bull,
which he takes to Michael's country to sell, meets him,
implores him to give up his mistress and come back
to Mary, who is wasting away for want of him, all,
however, to no purpose. Lion returns to Mary with his
woeful tale, and after months of pleading he manages
to make her marry him.

Michael hears of the wedding and immediately
realising all that he is losing, impetuously rushes home,
and after failing to find her in her own house, into
which he crept, his better nature urges him to go away ;
he meets her by accident and the tragedy hastens to its
finish. At once Mary returns to Lion's house, throws
her ring on the table and, deaf to all entreaties and
threats, goes off to live with Michael. Lion is then
roused and the end, though curiously protracted, is near.

One day Lion meets Michael and offers him his
hedging-hook as a weapon, himself using a stake drawn
from the hedge. Michael, who has obviously some-

thing of vast importance to say, is effectually prevented
from uttering it until each has mortally wounded the
other : then only has he time to gasp out in his dying
breath that Mary and he had agreed to separate, that
she was at that moment on her way to rejoin Lion.

She comes, sees Michael dead and, weeping bitterly,
laments the murder of her only real love : her heart
breaks and the tragedy bed is loaded with three corpses.

A gruesome story, curiously uneven. The language
which the disputants employ is half that of the cultured
scholar, half that of the farmer ; never consistent.

There is, too, the quaint conceit of the daffodil fields
brought in as a last line to every canto, quite unnecessarily : the title has really no bearing on the tale whatever, except that Mr Masefield likes to digress as to a
point of seasons whenever a fresh nail is driven into the
coffin of the luckless trio.

There is again much carelessness and a redundancy
that threatens to become an obsession. Here is one
example out of about thirty :

" A spring comes bubbling up there, cold as glass,
   It bubbles down, crusting the leaves with lime,
   Babbling the self-same song that it has sung through
      time.

Here is one even worse :

" Counting the dreary time, the dreary beat
   Of dreary minutes dragging through the day."

Surely Mr Masefield cannot believe that such tricks
make for effectiveness. His powers of description are
not dulled, he has wonderful fertility of language and
brings his characters to play their puppet parts with
the best possible skill that verse can command, but
there is still something lacking.

It is not these long poems at all that make Mr Masefield the great poet. I have purposely left his great work, and curiously enough his least known and earliest, till the last.

Ballads and Poems was published years before any of the long poems, and some of the best stuff in them was written, he tells us, in his adolescence, under the influence (it is obvious) of Rudyard Kipling.

This little volume, containing just one hundred pages, has more real poetry in it than all his other output added together : the true magic is rung in nearly every line : words of most ordinary significance assume a heightened sense, and music of a more poignant and haunting fragrance than we meet with elsewhere in his writings, so much so that, admire as we do his narrative poems, we feel (most of us) certain that his true vocation is the short lyric, not the metric annals of the sordid and the wretched.

On the first page we light on a verse totally unlike anything in the longer poems. It is called *The Ballad of Sir Bors*.

" Would I could win some quiet and rest and a little ease,
    In the cool grey hush of the dusk, in the dim green
      place of the trees,
    Where the birds are singing, singing, crying aloud
    The song of the red, red rose that blossoms beyond
      the seas."

There is more than a flash of resemblance to *La Belle Dame Sans Merci* in that stanza. Further on in the same poem we come across the line,

" A star will glow like a note God strikes on the silver
    bell,"

a line that lives in the memory when all thought of Jim
Gurney, Saul Kane, Michael Gray, and the rest of them,
is entirely obliterated. How different, again, is *Cargoes*,
now better known owing to the music that has been
written for it.

" Quinquireme of Nineveh from distant Ophir,
  Rowing home to haven in sunny Palestine,
  With a cargo of ivory,
  And apes and peacocks,
  Sandalwood, cedarwood and sweet white wine. . . .
  Dirty British Coaster with a salt-caked smoke-stack,
  Butting through the Channel in the mad March days,
  With a cargo of Tyne coal,
  Road-rails, pig-lead,
  Firewood, iron-ware and cheap tin trays."

It is easy to cavil at this sort of thing because it is
new and offends the susceptibilities of some critics, but
there can be little doubt that no truer picture has been
painted in less words.

Then there are ballads, *The Old Bold Mate of Henry
Morgan*, that John Silver ought to have sung.

Sir Arthur Quiller-Couch recognised the durability
of one of his poems when he included *Beauty* in *The
Oxford Book of Victorian Verse*.

" I have seen dawn and sunset on moors and windy
      hills
    Coming in solemn beauty like slow old tunes of
      Spain :
  I have seen the lady April bringing the daffodils,
    Bringing the springing grass and the soft warm
      April rain.

I have heard the song of the blossoms and the old chant
    of the sea,
And seen strange lands from under the arched white
    sails of ships :
But the loveliest things of beauty God ever has showed
    to me,
   Are her voice and her hair and eyes, and the dear red
        curve of her lips."

The whole feminine race may envy the woman to whom
that, in common with everything he has written, is
dedicated.   Panegyric and love could rise no higher.

His three sonnets :—

   (i) " Her heart is always doing lovely things,"
   (ii) " Being her friend I do not care, not I,"

and

   (iii) " Born for nought else, for nothing but for this,"

just accentuate the beauty of the quoted hymn of
adoration.

True poetry has been defined as the retelling of great
events remembered in passivity, heightened by language
that could be uttered in no other way, musical, magic,
from the soul.

For Mr Masefield this is the true touchstone.   Each
event seen and lived through, leaves its impress on his
poetic soul, and he strives to express in words what has
thrilled him through and through with beauty.

He may thank God for the perceptive vision, he is
endowed with divine powers ; those of us who love him
most watch with trepidation lest he should be led from
the path in which his real genius lies to prostitute
his talents and pander to a taste which revels in his

"bloodies," his audacious sensuality, his excerpts from the lowest Sunday papers.

Meanwhile we cling to the *Ballads and Poems*, reading and rereading them until he comes back to us.

We would leave him with one final warning. Could he but read the reams of rubbish with which his so-called imitators are flooding their studies, he would pause before pursuing his present path further.

As a playwright of poetic drama, he has no living equal, neither has he peer in ballad or lyric. Let him realise his limitations, and give us in the years to come more of the Coram Street and Tettenhall genius and less of the world-famous original poet of these last few years.

X

RUPERT BROOKE

"A young Apollo, golden-haired,
   Stands dreaming on the verge of strife,
Magnificently unprepared
   For the long littleness of life."

IN the first throes of anguish which every man who knew the poet experienced on hearing that Rupert Brooke was dead it seemed incredible that one so absolutely the incarnation of youth and spring could have vanished from us for ever ; but later this feeling gave way to another which will probably remain as the more lasting ; it now seems equally impossible that he could ever have lived ; he was almost too good to be true ; he was certainly one of those whom the gods love, εὐφυὴς καὶ εὐμαθής.

The son of a house-master at Rugby, he was himself educated there, and was successful both as a youthful poet and as an athlete, for he gained his colours for cricket and football in addition to winning the school English Verse Prize. In after years, at King's College, Cambridge, he took a second-class in the Classical Tripos, and was elected to a fellowship as the result of a thesis on Webster.

Deciding to travel, he was led by the spirit of Stevenson "across the plains" to the South Sea Islands, and wrote vivid prose impressions, which were printed in *The Westminster Gazette*. He eventually returned with

the idea of settling down at the old Vicarage, Grantchester, in order to lecture to undergraduates of his
university. The war put a stop to this, however, and
he joined the Royal Naval Division instead, underwent
the horrors of Antwerp, came back unscathed, and
after a short training at Blandford was sent out to the
Dardanelles. Early in April, 1915, he contracted sun-
stroke; septicæmia then mysteriously set in, and he
died aboard a French hospital ship on Shakespeare's
supposed death-day, and lies buried in the Island of
Scyros. It reads like legend; it is so exactly what
each of us would have demanded of our fairy god-
mother had we had the chance.

In common with many thinking men of his age (he
was only twenty-seven when he died), he lived in a
state of continual protest against the merely pretty;
he was in deadly fear of falling into a flattered literary
career, of winning fame as one more beautiful poet of
beautiful themes, so he ran counter to the accepted
tradition into violence and coarseness for salvation.
The same tendency may with equal certainty be traced
in the work of Masefield, Cannan, D. H. Lawrence and
Wilfrid Gibson.

The temptation to generalise on this point is insidious
but futile. I will, however, attempt to sum up in one
sentence what I believe to be the guiding principle of
the twentieth-century poet with regard to this: " A
thing is not necessarily beautiful because the majority
think it to be so; the only way to arrive at a sense of
real beauty is to cast out fear, become an iconoclast, to
prove all things and to hold fast that which we find to
be good."

The result of such a point of view on the world can
easily be imagined; strange labels are attached by the
conventional critic to the poetry which makes him

uncomfortable, to the work which he cannot understand.   Cannan is alliteratively styled cynic, Lawrence bourgeois, Masefield blasphemous and Brooke hard, savage, realistic, loveless. " Shamelessly undodgy," said Henry James of the younger generation.   It is worth while seeing how far this applies to Rupert Brooke.

He will write a sonnet on *Dawn*, starting with the arresting line :

" Opposite me two Germans snore and sweat,"

written in the train between Bologna and Milan, second-class.   He describes the windows, slimy-wet with a night's fœtor, the age-long night in the stuffy, foul carriage, the effect on his companions :

" One of them wakes and spits and sleeps again."

In *Wagner* he pictures the effect of music on the fat, greasy sensualist :

" The music swells.   His gross legs quiver. . . .
    And all the while, in perfect time,
    His pendulous stomach hangs a-shaking."

Menelaus and Helen is a gross attack on all that we hold most precious in legend and myth.   No Darby and Joan about this famous pair when they fall into the sere and yellow leaf :

" Often he wonders why on earth he went
    Troyward, or why poor Paris ever came.
Oft she weeps, gummy-eyed and impotent ;
    Her dry shanks twitch at Paris' mumbled name.
So Menelaus nagged ; and Helen cried ;
And Paris slept on by Scamander side."

Even more famous are his *Channel Passage*, with its physically disgusting descriptions of the sea-sick lover, and *Jealousy*, where we are shown unlovely love-making grown old.

To Brooke it was hypocrisy to restrain the direct expression of himself out of consideration of others. This side of his work is important as reflecting the natural ebullition of youthful spirits. Mr Harold Monro calls all these poems " jokes " ; a good joke, he says, is, after all, more stimulating than the best piece of advice. It is the most necessary thing for a poet to be able to laugh well. His principal failing seems to have been a sort of fear lest he should be taken seriously. If he thought he had loved too well he would laugh away his feelings in a horrible poem like *Jealousy* or *Ambarvalia*.

In point of fact, despite Henry James's label of " shamelessly undodgy " as applied to the youthful poets of to-day as if it were a new thing, not one of these poems in conception is new at all. I know that it is commonly accepted that the genius of the twentieth century owns to no masters in his craft ; he must be above all things a pioneer, hacking his way ruthlessly through virgin jungle ; but Rupert Brooke, at any rate, is in this entirely at variance with his contemporaries. What makes his work shine so far beyond that of any other man of his age is just this characteristic : he does lean upon two giants, John Webster and John Donne, each, unfortunately for his reputation, overshadowed by a greater man. Webster is only second to Shakespeare in tragic intensity ; Donne is only not the finest poet of the seventeenth century because Milton happened to live about the same time.

Neither man is even yet recognised at his true worth,

although Charles Lamb did his best for the one, and Browning for the other.

In Webster, Rupert Brooke found realism—there are passages in *The White Devil* and *The Duchess of Malfi* much more shamelessly undodgy than anything in Brooke—vigour, and an intellect as scintillating as his own, a writer whose thoughts toppled over pell-mell into a wealth of simile and metaphor as sane and apt as those of Shakespeare and Arnold, an exuberance of beauty made all the more conspicuous by the brusque, harsh, unmusical lines that compassed it about, a genius so audacious that he could afford, like Shakespeare in his famous five " nevers " in *King Lear*, to rise to those heights of sublimity that are so perilously near the ridiculous as to make us shiver with apprehension while we read, only to thrill with ecstasy afterwards when we realise that the dramatist has o'ertopped man's expectations and for a moment given us a glimpse into the unknown.   Everyone knows the lines :

> " *Vittoria.*   I am lost for ever.
> *Brachiano.* How miserable a thing it is to die
>   'Mongst women howling."

or the :

> "I have caught an everlasting cold : I have lost my voice most irrecoverably,"

in *The Duchess of Malfi*.

Rupert Brooke owed much to a dramatist whose sureness of touch could lead him to write the line that has been said to be the high-water mark of Romanticism :

> "Cover her face : mine eyes dazzle : she died young,"

to a man who could heap horror on horror, gloomy fatalism on melancholic madness, and yet know that

he was one of those rare spirits who had achieved the
supreme ideal of tragedy in purging the emotions by
terror and pity.

You can trace quite easily all these different facets
of Webster's craft in Rupert Brooke's work, but his
allegiance to John Donne was even more loyal, his debt
infinitely greater.

When justice is done to the burning vitality, the
clarity of vision, the fertility of imagination, the intellectual versatility, the heightened humour, and the
true sense of beauty pervading Brooke's work, then
will the part that Donne played in the making of
Rupert Brooke be adequately understood.

What drove Brooke to Donne was, of course, his
recognition of the similarity of their tastes ; just as
the Victorians saw nothing in Donne, because he was
as diametrically opposed to their point of view as
Samuel Butler and Meredith were, so any individual
man or clique will, in spite of Ruskin's advice, try to
find inspiration in the genius to whom he or it most
naturally approximates. Though this is a truism, it
needs saying ; for there is every likelihood of some such
absurd myth as the following becoming part of the
stock-in-trade of Brooke's critics.

Donne's first published poem was written while
serving in the Royal Naval Division under the Earl of
Essex before Cadiz, and is dedicated to a Cambridge
man whose name was Brooke : " A unique coincidence
with scarcely a parallel in the world of letters. This is
what drove Brooke of 1914 to Donne " ! Of course
it is unique ; all coincidences are ; but it is most
decidedly not what drove Rupert to John. Rupert
Brooke is simply John Donne come to life again, a
reincarnation. We are told by Professor Grierson that
Donne's intense individuality was always eager to find

a North-West Passage of its own, pressed its curious and sceptical questioning into every corner of love and life and religion, explored unsuspected depths, exploited new discovered paradoxes, and turned its discoveries always into poetry of the closely packed, artificial style which was all his own. Here is a poem of Brooke's called *Heaven* :

" Fish (fly-replete, in depth of June,
    Dawdling away their wat'ry noon)
    Ponder deep wisdom, dark or clear,
    Each secret fishy hope or fear.
    Fish say, they have their Stream and Pond :
    But is there anything Beyond ? . . .
    We darkly know, by Faith we cry,
    The Future is not Wholly Dry. . . .
    But somewhere, beyond Space and Time,
    Is wetter water, slimier slime. . . .
    Unfading moths, immortal flies,
    And the worm that never dies.
    And in that Heaven of all their wish,
    There shall be no more land, say fish."

Doesn't this exactly fit the criticism applied to Donne ? Here, too, are what Doctor Johnson called " the quaint conceits " and " the blasphemous obscenity of the metaphysical school." " Almost too clever," says Gilbert Murray, " to be poetry at all " ; there is in this that astringency which we associate with ammonia in the bath ; we find it in Donne, Meredith, Swift, Browning, Dryden, Pope, Churchill, Byron, Butler and Burns (a mere handful of names) and practically nowhere else in English literature. To label it as satire and merely to leave it at that is to miss half the point of it. It is worth noting that Donne, too, had looked not at heaven but at love from the fish's point of view in a parody of Marlowe's exquisite *Come live with me and be my love*, for it but adds a fresh rivet to my theory of debts and reincarnation.

It has also been said of Donne that he burst passionately and rudely into the enclosed garden of sentiment and illusion, pulling up the gay-coloured tangled weeds that choked thoughts, planting the seeds of fresh invention. Where his forerunners had been idealist, epicurean, or adoring, he was brutal, cynical and immitigably realist.

> "How can we find ? How can we rest ? How can
> We, being gods, find joy, or peace, being man ?
> We, the gaunt zanies of a witless Fate,
> Who love the unloving, and the lover hate,
> Forget the moment ere the moment slips,
> Kiss with blind eyes that seek beyond the lips,
> Who want, and know not what we want, and cry
> With crooked mouths for Heaven, and throw it by."

You can see it in *Kindliness*:

> " When Love has changed to kindliness. . . .
> That time when all is over, and
> Hand never flinches, brushing hand :
> And blood lies quiet, for all you're near ;
> And it's but spoken words we hear,
> Where trumpets sang : when the mere skies
> Are stranger and nobler than your eyes ;
> And flesh is flesh, was flame before ;
> And infinite hungers leap no more
> In the chance swaying of your dress."

Or in *The Wayfarers* :

> " Each crawling day
> Will pale a little your scarlet lips, each mile
> Dull the dear pain of your remembered face."

In *The Beginning* :

> " I'll curse the thing that once you were,
> Because it is changed and pale and old,
> (Lips that were scarlet, hair that was gold)."

The underlying thought in all these comes straight from Donne. I could quote a thousand instances. Here is one :

> "Who would not laugh at me if I should say
> I saw a flash of powder last a day ? "

or :

> " Changed loves are but changed sorts of meat :
> And when he hath the kernel eat
> Who doth not fling away the shell ? "

Or, to hark back for a moment to the series which I quoted on Brooke's realism, does not this strike a harmonious chord :

> " And like a bunch of ragged carrots stand
> The short swollen fingers of thy gouty hand ? "

How he huddles a new thought on the one before it, before the first has had time to express itself ; how he sees things and analyses emotions so swiftly and subtly himself that he forgets the slower comprehensions of his readers ; how he always trembles on the verge of the inarticulate ; how his restless intellect finds new and subtler shades of emotion and thought invisible to other pairs of eyes, and cannot, because speech is modelled on the average of our intelligence, find words to express them. This might be a criticism of Browning; it really is a criticism of Donne, and it exactly describes such a poem of Brooke's as *Dining-Room Tea*.

But you will have noticed here that a new note has crept in. I have already commented on his fear of becoming the beautiful poet of beautiful themes; he hated most, I imagine, the decadents and their school; but he has another not less awful dread; you see it in *Menelaus and Helen* and in *Kindliness*: the thought that he might one day grow old, that a time might conceivably come " when infinite longings leap no more," terrified him.

This constantly recurring obsession would have driven him mad (he was, in common with many other young men of great strength, given to appalling fits of nervous breakdown) had it not been that, like Shakespeare, who was probably as restless as he was, and unlike Milton, who most decidedly was not, he had the saving grace of a sense of humour; I say " saving " advisedly, for I believe that humour is the only antidote known to this form of mental depression.

In the hills north-west of Ottawa, he wrote, there grows a romantic light purple-red flower which is called fireweed, because it is the first vegetation to spring up in the prairie after a fire has passed over, and so might be adopted as the emblematic flower of a sense of humour. A parable—a piece of pure autobiography. Ever, and always you will see in Brooke's poems how fascinating, how explanatory, how wistful and faithful a follower is this will-o'-the-wisp, humour. It brings him back with a jerk from the inane pursuit of the abstract (" there's little comfort in the wise ") to the direct simplicity of actualities.

Think how Gray or Collins would have treated this threnody on *The Funeral of Youth* :

" *Folly* went first,
   With muffled bells and coxcomb still revers'd ;
   And after trod the bearers, hat in hand—
   Laughter, most hoarse, and Captain *Pride* with tanned
   And martial face all grim, and fussy *Joy*,
   Who had to catch a train, and *Lust*, poor, snivelling
       boy ; . . .
   The fatherless children, *Colour*, *Tune*, and *Rhyme*,
   (The sweet lad *Rhyme*) ran all-uncomprehending. . . .
   Beauty was there,
   Pale in her black ; dry-eyed ; she stood alone. . . .
   Contentment, who had known *Youth* as a child
   And never seen him since. . . .
   All, except only *Love*.   *Love* had died long ago."

Webster is here in the line on *Beauty* ; Donne too, the Donne of the general reader, the Donne known of all, the Donne of " a bracelet of bright hair about the bone."

This poem really marks a sharp cleavage in Brooke's work. It appears probable that two schools, widely divergent, are likely to rise in the future : those who pin their faith to the later Brooke and look on all his early work as so much youthful excrescence, a sort of impurity which had to be sweated out before the poet could express the greatness which he undoubtedly had in him but which perforce lay dormant, weighted under this savage, satiric bent of his ; and those who look on his early work as the final expression of his genius, who regard the last poems as a sad falling away into a distorted romanticism consequent upon untoward circumstances.

It all depends upon what you expect to get out of poetry. Most of us would agree that our object in reading it is to ascertain what the seer has to say about the vastly important matters of Death, Beauty and Love ; if Rupert Brooke had nothing strikingly sincere to say about these things he would have no claim, however brilliant his brain-power might be, upon our attention as a great poet.

As it happens, however, he has something poignant, refreshing and inspiring to say on all these three.

In this part of his work he reminds me of three other geniuses in English literature. He has the same passionate sense of rhythm and beauty that Marlowe had, the same tendency to extravagant hyperbole, as can be seen at once in a poem like *Mummia* :

> " Helen's the hair shuts out from me
>   Verona's livid skies ;
>   Gypsy the lips I press ; and see
>   Two Antonys in your eyes,"

the same unlawful desires to pry into the hidden recesses even at the risk of losing his own soul ; the same love of words for words' sake only.

It is not because of the fortuitous accident of dying young and in Greece, not because he was inordinately fond of swimming in the dark, that he reminds me of Byron ; he was possessed by the same exuberant and defiantly adventurous spirit, the same protesting passion of revolt, and the same delight in real existence :

> " I shall desire and I shall find
>   The best of my desires ;
>   The autumn road, the mellow wind
>   That soothes the darkening shires.
>   And laughter, and inn-fires."

His claim to be called the Shelley of our day has aroused a good deal of scoffing ; there is no doubt, however, that he had in him much of that clear, ethereal vision that so endears Shelley to us, much of that intellectual hypersensitiveness peculiar to Shelley which acts as so strong and biting an antidote to sentimentalism in thought and melodious facility in writing ; there are, moreover, times when we feel that had Rupert Brooke lived he could have left just such another poem as *The Cenci*. But the Shelleyan influence is most noticeable in two sonnets dealing with the Beyond :

"Not with vain tears, when we're beyond the sun,
We'll beat on the substantial doors, nor tread
Those dusty high-roads of the aimless dead
Plaintive for Earth ; but rather turn and run
Down some close-covered by-way of the air,
Some low sweet alley between wind and wind,
Stoop under faint gleams, thread the shadows, find
Some whispering ghost-forgotten nook, and there
Spend in pure converse our eternal day ; . . ."

In another sonnet he compares the dead to clouds :

"I think they ride the calm mid-heaven, as these,
  In wise majestic melancholy train,
And watch the moon, and the still raging seas,
  And men, coming and going on the earth."

When the war broke out he began naturally to write more and more about Death ; he felt certain that he was not to be permitted to return alive, and he has left behind a series of sonnets which threaten to become his best-known work, so often have they been quoted of late :

" War knows no power.   Safe shall be my going,
Secretly armed against all death's endeavour :
Safe though all safety's lost ; safe where men fall ;
And if these poor limbs die, safest of all."

Even here he has not forgotten his master ; the
sonnet is almost a direct plagiarism from Donne :

" Who is so safe as we ? "

In another he begins characteristically :

" Now, God be thanked Who has matched us with His
        hour,
To turn . . . glad from a world grown old and cold
        and weary,
Leave the sick hearts that honour could not move
And half-men, and their dirty songs and dreary,
And all the little emptiness of love."

You see what a hold this early hatred of false love
keeps on a man of fastidious delicacy like Brooke.
There is a touch reminiscent of Shelley's " love's sad
satiety " in the comparison of love's emptiness with the
dirty, dreary songs of half-men.

But by far his most famous war sonnet is *The Soldier*,
which recalls exactly Masefield's verse about those who

" Died (uncouthly; most) in foreign lands
For some idea, but dimly understood,
Of an English city never built by hands,
Which love of England prompted and made good."

Rupert Brooke's poem runs thus :

" If I should die, think only this of me :
    That there's some corner of a foreign field
    That is for ever England.   There shall be
    In that rich earth a richer dust concealed ;

A dust whom England bore, shaped, made aware,
Gave, once, her flowers to love, her ways to roam,
A body of England's, breathing English air,
Washed by the rivers, blest by suns of home. . . ."

It has been said that in this poem he fell a victim
to that very romanticism which he so detested ; a
notable successor of Donne's at St Paul's has commented adversely on the "materialism" underlying
the thought ; it has also been described as infinitely
the most inspired poem written since August, 1914.
I do not know ; we are, perhaps, a little too near the
big event to be able to judge calmly or rationally of the
lasting power of war poetry.   What there can be no
possible doubt about is the beauty of the conception
and the perfection of the execution.   The very repetition of the word " England " here is like the repetition
of a majestic chord in a peculiarly fine piece of music.
It should be noted, however, that his love of country
found expression in *Grantchester* as long ago as 1912,
and at the very beginning of the war he wrote in a prose
essay in *The New Statesman* :

" The word ' England ' seems to flash like a line of foam."

But for myself I must confess that I prefer *The
Treasure*, which is comparatively unknown, to any of
the five sonnets :

" When colour goes home into the eyes,
And lights that shine are shut again
With dancing girls and sweet birds' cries
Behind the gateways of the brain ;
And that no-place which gave them birth, shall close
The rainbow and the rose :—

Musing upon them ; as a mother, who
Has watched her children all the rich day through,
Sits, quiet-handed, in the fading light,
When children sleep, ere night."

This poem is all the more precious when we compare
it with his no less beautiful but more juvenile description of the orthodox heaven :

" All the great courts were quiet in the sun,
And full of vacant echoes : moss had grown
Over the glassy pavement, and begun
To creep within the dusty council-halls.
An idle wind blew round an empty throne
And stirred the heavy curtains on the walls."

Or contrast it with that restrained, agonising cry (so
like T. E. Brown's *Dora*) in *The Vision of the Arch-
angels* :

" (Yet, you had fancied, God could never
Have bidden a child turn from the spring and the sun-
light,
And shut him in that lonely shell, to drop for ever
Into the emptiness and silence, into the night). . . .
God's little pitiful Body lying, worn and thin,
And curled up like some crumpled, lonely flower-
petal. . . ."

He seems to have cast off that preciosity so dear to
the heart of the intellectual young graduate, that hard
brilliance which almost becomes synonymous with soul-
lessness ; his beauty becomes deeper and more mellow
with advancing years ; the outspokenly sensual and
cruelly cynical stage with him, as with Donne, was
not lasting ; it just marked the stage of transition from

scintillating coruscations of wit to the tranquil heights of recollected emotions made trebly more tender by the calm peacefulness that permeates them; now indeed does he feed on thoughts that voluntarily move harmonious numbers.

You see it in *The Charm* :

> " You, asleep,
> In some cool room that's open to the night
> Lying half-forward, breathing quietly,
> One white hand on the white
> Unrumpled sheet, and the ever-moving hair
> Quiet and still at length."

You see it in *Day that I have Loved* :

> " From the inland meadows,
> Fragrant of June and clover, floats the dark, and fills
> The hollow sea's dead face with little creeping shadows,
> And the white silence brims the hollow of the hills."

But you see it most of all in *Grantchester*, the one poem by which the poet was generally known before the war :

> " Just now the lilac is in bloom,
> All before my little room ;
> And in my flower-beds, I think,
> Smile the carnation and the pink ;
> And down the borders, well I know,
> The poppy and the pansy blow. . . .
> Oh ! there the chestnuts, summer through
> Beside the river make for you
> A tunnel of green gloom, and sleep
> Deeply above ; and green and deep
> The stream mysterious glides beneath, . . .

Du lieber Gott!
Here am I, sweating, sick, and hot,
And there the shadowed waters fresh
Lean up to embrace the naked flesh. . . .
εἴθε γενοίμην . . . would I were
In Grantchester, in Grantchester !— . . .
Oh, is the water sweet and cool,
Gentle and brown, above the pool ?
And laughs the immortal river still
Under the mill, under the mill ?
Say, is there Beauty yet to find ?
And Certainty ? and Quiet kind ? . . ."

Here is the seeing eye, the inevitable word, the god
speaking through the lips of man ; it is true magic,
gossamer-like, almost unbelievably beautiful. It
makes one get a faint glimmering of what that critic
meant who said that had it not been for Keats we should
have had no Brooke. If the process of pruning on
which I touched at the beginning of this paper enables
a man to rebuild his conceptions of beauty as effectively
as this, from henceforward I belong to the iconoclasts.

I come now to my final stage, the discussion of
Brooke's attitude to Love.

It is by no mere coincidence that Browning was the
greatest love poet England has ever had ; that Browning
was merely the Victorian edition of Donne ; that
Brooke is the Georgian reincarnation of the same man ;
there is no fallacy in these premises. Doctor Johnson
would not have been alone in stigmatising these lines,

" I'll write upon the shrinking skies
The scarlet splendour of your name,"

as " extravagantly hyperbolical," but that does not
prove that they are not true. There can be no

hyperbole in real love. These lines are no more than the naked truth to a man of Rupert Brooke's temperament. Just as he only discovered real beauty by smashing up the seemingly beautiful, so he found real love only after many ghastly experiments with the false.

> "I said I splendidly loved you ; it's not true.
> Such long swift tides stir not a land-locked sea.
> On gods or fools the high risk falls—on you—
> The clean clear bitter-sweet that's not for me.
> But—there are wanderers in the middle mist,
> Who cry for shadows, clutch, and cannot tell
> Whether they love at all. . . .
>   They doubt, and sigh,
> And do not love at all. Of these am I."

How Donne-like is this almost too clever twist in the tail. You see it again in this favourite selection of two such different critics as Gilbert Murray and Charles Whibley :

> "Breathless, we flung us on the windy hill,
> Laughed in the sun, and kissed the lovely grass.
> You said, 'Through glory and ecstasy we pass ;
> Wind, sun, and earth remain, the birds sing still,
> When we are old, are old. . . .'
> Life is our cry. 'We have kept the faith!' we said ;
> 'We shall go down with unreluctant tread
> Rose-crowned into the darkness!' . . . Proud we were,
> And laughed, that had such brave true things to say
> —And then you suddenly cried, and turned away."

In *Mummia*, another love poem which would have caused Doctor Johnson qualms, he says :

"So I, from paint, stone, tale, and rhyme,
    Stuffed love's infinity,
And sucked all lovers of all time
    To rarefy ecstasy,"

and goes on to pray that his love may be the quint-
essence of all the great lovers of distant ages :

"For the uttermost years have cried and clung
    To kiss your mouth to mine."

At another time he imagines himself to be a paralytic
in love—Brooke, of all people !

"—And you
Flower-laden, come to the clean white cell,
And we talk as ever—am I not the same ?
With our hearts we love, immutable,
You without pity, I without shame."

But the most pregnant of all these is *The Voice*, where
the lover goes out into the woods :

"And I knew
That this was the hour of knowing,
And the night and the woods and you
Were one together, and I should find
Soon in the silence the hidden key
Of all that had hurt and puzzled me—
Why you were you, and the night was kind,
And the woods were part of the heart of me.

You came and quacked beside me in the wood.
You said, 'The view from here is very good !'

You said, ' It's nice to be alone a bit ! '
And, ' How the days are drawing out ! ' you said.
You said, ' The sunset's pretty, isn't it ? '

.   .   .   .

By God ! I wish—I wish that you were dead ! ' "

I know of nothing quite so stirring as this in his
many poems where he harps on the insatiable wants of
man, who knows not what he wants but cries with
crooked mouth for heaven, only to throw it by. But
love of women was not Rupert Brooke's greatest love :

" I have been so great a lover : filled my days
  So proudly with the splendour of Love's praise,
  The pain, the calm, and the astonishment,
  Desire illimitable, and still content. . . ."

You tremble here, as one critic has said, on the verge
of the hectic nineties ; you imagine that he is about
to describe his Cynaras and Jennys. Not so.

                    " These have I loved :
White plates and cups, clean-gleaming,
Ringed with blue lines ; and feathery, faery dust ;
Wet roofs, beneath the lamp-light ; the strong crust
Of friendly bread ; and many-tasting food ;
Rainbows ; and the blue bitter smoke of wood ;
And radiant raindrops couching in cool flowers ;

O dear my loves, O faithless, once again
This one last gift I give ; that after men
Shall know, and later lovers, far-removed,
Praise you, ' All these were lovely ' ; say, ' He loved.' "

Walt Whitman himself never exulted in so sustained an anthem ; it is the *benedicite* of all lovers of Nature. How instantly and surely does Brooke show us the captivation of the sudden flowering miracle of the ordinary.

We, too, go out after reading this, and for a moment gaze spellbound in ecstasy with new eyes at the beauty of boys bathing in a pool, of the lighted cottage window at dusk, the dim religious light of an abbey crowned by the crescent moon ; we, too, have our immortal moment in lilac and laburnum time, when we picture some old song's lady, a snatch of a forgotten tune, the echoing laughter of our best beloved who may be far away or dead ; we, too, stand on the heights unpinioned and gaze out over the empurpled hills, razor-like in their majestic nakedness, and for a million years enraptured, god-like, appreciative ; we, too, can see visions of Arthur setting out for that distant vale of Avilion, where falls not hail, or rain, or any snow, nor ever wind blows loudly ; we, too, can hear the voice of many waters, of the breeze, of the lark ; the scent of sweetbrier and of peach has the power to drive even us almost mad with infinite longings . . . but for the most part we are content to crawl homewards with downcast eye, oblivious of beauty, forgetful of love ; it is in these arid, never-ending, viewless deserts that we need most of all the poets, that we may open our eyes to see, our ears to hear ; to see in the long melancholic train of clouds our dead friends hovering, to hear in the joyous trilling of birds our loved ones' happy laughter. We, too, need to have something of that magnificent unpreparedness for the long littleness of life which is only to be learnt of poets. Rupert Brooke, perhaps more than any poet of our era, is able to teach us something of the things that matter. It was not for nothing that Ben Jonson styled Donne the first poet in the world for some things. So is his disciple Brooke. If you require a corrective for lazy thinking and facile writing, turn to Donne or Brooke ; if that kind of wit which is one long succession of disconcerting surprises refreshes you and inspires you, you will find it in each of these ; if you are willing or able to let beauty come to you as it comes to the Alchemist who " Glorifies his pregnant pot, If by the way to him befall, Some odoriferous thing or medicinal," you will be helped again by reading these two men, you will forgive the frequently bizarre, the sometimes even repellent tone that creeps in almost unconsciously, because of that rare intensity of feeling which pervades their whole outlook on life. If you love Browning, but are too troubled to acquiesce without question in his too comfortable " God's in His Heaven—All's right with the World," or his non-proven optimism about reunion, " I shall clasp thee again, O thou soul of my soul, and with God be the rest," turn to Brooke and you will find the same erudition, the same packed intricacies, the same multitudinous beauties and whimsical phraseology, but none of his annoying sophistry. There is always latent that surest of all foundations, a perfect blend of reason and imagination, each restraining the other so that reason does not become unsympathetic hardness nor imagination degenerate into what Wordsworth so well called mere fancy.

If your criterion of a poet be that he should possess fire, a joy in life, a classical taste, an Hellenic eye for beauty and grace, a sense of the lovely, and be able to differentiate that best of all things, Love, from that worst travesty, Sentimentalism, you will be among those who will turn for solace and true enjoyment to Rupert Brooke.

There has passed away through his death a glory from the earth; each of us is the poorer by the loss of a man whom all his friends idolised and his readers revered. He died as he had lived; as England had lavished on him all the gifts that mortal man can desire, so he was willing to renounce them as a sacrifice on the altar of honour. "Proud then, clear-eyed and laughing, go to greet Death as a friend." Of him it can truly be said:

"Nothing is here for tears, nothing to wail
Or knock the breast; no weakness, no contempt,
Dispraise or blame; nothing but well and fair,
And what may quiet us in a death so noble."

XI

THE POETRY OF THOMAS HARDY

W E have always regarded the Golden Treasury
Series as a garner-house in which was stored
all the choicest flowers from the classics.
Messrs Macmillan have now extended their scope to
include (for the first time) selections from the work
of a genius still, happily, alive, and it is a compliment
to a great poet that his work should be considered
worthy to find a place in this august library, and also a
tribute to the critical powers of the publishers that they
should have chosen so rare and precious an artist as
Thomas Hardy with whom to inaugurate their departure
from their original scheme. For it may be confidently
stated that for every hundred of his readers as a novelist
he has but one as a poet. Even the most cultured
among us would think twice before daring to assert
that Thomas Hardy, the greatest living writer of fiction
(which few would dispute), was also among the first
three poets of his age.

It is curious how many novelists are also poets. It
would be hard to recall many instances of famous poets
who were also novelists, but there are numerous cases
of the converse of this. D. H. Lawrence, who made
his name as a novelist, has yet written much poetry
which would be included in any anthology of contemporary poetry. St John Lucas, who has earned our
lasting gratitude in *The First Round* and *April Folly*, is
also a poet of no inconsiderable merit. Ivy Low . . .

but there are far more famous instances than these ; Robert Louis Stevenson and George Meredith, George Eliot and the Brontës, Kipling and Goldsmith, Scott —the list is unending. The difficulty is to find an exception, whereas it is hard to imagine those who are primarily poets writing novels at all. What sort of a novel should we expect from Wordsworth, Keats, Shelley, Rupert Brooke, Swinburne, Tennyson, Browning, Robert Bridges, Yeats, Noyes, Drinkwater or Flecker ?

Naturally we read with unqualified delight and interest all that our favourite novelists put into poetry, for we there find their philosophy crystallised, we find more of themselves, for, broadly speaking, the average novel is objective and dramatic, whereas poetry is subjective and reflective. We get a far closer insight into the workings of our novelist's mind if he writes poetry, for there at least we can be certain of finding the man himself. So just as all true lovers of Meredith read his poetry with no less avidity than his novels, so all disciples of Hardy will be grateful for this collection of his poems now published.

The book, which is all too slim, and contains less than one hundred and fifty short poems, is divided into three parts—Lyrical, Narrative and Martial—written in every conceivable sort of metre. For Hardy is nothing if not experimental ; he ranges from the severely classical Sapphic to the most formless of modern metric devices ; he achieves beauty in nearly every case, but he is obviously never satisfied that he has found the best mould in which to cast his thoughts ; he repeats himself less than any contemporary poet, whether in language or form. On the other hand, his philosophy, the essence of his work, is stable and uniform ; the fatalism which we have come to regard as his most

284 FROM SHAKESPEARE TO O. HENRY

pronounced characteristic is softened to a considerable extent. We could no longer imagine Mr G. K. Chesterton, for instance, comparing him in this instance with " the village atheist blaspheming over the village idiot."

Browning, to take a typical example, might well have written *On the Departure Platform*, with its theory of the transitory nature of human happiness :

> " And why, young man, must eternally fly
> A joy you'll repeat, if you love her well ?
> —O friend, nought happens twice thus ; why,
> I cannot tell ! "

—and Browning above all men was dear to the heart of Chesterton. It is a mistake to suppose that Hardy has not experienced his ecstatic moments in common with the most thoughtless of us.

> " A Day is drawing to its fall
> I had not dreamed to see ;
> The first of many to enthrall
> My spirit, will it be ?
> Or is this eve the end of all
> Such new delight for me ?
>
> I journey home : the pattern grows
> Of moon shades on the way :
> ' Soon the first quarter, I suppose,'
> Sky-glancing travellers say.
> I realise that it, for those,
> Has been a common day."

This scarcely fits in with our preconceived theories about the pessimistic ugliness of the author of *Tess*.

The truth is rather that Hardy is of all living poets

the most sensitive to the appeal of beauty ; out of
the simplest hack phrases of conversation he seems
to evolve a magical melody.

> " Let me enjoy the earth no less
>   Because the all-enacting Might
> That fashioned forth its loveliness
>   Had other aims than my delight . . ."

is a brave verse, and certainly not the despairing cry
of the village atheist blaspheming. " Life offers—to
deny," he sings in *Yell'ham-Wood's Story*, but that is
merely the cry of a heart that will not allow reason to
be overpowered by plausible blind emotion ; he refuses
to blink the fact that life is tragic, poignant, illogical
and uncomfortable.

He merely wishes to put on record his experience
that, given the time and the place and the loved one
all together, there still lurks some secret thing which
prevents man from seizing the golden opportunity. He
pictures in *At an Inn* two lovers left alone as " Love's
own pair " who had resigned all for " love's dear ends."

> " The kiss their zeal foretold,
>   And now deemed come,
> Came not ; within his hold
>   Love lingered numb.
> Why cast he on our port
>   A bloom not ours ?
> Why shaped us for his sport
>   In after-hours ?
>
> As we seemed we were not
>   That day afar,
> And now we seem not what
>   We aching are.

O severing sea and land,
        O laws of men,
    Ere death, once let us stand
        As we stood then ! "

At times he jerks out uncouth words at us with
malicious intent; " unsight," " enray," " enarch,"
" unease " and " disennoble " all occur in two sequent
stanzas, but when he employs terms like these we feel
somehow that he does so for some hidden purpose of
his own, not from slackness, not because he is deaf to
their sound, not because there were no other more
legitimate and pleasant-sounding words that would
do instead, but because by them alone could he attain
exactly the atmosphere he required at that moment.

His most intimately personal, beautiful and moving
poems are those written on his wife's death. Here we
have sheer beauty of sentiment allied with perfect,
simple expression :

" Why did you give no hint that night
    That quickly after the morrow's dawn,
  And calmly, as if indifferent quite,
      You would close your term here, up and be gone
          Where I could not follow
          With wing of swallow
      To gain one glimpse of you ever anon !

  Never to bid good-bye,
    Or give me the softest call,
  Or utter a wish for a word, while I
      Saw morning harden upon the wall,
          Unmoved, unknowing
          That your great going
      Had place that moment, and altered all.

Why do you make me leave the house
And think for a breath it is you I see
At the end of the alley of bending boughs
Where so oft at dusk you used to be :
    Till in darkening dankness
    The yawning blankness
Of the perspective sickens me ! ''

Even more, harping on the same strain, that of his
wife's death, in *Without Ceremony*, do we see how he
gets a supremely exquisite effect with the common
phraseology of every day transmuted into music by
the genius of the poet :

    " It was your way, my dear,
    To be gone without a word
    When callers, friends, or kin
    Had left, and I hastened in
    To rejoin you, as I inferred.

    And when you'd a mind to career
    Off anywhere—say to town—
    You were all on a sudden gone
    Before I had thought thereon,
    Or noticed your trunks were down.

    So now, that you disappear
    For ever in that swift style
    Your meaning seems to me
    Just as it used to be :
    ' Good-bye is not worth while ! ' ''

It is worth while analysing this poem in detail, if you
would discover Hardy's mastery over the commonplace.   Notice   the   intricate   rhyme-scheme,   the

ordinariness of " when you'd a mind to career off anywhere—say to town " ; could anything be more con-
versational, more like the speech of every day ?   How
Wordsworth would have delighted in this consummate
proof of the efficacy of his theory of poetic diction : it
requires more than common courage to risk such bare
simplicity, for if you fail, your fall is seen at once by
even the dullest critic ; conversely, if you succeed, as
there is no doubt Hardy does here, your success is due
to genius alone, unaided by any cloying sweetness, or
exotic, fair-sounding words that lull the senses and put
all one's critical faculties to sleep.

Could anything be more simple than his two superb
poems to his dead wife, *At Castle Boterel* and *The
Phantom Horsewoman* ?

> " Queer are the ways of a man I know :
>   He comes and stands
>   In a careworn craze,
>   And looks at the sands
>   And the seaward haze
>   With moveless hands
>   And face and gaze,
>   Then turns to go. . . .
> And what does he see when he gazes so ?
>
> They say he sees as an instant thing
>   More clear than to-day,
>   A sweet soft scene
>   That once was in play
>   By that briny green :
>   Yes, notes alway
>   Warm, real, and keen,
>   What his back years bring—
> A phantom of his own figuring.

A ghost girl-rider.   And though, toil-tried,
   He withers daily,
   Time touches her not,
   But she still rides gaily
   In his rapt thought
   On that shagged and shaly
   Atlantic spot,
   And as when first eyed
Draws rein and sings to the swing of the tide."

It will surprise many of those people who for years
have denounced Hardy for his miserable lack of hope
or faith to find that he comes into line with all the
youngest soldier-poets of to-day, who sing incessantly
of the future life when their spirits will return to the
places they had learnt to love best.

   " My spirit will not haunt the mound
     Above my breast,
   But travel, memory-possessed,
   To where my tremulous being found
     Life largest, best."

This scarcely fits in with the accepted ideas about
pessimism. The truth is, Hardy was as capable of
experiencing the finest passions as any great genius is ;
life's peerless moments of bliss had come his way too
and he had not despised them. His love for his wife
is as self-evident as Browning's was ; only the inevitable reaction came. " Too fragrant was Life's early
bloom, Too tart the fruit it brought." Just as he
was capable of loving much so was he condemned,
as all great lovers are, to suffer in exactly the same
proportion.

"Brush not the bough for midnight scents
  That come forth lingeringly,
And wake the same sweet sentiments
  They breathed to you and me
When living seemed a laugh, and love
  All it was said to be.
I did not know
That heydays fade and go,
But deemed that what was would be always so."

Is not this rather the awakening of the optimist to a sense of this world's shortcomings ?

I think it was Chesterton who first pointed out that the pessimist was really more optimistic than the optimist because he was not content with things as they are but saw in his visions a much finer world and spent his whole life in trying to bring it into being. In *To an Unborn Pauper Child* we get this point of view exactly :

"and such are we—
Unreasoning, sanguine, visionary—
  That I can hope
  Health, love, friends, scope
In full for thee ; can dream thou'lt find
Joys seldom yet attained by humankind."

"Unreasoning, sanguine, visionary" are not the adjectives we should normally apply to Hardy, but no picture of him can claim to be complete which harps only on his fatalistic side, the side that produced that terrible poem on *The Titanic*:

"Well—while was fashioning
  This creature of cleaving wing,
The Immanent Will that stirs and urges everything

Prepared a sinister mate
For her—so gaily great—
A Shape of Ice, for the time far and dissociate.
    And as the smart ship grew
    In stature, grace, and hue,
In shadowy silent distance grew the Iceberg too.
    Till the Spinner of the Years
    Said ' Now ! ' and each one hears,
And consummation comes, and jars two hemispheres."

There shines forth the intellect that refuses to be hoodwinked, that will not allow itself to be soothed with vain, false words of comfort.

How perfectly he merges that clear, critical faculty into the musical can be seen at once in his tribute to Swinburne :

" —It was as though a garland of red roses
Had fallen about the hood of some smug nun
When irresponsibly dropped as from the sun,
In fulth of numbers freaked with musical closes
Upon Victoria's formal middle time
    His leaves of rhythm and rhyme."

He is like Wordsworth in this, that he does mean so very much more than he says. There is a whole parable of life in the poem on the tradition of the oxen kneeling on Christmas Eve.

    " I feel
If someone said on Christmas Eve,
  ' Come ; see the oxen kneel
In the lonely barton by yonder coomb
  Our childhood used to know,'
I should go with him in the gloom,
  Hoping it might be so."

How Wordsworthian, again, is *The Dear*, in which he describes his chance meeting on the hill-tops with a maiden, " one fain would guard from every hazard and every care " :

> " I wondered how succeeding suns
>   Would shape her wayfarings,
> And wished such Power might take such ones
>   Under its warding wings."

He then greeted her : " Commiserate still. ' Good morning, my Dear ! ' I said." She replied that she was not *his* dear and passed him by . . . and . . . " I did not try to make her understand."

It is easy enough to misread such a poem altogether and dismiss it with a sneer, but it is a mistake into which we often fall, this of attributing to genius intellects not very far superior to our own. We have to remember too, that, unlike many great poets, Hardy has a very finely developed sense of humour and is not likely to be led astray into writing rubbish.

Some of his narrative poems have as their theme the most commonplace incidents, which yet become pregnant with meaning when seen through the eyes of the seer. Few who have read *Beyond the Last Lamp : beyond Tooting Common* (of all unpoetic places) will easily forget the impression made on them by the story of the miserable couple pacing up and down " heedless of the night and rain."

> " One could but wonder who they were
> And what wild woe detained them there."

Thirty years after, the poet still sees them when nights are weird and wet . . . it is this interest in all

the world about him that makes the only true criterion
by which we can judge our poet.

The Face at the Casement is more definitely tragic.
The lover passes with his beloved under the window
of the dying man, who had also loved her, but in vain.

> " He wished to marry me,
>   So I am bound, when I drive near him,
>   To enquire, if but to cheer him,
>   How he may be."

Her message is sent up to the sick man, who thanks
her extravagantly for coming, and they drive on.
The favoured lover then designs a deed of hell : knowing his rival to be gazing out of the lattice upon their
receding figures, he puts his arm about her that he
might see, nor doubt her " my plighted Love." The
poem then ends on a note quite foreign to our old idea
of Hardy :

> " Love is long-suffering, brave,
>   Sweet, prompt, precious as a jewel :
>   But O, too, Love is cruel,
>   Cruel as the grave."

It seems hard to believe that he would concede so
much to Love as to allow her those five all-conquering
attributes, especially when we remember that in an
earlier poem he had definitely stated that it would be
better for mankind to cease without Love's kindling
coupling-vow rather than to learn what her sway
meant.

A third narrative poem, longer than the others,
called *The Burghers* (Casterbridge, 17—), tells of a man
who caught his wife on the point of running away with

a man ; instead of killing them, as his friend advises, he heaps on her all his possessions and sees them quietly off the grounds.

"It was my friend. 'I have struck well. They fly,
  But carry wounds that none can cicatrize.'
  'Not mortal ? ' said he. 'Lingering—worse,' said I."

Once only, in *In Tenebris*, does he lament his loneliness and separation from mankind ; once only, just as Meredith let us see his deep agony in his letters.

The poem is more self-revelatory than anything else Hardy ever wrote—it is wrung out of him.

He begins by quoting Psalm 141 : " Considerabam ad dexteram, et videbam ; et non erat qui cognosceret me."

"When the clouds' swoln bosoms echo back the shouts
    of the many and strong,
  [The things are all as they best may be, save a few to
    be right ere long,
  And my eyes have not the vision in them to discern
    what to these is so clear,
  The blot seems straightway in me alone ; one better
    he were not here.
  Let him in whose ears the low-voiced Best is killed
    by the clash of the First,
  Who holds that if way to the Better there be, it
    exacts a full look at the Worst,
  Who feels that delight is a delicate growth cramped
    by crookedness, custom, and fear,
  Get him up and be gone as one shaped awry : he
    disturbs the order here."

So we get our Hardy humanised even more than we thought ; he does care, he does suffer horribly under

the false accusations made against him. It is the lot
of the seer, the prophet and the teacher, " to disturb
the order here " ; the whole of progress lies in our
poets' capacity for making us readjust our values and
test our standards anew from time to time ; were it not
for the many severe shakings that they administer
we should contentedly settle down, apathetically take
things as they come, and give assent to that immoral
doctrine that all is for the best in this best of all possible
worlds ; if that is so we must be pessimists indeed.
Like Alexander we might be forgiven if we sat down
and wept as there are no môre worlds to conquer. It is
the optimist who forges ahead, feeling that delight is a
delicate growth, cramped by crookedness, custom, and
fear, to worlds where delight may be pure and unalloyed.

But after all *In Tenebris* is only a mood ; luckily all
poets know in their hearts that they are right and the
world is wrong. In the final poem of Part II. of this
volume we see him once more his true self, out of the
depths, serene :

> " For loud acclaim he does not care
>   By the august or rich or fair,
>   Nor for smart pilgrims from afar,
>   Curious on where his hauntings are,"

and he finishes on this triumphant note of thankfulness :

> " Whatever his message—glad or grim—
>   Two bright-souled women clave to him."

There is little here of the village atheist blaspheming
over the village idiot.

The last part of the book is given up to war poems
and lyrics from *The Dynasts.*

Here again he refuses to blink his eyes to the facts, and just because he is clear-sighted he can foresee a time when patriotism, grown God-like, will scorn to stand bondslave to realms, but circle earth and seas. War is so amazingly futile and purposeless.

> " Yes ; quaint and curious war is !
>   You shoot a fellow down
>   You'd treat if met where any bar is
>   Or help to half-a-crown.''

And yet . . . and yet . . .

> " Is it a purblind prank, O think you,
>   Friend with the musing eye,
>   Who watch us stepping by
>   With doubt and dolorous sigh ?
>   Can much pondering so hoodwink you !
>   Is it a purblind prank, O think you,
>   Friend with the musing eye ?
>
>   Nay.   We well see what we are doing,
>   Though some may not see—
>   Dalliers as they be—
>   England's need are we :
>   Her distress would leave us rueing,
>   Nay.   We well see what we are doing,
>   Though some may not see.''

This is a good note on which to leave this all too slim volume.   Hardy himself has never been in any doubt as to his aims—it is only we who are in blinkers when we attribute to such an intellect " purblind pranks '' or the inspissated gloom of the cursing atheist.

He has found life very sweet, and as a quite natural corollary he has also found it exceeding bitter ; he

reveals himself in all his moods; at one moment he
turns from the trees to human companionship :

> " Since, then, no grace I find
>   Taught me of trees,
> Turn I back to my kind,
>   Worthy as these.
>
> There at least smiles abound,
>   There discourse trills around,
> There, now and then, are found
>   Life-loyalties."

At another he seeks the Wessex Heights to escape
from the ghosts that continually haunt him in the
lowlands :

> " Mind-chains do not clank where one's next neighbour
>   is the sky.
> There are some heights in Wessex, shaped as if by a
>   kindly hand
> For thinking, dreaming, dying on, and at crises when
>   I stand,
> Say, on Ingpen Beacon eastward, or on Wylls Neck
>   westwardly,
> I seem where I was before my birth, and after death
>   may be.
> So I am found on Ingpen Beacon, or on Wylls Neck
>   to the west.
> Or else on homely Bulbarrow, or little Pilsdon crest,
> Where men have never cared to haunt, nor women
>   have walked with me,
> And ghosts then keep their distance : and I know
>   some liberty."

Curiously enough, Hardy's superb descriptions of the
beauties of the Dorset which he has made all his own

are reserved for his prose epics ; he never approaches the majesty of the opening chapters of *The Return of the Native* in any of his descriptive poems ; he is rarely in his poetry merely descriptive at all.   At his sweetest, he uses the scenery, say, of the Cornish coast as a background and a setting for his wife's portrait.   Not that he cannot crystallise in the most exquisite form any mood of Nature which he wants to pin down, more particularly, of course, her harsher ones.

> " I leant upon a coppice gate
>   When Frost was spectre-grey,
> And winter's days made desolate
>   The weakening eye of day.
> The tangled bine-stems scored the sky
>   Like strings of broken lyres,
> And all mankind that haunted nigh
>   Had sought their household fires.
> The land's sharp features seemed to be
>   The Century's corpse outleant,
> His crypt the cloudy canopy,
>   The wind his death-lament.
> The ancient pulse of germ and birth
>   Was shrunken hard and dry,
> And every spirit upon earth
>   Seemed fervourless as I."

His wonderful manipulation of diverse metrical forms, his passionate love for his wife and his never-to-be-forgotten sense of loss when she died, beautifully expressed in imperishable verse, his keen, penetrating philosophy, his delight in the mere telling of a story, all combine to make this all too slim body of work of rare and lasting value.

His sense of the musical was evident to anyone who

studied the lyrics in *The Dynasts*, but his amazing successes with every sort of metrical and rhythmical experiment that he tried are not so commonly recognised. The point most to be kept in mind is that he attains that success with the ordinary, everyday speech of us all. Here is none of the dreamy, sensuous language of Keats or Coleridge, heavy with romance words ; his is the vocabulary of the satirist, of Swift, Anglo-Saxon, monosyllabic, intellectual, bare . . . he has followed no school and founded none. He disdains to employ any tricks to cajole the multitude to listen to his pipings ; consequently, the Cæsar to whom he appeals for judgment is posterity. He will never create a furore among his contemporaries ; he has remained isolated and aloof all these years and may be well content to remain so for the remainder of his life. He already has to suffer, while alive, the doom of being a classic, and therefore talked about and not read by the million, in his novels. He has to endure the vitriolic abuse of the orthodox, who see in his intellectual straightness and hard-won theories of life only the vapourings of a village atheist, and finally, like so many other great poets, he has failed altogether to obtain recognition for his purest work owing to the blindness or slackness of contemporary criticism.

XII

O. HENRY

I CANNOT claim to be among that select band who found and loved O. Henry's short stories before the present boom set in. I owe my knowledge of him entirely to Stephen Leacock's eulogistic essay, in which he prophesies that the time is coming when the whole English-speaking world will recognise in O. Henry one of the great masters of modern literature. I read him to refute this amazing pæan ; I read every word he published ; I read a great deal of him aloud, and I may say, in passing, that he gains infinitely by being read aloud. Now comes an authentic biography of him from a Professor of English in the University of Virginia, who says that in O. Henry non-critical readers find a range of fancy, an exuberance of humour, a sympathy, an understanding, a knowledge of the raw material of life, an ability to interpret the passing in terms of the permanent, an insight into individual and institutional character, a resolute and pervasive desire to help those in need of help—in a word, a constant and essential democracy that they find in no other short-story writer.

I fear that the two professors, in their enthusiasm over their hero, are likely to overshoot the mark and drive away many timid readers who, carefully enticed, might have become devotees of this remarkable writer ; for however much the method of " thrusting down the throat " may succeed in America, it " cuts very little ice " in England.

We are told that his adherents across the Atlantic can be counted in millions, which rather tends to make the cultured, academic mind of this country avoid so successful a genius. He thinks fretfully of those writers who count as best sellers in the British Isles. So far from being a point in their favour, such evidence only militates against them here, for the most popular writers are rarely the masters and are but seldom among those who have any new message to deliver.

Respecting, however, the calm verdict of so obviously sane a critic as Professor Leacock, they buy one volume of O. Henry's, ready to find fault, and within a few minutes they have found a dozen or a score of tactical errors that rankle.

They object to his slap-dash style, his far-fetched metaphors and similes with which he besprinkles nearly every sentence. He is as fond of a ridiculous illustration as Shakespeare was of puns. They cavil at his impossible exaggerations as palpable and false as Falstaff's; his wit, which degenerates only too often into buffoonery; at a thousand things which an English writer would have left unsaid; at the constant irruption of the narrator into the story; the "take it or leave it," high-handed tone which he takes with his readers; at the blatancy of the tricks he plays upon the imagination—at a thousand little details.

Many quite acute critics never get beyond this stage, and give O. Henry much too short a trial, only to turn from him in disgust before they penetrate to the real writer at all. It must be allowed at once that the pure gold, of which there is much, is hidden beneath a good deal of dross. There are twelve volumes of these stories, and in each volume there are over two dozen separate tales. It is not to be expected that of these two hundred and seventy odd experiments all will

succeed. I would guarantee to select fifty which
would make an irresistible appeal to the most exacting
and captious critic, but these fifty would have to be
chosen with great circumspection, and they are to be
found in no two or three volumes. They are scattered
haphazard in between stories that are merely dull,
pointless or insipid, and to the full appreciation of them
a knowledge of the salient points of O. Henry's life
would be necessary ; so this I propose to give now.

His biographer, Professor Alphonso Smith, devotes
a great many unnecessary pages to his ancestors and
other irrelevant matter. He has written a book which
is not at all to be commended to those who would
understand the true Henry, and yet without it we
should be apt to miss a great deal that is important if
we wish fully to understand the appeal that his best
stories ought to make.

In the first place, as most people know, his name was
not O. Henry at all, but William Sydney Porter. He
was born at Greensborough, North Carolina, in 1862,
and as a boy in his native town gained a good deal of
local approbation as a cartoonist. After leaving school
he became apprenticed to his uncle, and spent five years
in a drug store, and completed his education by reading
omnivorously. Among his favourite books were *The
Arabian Nights*, *The Anatomy of Melancholy*, the novels
of Scott, Dickens, Thackeray, Charles Reade, Bulwer
Lytton, Wilkie Collins, Victor Hugo and Dumas. His
health, however, was not strong (he came of a con-
sumptive stock), and so at the age of eighteen he was
sent to Texas in order to learn the art of ranching.
His thirst for knowledge during this period seems to
have been unquenchable. History, fiction, biography,
science and magazines of every sort were devoured and
talked about with eager interest. Tennyson and

Webster's *Unabridged Dictionary* were his two most
frequent companions. Though he was always shy and
somewhat of a dreamer, he absorbed, apparently with
little effort, the different accomplishments which he
was now called upon to learn—lassoing cattle, dipping
and shearing sheep, shooting and the management of
horses.

Just as the confinement in the Greensborough drug
store had whetted his appetite for the freedom of the
ranch, so now, after two years, the isolation of ranch life
began to pall and he became eager for the social contact of city life. So he now migrated to Austin, where
he became, in turn, occasional clerk in a tobacco store
and later in a drug store, book-keeper for a real estate
firm, draftsman in a land office, paying and receiving
teller in a bank, member of a military company, singer
in the choirs of the Presbyterian, Baptist and Episcopal
churches, actor in private theatricals, editor of a
humorous paper, serenader and cartoonist.

It was at this time that he acquired his lifelong taste,
which was afterwards to stand him in such good stead,
of going "bumming"—that is, of night-prowling in
the streets. He used to watch and get into conversation with every sort of person in the streets, with the
result that out of work hours he lived in a constant
state of adventure.

Like Dostoievsky and all the great Russians, he was
an incorrigible romancist, and was always on the look-
out for what was "round the corner" in life.

In 1887 he married Miss Athol Estes, a seventeen-
year-old girl, unfortunately, like himself, of con-
sumptive parentage. Owing to the refusal of the girl's
parents, on the ground of health, to allow the couple to
get married, they eloped, but were ultimately recon-
ciled. Mrs Porter appears to have given him exactly

the incentive he needed. The year of his marriage was also the year in which he began to rely on his pen as a supplementary source of income. There was born during this period his only daughter, Margaret Worth Porter, who is now herself making a name in America as an author.

In 1894 he started a paper called *The Rolling Stone*, which lived for exactly a year. He then accepted a job on the staff of *The Houston Daily Post*, which he held from October, 1895, to June, 1896, when he was suddenly recalled to Austin to answer a charge of embezzlement while acting as teller at the bank. That he was innocent no one now doubts, but he committed what he afterwards called the one irretrievable error of his life by running away. He took train from Houston, obviously with the intent of standing his trial, but at Hempstead his too imaginative mind betrayed him, and he got out and took the night train to New Orleans, a fugitive from justice. He went on by fruit steamer to Honduras, and there met the leader of a notorious gang of train robbers,[1] whom he joined, and together this strange pair circled the entire west of South America. He wrote regularly to his wife, and was full of plans for the education of his daughter in Honduras, when suddenly he learnt that his wife was dangerously ill. He immediately returned and gave himself up in order to be near her. She died in July, 1897, and his trial was held in February of the following year. He pleaded not guilty, but appeared to be indifferent as to the result.

One peculiar feature of the indictment was that he was accused of stealing money in November, 1895, nearly a year after he had left the bank ! This appears

---

[1] Al Jennings, who has described, in *Through the Shadows with O. Henry*, their remarkable friendship.

not to have been commented on at all. Like "Lord Jim," O. Henry appears to have been crushed by his one great mistake, in running away. The rest of the matter did not appear to concern him. He was sentenced to five years' imprisonment, but came out in 1901, after three years, owing to his flawless record in prison. He acted during these years as drug clerk in the penitentiary, and Professor Smith includes in his biography a great number of letters written to his daughter during this time, over which it is not necessary now to dwell. He retained no trace of bitterness at the hardness of his lot. The years had left an ineradicable mark upon his character, and he came out into the world again a changed man, nobler, of infinite charity and kindliness, with an intense sympathy for all his fellow-creatures.

It was at this time that he began to write under an assumed name, the name by which he is now known to practically every intelligent person in the English-speaking countries.

The stories that were written in prison, under the stress of so great suffering, mark the transition from journalism to the domain of literature proper.

In the spring of 1902 came the call to him to go to New York. From that time forward he found that he could not work outside of the city which he now made his own and which claims him as her most inspired lover. "If ever," writes Professor Smith, "in American literature the place and the man met, they met when O. Henry strolled for the first time along the streets of New York."

Conqueror-like, he began to rechristen the city of his choice. "Little Old Bagdad-on-the-Subway," "The City of Too Many Caliphs," "Noisyville on the Hudson," "Wolfville on the Subway" and "The City of Chameleon Changes " will give some idea of the impression this vast Manhattan made on its greatest lover. He made many and valuable friends, but was very much averse from any tendency that might be shown to lionise him.   He was nearly always penniless, owing to his lack of thrift and his incurable habit of promiscuous charity, but he was never tempted by golden offers to swell his coffers.   On one occasion a very famous publishing firm, who had refused many of his short stories when he was unknown, now came forward and sent him a cheque for a thousand dollars, asking him for something from his pen—anything.   His reply was to send back the cheque without further comment.

There were but two things that could be really counted upon to offend him—a salacious story and the proffer of a plot.   He preferred to get his plots for himself by mixing with shop-girls and salesmen, by roaming at all hours of the day and night along the river front and talking with anyone who would condescend to do so.   He seems never to have wanted " copy."

" If I could have a thousand years," he writes, in one of his short stories—" just one little thousand years —more of life, I might, in that time, draw near enough to true Romance to touch the hem of her robe.

" Up from ships men come, and from waste places, and forest and road and garret and cellar to maunder to me in strangely distributed words of the things they have seen and considered.   The recording of their tales is no more than a matter of ears and fingers.   There are only two fates I dread—deafness and writer's cramp."

To one of his stories, *Madame Bo-Peep, of the Ranches*, he owes his second wife, Miss Sallie Coleman of Asheville, North Carolina.   She had written to him about this story and told him of her own ambition to write.

His reply is illuminating and quite extraordinarily helpful, not only to a true understanding of the romantic trait which is O. Henry's predominant and most charming characteristic, but also as a piece of advice to the thousands of young adventurers of to-day who, like the cat in the adage, are hesitating.

"Now I'll tell you what to do," he says. "Kick the mountains over and pack a kimono and a lead-pencil in a suit-case and hurry to New York. Get a little studio three stories up with mission furniture and portières, a guitar and a chafing-dish and laugh at fate and the gods. There are lots of lovely women here leading beautiful and happy lives in the midst of the greatest things in this hemisphere of art and music and literature, on tiny little incomes. You meet the big people in every branch of art, you drink deep of the Pierian spring, you get the benefit of the earth's best."

Was ever good advice more succinctly or more charmingly given? It is the root of the whole matter. Seize your opportunity, he seems to say, in both hands; don't fear for the result. Vegetate no longer in the country, where your talents will only run to seed, but come up to town, where real life is to be lived and enjoyed. Those only live who are willing to take the risk.

This wise maiden took the risk, and in November, 1907, she became the second Mrs Porter. He now entered upon his most prolific period.

In 1904 he produced sixty-five, and in 1905 fifty short stories. In 1906 appeared the volume entitled *The Four Millions*, with this illuminating foreword:

"Not very long ago someone invented the assertion that there were only 'Four Hundred' people in New York City who were really worth noticing. But a wiser man has arisen—the census-taker—and his larger estimate of human interest has been preferred in marking out the field of these little stories of the ' Four Million.' "

Here we get the clue to O. Henry's greatness, his kinship with Dickens and Shakespeare and all great writers. He was the born, large-hearted democrat who, with the utmost sincerity, can lay his hand upon his breast and say : " Humani nihil a me alienum puto."

Each succeeding year, until 1911, saw the publication of two collections of his stories touching on every sort of topic, treating of every kind of life.

In 1909 he showed signs of breaking up, and in the autumn of that year he returned to Asheville, only to return to his beloved city in the following March. On the evening of the 3rd of June he was taken to the Polyclinic Hospital, and on the following Sunday morning, just before sunrise, with a whimsical smile and a jest upon his lips—" Turn up the lights : I don't want to go home in the dark "—he died.

Such is the life story of a man who has been variously styled " The American Kipling," " The American de Maupassant," " The American Gogol," " Our Fielding à la mode," " The Bret Harte of the City," " The Y.M.C.A. Boccaccio," " The Homer of the Tenderloin," " The Twentieth Century Haroun Al-Raschid," " The Greatest Living Master of the Short Story."

It remains to see how far he has justified these extraordinary titles.

First, then, as to technique.

No man has made so much his own the art of the unexpected ending. He begins quietly, yet arrestingly, but you are unable to tell whether you are to be let in for a tragic or comic *dénouement*, a defeat or victory. In the second stage, that of the first guess, you begin to discover the plot ; something definite and resultant seems to be on the way ; you can't guess the end, but you can't help trying to.

The third stage shows you that your guess was wrong. This is the stage of the first surprise. Something has happened that ought not to have happened if the story was to end according to your expectations.

The last stage is marked by light out of darkness.

We are surprised, happily surprised, and then surprised again that we should have been surprised at first.

> " He always worked a triple-hinged surprise
> To end the scene and make one rub one's eyes."

The sting in the tail, the entire *volte-face* from what one expected, is amazingly in the vein of Rupert Brooke, and adds tremendously to the charm of the narrative, but it is, after all, a trick, mechanical and often tiresome after one gets accustomed to it. But there is something much deeper than this : there is the art which yet makes the unexpected the inevitable. You go over the stories a second time and then begin to perceive the mastery with which the tricks are forged. It is all of a piece. There are no loose ends, no irrelevancies. All O. Henry's stories are marked by a fierce economy of detail which at once put him on a plane far different from that occupied by the average teller of short stories.

The next point to be noticed is his gift of observation mingled with what Bagehot called the experiencing mind. Not only did he watch with meticulous carefulness all the idiosyncrasies of every sort of person with whom he came into contact, but he was further obsessed with a passionate interest in and sympathy with every type of man.

He is particularly fond of turning the tables on

Haroun Al-Raschid. Not only does he let the rich wander incognito among the poor, but he gives his imagination rein and, Pippa-like, bestows upon the poverty-stricken clerk a day when he can become one with the rich. Again and again he returns to this subject, every time to treat of it from a fresh and inspiring point of view.

We see it in the story of the salesman who saved up ten dollars every seventy days in order to masquerade as a man about town for one night. He meets a girl who is masquerading as a shop-girl for amusement; he takes her out to dinner and talks of his bridge and yachts and golf . . . and other aimless amusements of the life that he pretends to belong to. They separate, and we see her at the close of the story lamenting that she could find it in her heart to love a man who was chivalrous and kind to poor shop-girls, but never one who wasted his life in expensive amusements.

Habit was another favourite topic. O. Henry was very interested in the question of relapse.

The Pendulum is perhaps the best in this vein.

There we have a man who gets tired of the monotony of home life, and so forms the habit, at eight-fifteen every night, of leaving his wife alone and going off to a game of " pool " with his male companions.

One night on returning from work he finds a note from his wife saying that she has been called away to see her mother, who is ill. He immediately begins to feel conscience-stricken; he has treated his wife abominably. When she comes back he will spend the rest of his life in making up for his desertions. He is ruminating on all this when she suddenly returns; her mother was not so bad as she had been led to expect. Immediately the husband looks up at the clock. Eight-fifteen! He gets up, preparatory to leaving the house. Querulously his wife asks where he is going. "Thought I'd drop up to M'Closkey's," he replied, "and play a game or two of pool with the fellows."

But by far the most insistent note in O. Henry's stories is that searching for what is "round the corner," as I indicated before : the insatiable thirst for romance which every right-thinking man ought to encourage. "At every corner," he writes, "handkerchiefs drop, fingers beckon, eyes besiege, and the lost, the lonely, the rapturous, the mysterious, the perilous, changing clues of adventure are slipped into our fingers. But few of us are willing to hold and follow them. We are grown stiff with the ramrod of convention down our backs. We pass on ; and some day we come, at the end of a very dull life, to reflect that our romance has been a pallid thing of a marriage or two, a satin rosette kept in a safe-deposit drawer, and a lifelong feud with a steam radiator."

In the story from which this is taken we have an incorrigible romantic who is given, by a negro in a street, a ticket with "The Green Door" written on it. He passes him again in the crowd, and is again given a ticket with the same name on it. He enters the house opposite which the negro is standing, and upstairs finds a door of the right colour, opens it, and finds a pretty shop-girl fainting for want of food. This he instantly procures for her, and promises to come and see her again. As he goes out he notices that all the doors in the house are painted green. He accosts the negro outside and asks him why he gave him the ticket. The negro points down the street to a neighbouring theatre, over which is flashed out the title of the play then running, *The Green Door*.

Another favourite theme is Destiny.

> " I go to seek on many roads
>   What is to be.
> True heart and strong, with love to light—
> Will they not hear me in the fight
>   To order, shun or wield or mould
>   My Destiny ? "

The answer is : No. Destiny awaits you. You cannot " order, shun or wield or mould " it.

" It ain't the roads we take : it's what's inside of us that makes us turn out the way we do."

But Henry's true venturer dares Fate in its blindest manifestations : the true venturer does not ask a schedule and map from Fate when he begins a journey. What he wants is to encounter an adventure to which he can predict no conclusion.

But he attains the topmost pinnacle of his fame only when he writes about the shop-girl. It is as the little shop-girl's true knight-errant that O. Henry stands most vividly before us.

Of all social problems (and social problems were the very life blood of O. Henry), that of the conditions under which the shop-girl lives, and of her outlook on life, interested him most.

In *A Lickpenny Lover* we see her, beautiful, shrewd, cunning, with vision limited behind the counter in a glove store. To her comes Irving Carter, painter, millionaire, gentleman, and falls immediately in love with her. Summoning up courage, he suggests that he should call on her people.

" Carter did not know the shop-girl. He did not know that her home is often either a scarcely habitable tiny room or a domicile filled to overflowing with kith and kin. The street-corner is her parlour, the park is

her drawing-room ; the avenue is her garden walk ; yet
for the most part she is as inviolate mistress of herself
in them as is my lady inside her tapestried chamber."

He meets her in the streets and implores her to marry
him, drawing a perfect picture of Venice and India,
Persia and the ends of the earth to which he will take
her.

To her bosom friend she recounted the episode.

" Say, Lu, what do you think that fellow wanted me
to do ?   He wanted me to marry him and go down to
Coney Island for a wedding tour."

In *Elsie in New York* we have the story of a girl looking for work, who is met on the threshold of each place
by some self-styled charity organisation which prevents
her from accepting without providing her with anything
else.   In the end she falls a victim to the worst type of
scoundrel.

In *The Guilty Party* Liz is driven to the streets and
ruin simply because her father would do nothing to
make her home attractive for her.

An Unfinished Story dwells on the underpayment of
working girls and their ultimate ruin owing to their
quite natural love of adornment.   It finishes thus :

" I dreamed that I was standing near a crowd of
prosperous-looking angels, and a policeman took me by
the wing and asked if I belonged to them.

" ' Who are they ? ' I asked.

" ' Why,' said he, ' they are the men who hired working girls, and paid 'em five or six dollars a week to live
on.   Are you one of the bunch ? '

" ' Not on your immortality,' said I.   ' I'm only the
fellow that set fire to an orphan asylum, and murdered
a blind man for his pennies.' "

In *Brickdust Row* we are reminded of Shaw in
Widowers' Houses.   The shaft is aimed at those who

compel girls to meet men on the boats, in church, in the park or on the street.

"A girl has got to meet the men," says Florence to the man who has fallen in love with her but doesn't understand the sort of life she is forced to live ; "the first time one spoke to me on the street, I ran home and cried all night. But you get used to it. I meet a good many nice fellows at church."

The hero finds that he owns the very block of flats in which the girl lives. His lawyer suggests making reception rooms.

"Man," replies the agonised lover, "it's too late, I tell you. It's too late. It's too late. It's too late."

In *The Trimmed Lamp* we see two shop-girls and the devoted lover. One of the girls, caring only for ostentation and finery, throws him over, and he mates with the other. At the end we are shown the flashy girl, led astray by baubles, expensively clad, with diamond rings and all the paraphernalia of her new profession, crouching down by a dark fence, sobbing, with a plainly dressed working girl by her side who was doing her best to console her.

Another main feature of O. Henry is his study of cities.

"He studied cities as women study their reflections in mirrors : a city was a thing with a soul, an individual conglomeration of life, with its own peculiar essence, flavour and feeling," he says of Raggles, in *The Making of a New Yorker*, "Chicago seemed to swoop down upon him with a breezy suggestion of Mrs Partington, plumes and patchouli, Pittsburg impressed him as the play of *Othello* performed in Russian in a railroad station by Dockstader's minstrels. New Orleans simply gazed down upon him from a balcony, Boston seemed to him a white, cold cloth that had been bound tightly round his brow to spur him on to some unknown but tremendous mental effort."

New York seemed to ignore him altogether until he had been knocked down by a motor car, when he discovered how, underneath the surface, she stood kindly, human, sympathetic, a veritable mother city.

In *A Municipal Report*, which Professor Leacock admires more than all his other stories, he tries to show that romance may be found in even the dullest and most unlikely remote corners of the globe. In Nashville, Tennessee, he found the most romantic story he ever wrote. To the seeing eye all cities are story cities.

He has painted for us Latin America, the South, the West and the North, all with consummate skill ; his sense of atmosphere is as sure as his sense of romance, satire or humour, on all three of which he is a past master.

He is as happy in his description of the land of the lotus-eaters, where " The climate was as balmy as that of distant Avalon ; the fetterless, idyllic round of enchanted days ; the life of the indolent, romantic people —a life full of music, flowers, and low laughter ; the influence of the imminent sea and mountains, and the many shapes of love and magic and beauty that bloomed in the white tropic nights," as he is in his truer home of Wall Street, where harassed brokers are so busy that they even forget that they are married the day after.

Whether the air was languorous with the scent of jasmine and orange blossoms, or cold and dank, as in Manhattan, he was equally able to make it live again in the pages of his books, so that you are transported there in a moment and feel the very climatic conditions as you read. Like our own English humorist, now, alas !

dead (Mr H. H. Munro), he had the gift of exactly fitting his characters with apt names.

Who does not conjure up at once an exact vision of Don Señor el Coronel Encarnacion Rios, Monteleon y Dolorosa de los Santos y Mendez, or John de Graffen-reid Atwood, from their names alone ?

He is for ever bursting out into the ridiculous, strain-ing humour beyond the bounds to which we as a nation allow it to stretch, as in " Omnia Gallia in tres partes divisa est : which is the same as to say ; we will need all of our gall in devising means to tree them parties."

Again he lets slip from time to time, usually apropos of nothing, little passages of philosophy which, once read, we are likely to carry with us to the grave.   Of these the one that I remember most clearly runs thus : " You can't write with ink, and you can't write with your own heart's blood, but you can write with the heart's blood of someone else.   You have to be a cad before you can be an artist."

In *The Country of Elusion* we see his hatred of the sham Bohemia of the New Yorker.

" You know how the Bohemian feast of reason keeps up with the courses.   Humour with the oysters ; wit with the soup ; repartee with the entrée ; brag with the roast ; knocks for Whistler and Kipling with the salad ; songs with the coffee ; the slapsticks with the cordials.   Freedom is the Tyrant that holds our Bohemians in slavery."

I notice that no writer on O. Henry dares to conclude without asserting violently his preference for one story over the rest.   Perhaps so great a choice (out of two hundred and seventy) eggs one on to do a thing like this.   Anyway, I will try my hand at the game too. For pure humour I place *Let Me Feel Your Pulse* easily first.   It has an appeal which none of the others has for the purely English reader. It is freer of exaggerated jargon ; it is purer in style (O. Henry was no stylist, at any rate, in diction), and has, as all good humorous stories should have, a quite pregnant climax. It obeys the laws laid down by Meredith for the Comic Spirit : it makes us laugh at human follies ; it satirises and ridicules and yet it does us quite active and appreciable good. It is an anodyne in itself for all bodily ailments, an infallible prescription from an unerring doctor.

For pathos I place *The Furnished Room* and *Past One at Rooney's* as exquisite examples of what drama it is possible to convey through the medium of the short story, and for a picture of the life which O. Henry was most fond of, that of the New York shop-girl, I think most readers might wander farther and fare worse than contenting themselves with *The Third Ingredient*, but all of the stories which I have mentioned are of the kind that one reads only to reread with greater enjoyment every time one comes back to them.

That O. Henry is one of the world's great geniuses is not true. That he was a vastly diverting raconteur, poignant in his pathos, terrible in his tragedy, witty, urbane and kindly in his humour, is an established fact which no sane critic can deny. Luckily (for us) his reputation is growing day by day, and whether the whole English-speaking world come to recognise in him one of the greatest masters or not, the time is not far distant when everyone will get to know him well enough to offer up a prayer of gratitude that we should have been privileged to come under the influence of so eminently sane, human, and healthy a writer.